Google
and the
Mission to
Map Meaning
and
Make Money

Bart Milner

Electric Book

ELECTRIC BOOK

Published by: The Electric Book Co Ltd, 20 Cambridge Drive, London SE12 8AJ, UK, *http://www.elecbook.com/* in association with:

fleetworks.info,
Malvern House, 15-16 Nassau Street, London W1W 7AB
(http://fleetworks.info)

Table of Contents

WebThreads   243

Index   267-275

Preface

If ever a book was written standing on the shoulders of a giant, it has to be this one. If only the said giant would keep still, rather than, as Google has been doing, running Olympic marathons against the likes of Microsoft. Just as I was about to index the final version of this book, Microsoft withdrew, hurt, after it became clear that its "Google-killing" version of Windows - Longhorn - was somewhere over the rainbow rather than waiting in the wings.

Google promptly tweaked the tiger's tail by publishing the Beta software of Google Desktop Search (GDS) for personal computers (pcs). Geoff Williams, one of the editors, found this "most impressive" on early test. With hypertext usually unavailable on the desktop, he reports that GDS generally uses dates to rank broad relevance, ignores passwords, but otherwise makes a cracking job of it.

So congratulations are probably in order; Google will have another global hit on their hands. The screendump provided by the O'Reilly experts network even showed an income-generating ad, albeit for a dating service, but it's early days, early days.

One of the things that this book does not provide is local color. If you want a picture of how Sergey drinks his coffee, you will have to try elsewhere. The intention was to write the biography of a technology, of which Google is an essential part, using Google Search and Google (News) Alerts to answer all questions.

In the end, there was only one question that Google was completely unable to answer from those two primary rivers of information, but it is quite silly and is included as a postscript to this preface. My experience is that this combination really is a magnificent research tool. For those who think the Web only consists of porn, holidays and second-hand motherboards, the exact wordings of Ovid, Jowett, Dodgson, Clemens, and Melville are free, legal and available with ten seconds of work in Google.

The electronic version of this book contains nearly 600 links to relevant articles gleaned out of the tens of thousands that Google have made available. The idea of these WebThreads is that any researcher, journalist or student should only be three clicks away from the centre of the debates and descriptions of any aspect of Internet Search. This is available from http://fleetworks.info, free, if you own a print version of the book.

During most of the time this book was being written, Google were in their SEC-determined quiet period and prohibited from discussing the company or giving interviews. Even if they had not been, the nature of IT competition means that Google should avoid doing anybody else's strategic research, and stick to their policy of keeping quiet about developments until they have been released as public Betas, and then only discuss them at public gatherings of developers or with journalists that they know they can trust. It may be useful for somebody like me to speculate, but it is a lot less useful if like Google you have responsibility for keeping the competition distanced from a company now worth $e billion.

This book is mainly the result of watching Google from a neighboring field. When Google's immensely powerful cyberspace ship appeared, I was working on natural language texts. It was immediately clear that Google had cracked context in HTML-organized web pages. But natural language texts are even more chaotic than HTML pages and the rules are probably going to be very different, or so I thought. Half right. As I began to understand more fully the problem of what had blocked the development of computer software able to process meaning from ordinary text, the significance and scale of Google's technical achievement also became clear.

This book started as a review of this technology, which is very exciting, but the context of Google's transformation into what will almost certainly be one of the flagship companies of the 21st century itself became a great story when their founders' political and commercial philosophy took them into deep conflict with Wall Street. People can take on Microsoft and win, but nobody, unless you count Eliot Spitzer, nobody goes up against Wall Street and wins. But finance depends ultimately on the maths and so far Google's maths has been better.

My own field appeared relatively barren, but I knew I had a couple of magic beans. Bill Gates had issued the challenge to get computers to understand their users' intentions. Pointless to compete with Microsoft's global resources, at one level, but anybody working on the problem would start at exactly the same place: what in purely binary and boolean terms is the logic for learning meaning and significance - Vannevar Bush's "associations"? Writing code costs little more than time, so the tools available are the same for Microsoft as they are for anybody else, beginning with Let x = x, as Laurie Anderson put it, or perhaps, Let x() = new Array.

There had to be a reason why software had failed to develop a capacity to learn and had failed to build an algorithm for learning context in natural language; a failure that has lasted thirty years, according to Marvin Minsky. The cause may be that binary logic, immensely powerful as it has proved, has an inherent inability to process meaning, probably because meaning almost always includes undefined variables, which cannot be stored in a binary system.

I do propose a way around this, but it may finally be a bodge, because it asks the user to define all the variables that remain unknown after all processing is completed. For a machine to handle this autonomously, its primary language would probably need to be at least ternary, and include a value of "undefined" as well as "true" and "false". A technology for this logic has not really been developed yet.

At the risk of "That's bloody obvious" comments from Google and maybe Stanford, I have to say that I am no mathematician. All the maths I understand is the result of having to solve logical problems in binary code in order to get a particular job done with software. Not unusually, to do this I have to be able to picture the logic as if it were some kind of working machine, so that I can visualise how all the parts fit together. Once the maths becomes more abstract than code, which is soon, I start to fade, but the binary "problem" is literally hard-wired into our systems, and it is there at the core of digital engineering, of which I have enough experience to feel confident about identifying its possible limitations.

I am very grateful to Steve Grand - the pioneer of genetic algorithms that cross-fertilise - for providing support when I started writing about this problem. He told me to keep going, but himself believed that I might be wrong because, if he will forgive me summarizing a complex argument, meaning may be organized holographically as perception, rather than using a ternary system. Maybe, but that would still leave the problem of how information is processed from a holographic memory system into meaning and significance.

A ternary system would only have the advantage of permitting the storage and manipulation of a third "undefined" value, as a primary element together with true or false. Other, more complex systems could also do the same, maybe better. It is possible that the way we store and exchange meaning is an analogue of the way that genetic information is stored and exchanged. Genetic communication uses three letter 'words' using a four letter alphabet. This might be a fruitful structural model for future computer systems, because like our genetic code, human communication contains a large proportion of "junk" information.

Apart from thanking Google themselves for providing almost all the research resources for this book, I should also thank the 10,000 journalists, developers, and bloggers who have written about Google and its context. There are far too many to name, but I hope that the Footnotes and Webthreads make most of the best of them available. Danny Sullivan at *Search Engine Watch* was a benchmark for Brin and Page in 1997, and we have every reason to treat his team, including Chris Sherman, with the same respect today. Robert X. Cringely is always great value. *Fortune*, the

FT, and **Wired** have been outstanding in their IT reporting since, at least in **Fortune**'s case, the Microsoft IPO. Stefanie Olsen and the team at **CNET**, particularly Jim Hu, have been similarly impressive.

I have also placed heavy reliance on Jack Schofield and colleagues at the **Guardian** and **Observer**, and remain grateful that there is a free online version of all the extremely strong business, IT and science reporting from those newspapers. Long may they continue to be able to afford it, but they need to worry if Google starts offering a good jobs finder service, because that is where a lot of their profit margins come from.

Special thanks must go to Geoff Williams, Wiseman Lee, for his support, close reading of most of the drafts and legal view of the text. Any mistakes have been added subsequent to Geoff's corrections. I have tried, and sometimes failed, to refer to Google and other companies as "they" rather than "it".

In case I do not make it clear in the text, I do not have a beef with honest solicitors or attorneys who are doing a difficult and necessary job. I do have a problem with company lawyers attempting to erect a tollgate on a technology by invoking a patent from a product that was never used in its actual development, and which they have probably acquired from the original author anyway.

Thanks to James Law for his advice, which was almost invariably right, and Jonathan Wine for his help. Any new ideas in this text are there because the publisher, Pat Coyne, has failed to shoot them down, even after a couple of glasses of London Pride and despite a huge knowledge of science journalism. Semantics is a family business, so thanks to John, Rosie, George and Judith Milner and Bede Constantinides for their help.

Finally thanks for help in the studio to Roy Flooks, Rick Pennington and to Dr Michael Coigley and Ricky Muir for their almost unfailing patience, and to Peter and the gang at DH Harris, Great Titchfield Street W1 for providing the best Italian diner on the planet.

The question that neither Google nor any other search engine could answer probably wins me the geek of the week award. Which mainstream sci-fi film has a water-based computer that breaks down at the plot's climax and repeats **"negative, negative, negative"** on an infinite loop? I cannot believe the answer is not out there on the Web, somewhere; the phrase "negative, negative, negative" certainly is.

Everything in Internet Search has changed utterly since Google first appeared, except for a basic technique for finding information which is essentially the same as the method we once taught for AltaVista: think of three words that *must* be on any page that you are interested in. Happy hunting.

Bart Milner, London October 2004

1

Roots2Fruits

Wherefore by their fruits (and roots) ye shall know them...

It was 3.15 am Greenwich mean time, hour of the wolf, 30th April 2004 when an email newsfeed finally appeared on Google's Initial Public Offering (IPO), which would take the company into public sale on Wall Street. The *Financial Times* had posted [1] up links to the IPO filing to the SEC (Security and Exchange Commission) and Larry Page's users' manual [2]. Sixty pages later, as dawn broke over London, it was clear that they had done their maths, and figured the engineering. They were safe and on their way.

At the same time, the spacecraft Cassini arrived at Saturn [3], having used the gravity of Venus and Jupiter to power its slingshot [4] trajectory since its launch in 1997. Google's pilots: founders Larry Page and Sergey Brin and Chief Executive Officer (CEO) Eric Schmidt, are undertaking a similar maneuver in cyberspace; instead of being sucked into what sf writer William Gibson [5] has called "a black hole... the unthinkable gravitic tug of Big Money" they are using the force of their multi-billion dollar IPO to power the next stage of their jaw-dropping journey into hypertext, context and meaning.

Although Cassini's flight had looked almost flawless, in 2004 fingers were still crossed for the success of its European Space Agency probe Huygens, particularly after the Genesis probe crashed into the Utah desert at 193 mph in September, because the parachute switches were installed backwards. When they discovered that Huygens was using a different radio frequency from Cassini, NASA remedied it by remote engineering over a billion miles, but might not have wanted advice from the world's press at the time.

Wobbling around Venus

Google were not so fortunate in their own transit of Venus. When they failed to schedule the publication of an Interview with *Playboy* outside the SEC-designated 'quiet period', they found, as in the Irish joke, that the eyes of the *Skibbereen Eagle* and every other news channel on the planet were upon them.

They should have enforced a later publishing date, but the *Playboy* interview is an American rite-of-passage, a mainstream statement that shows the jocks from high school who really calls the shots. More seriously their July price estimate and volume had to be diverted sharply downward for the August IPO, which jumped 18% on the first day of trading, finally giving Wall Street the bonus it craved, unearned unless you count the work done on the barrage of negative publicity, fueled by Google's own exaggerated errors, which helped scare off retail investors.

A new light

But it is probably fair to say that the Black Hole of an IPO did little more than rattle Google's insulation tiles, the real journey will now follow. After the first day of trading the *Wall Street Journal*'s headline was "Google's Debut is Considered a Success". (Their second headline was: "Google's Wealth Could Bring Woes" - gee, thanks, guys.) The *FT*'s Lex gave what the Trotskyists used to call 'Critical support in struggle':

> Wall Street will see the auction as a failure. Execution was poor. Strong vested interests and tough markets made life even harder. However, Google did get listed and its unconventionality shone light on important areas.

James Surowiecki of the *New Yorker* was even more forthright in an *FT* Comment article entitled Ignore Wall St's whining - Google's IPO worked:

> Wall Street can spin this however it wants. But Google went public without the marketing support of a major investment bank, without handing out favors to well-connected executives and without dictating a price in the manner of Soviet central planners. Because it did, it now has hundreds of millions of dollars that it would not otherwise have had. By any standard, this was one IPO that worked.

No concessions

Money loves only money, and if Google ever runs out of cash, expect the banks to be gleeful to the point of sadism as they dispatch the management and, almost certainly, break up the company. But, same difference really, even if Google had, like previous dot.coms permitted Wall street to make obscene profits out of its IPO, it would still get the same treatment if it ever mismanages its income flow.

The founders' founding ideals of free, unbiased, fast, public Internet Search would then be repeated publicly, before being ignored behind closed corporate doors, because the short-term profits from Search bias are so big, particularly if, like Google, you have a huge brand based on honesty. That remains a threat.

Yahoo! survived as a company following its IPO, true, but only after not only its founders had been replaced, but the "professional" management demanded by Wall Street had themselves been purged. That's not what Page and Brin intend to let happen, if they can fight to prevent it. So far so good.

This is partly a battle for America's soul; whether the country returns to the hugely ambitious, ingenious engineering, which has been its hallmark, or follows the Enron route to making money by gambling with its own, and other people's, primary assets. Having survived the dot.con boom, Google's management share with the whole IT industry the knowledge that financial speculation in tech shares has done nothing but damage to anybody except the tiny minority of individuals and companies who won the sweepstake of other peoples' investment.

The Comstock Lode

This IPO was in no way an attack on capitalism, but on financial speculation and short-term management objectives which prevent the growth of companies centered, like Google, on products which people want, and want enough to pay for, one way or another, over the long term.

It now looks like Google's management have pulled it off. This is partly because the quality of their products speaks for itself, even if the Google Press Office is on permanent sabbatical, but also because they have tapped into the mother lode, the equivalent of Gould and Curry's Comstock seam in Mark Twain's Nevada.

Google's success depends on many things, but part of it is a critical development of the concept of context. Context is at the heart of Stanford's work on IT theory under the leadership of Professor John McCarthy, as it has been at the centre of the late Jacques Derrida's philosophy.

John Hegarty, chairman of Bartle Bogle Hegarty, uses the concept of "Truth to Product" which suggests that the most striking advertising campaign in the world will turn out to be a total waste of budget if it does not tell an essential truth about the product as it is perceived by the consumer. He argues [6] that context is central to the development of a brand.

> Microsoft, rightly or wrongly, is perceived by many to be the evil empire and is therefore attacked by mindless viruses that distract the brand from its global domination. It is within this emotional context of domination that the brand must respond and organize its defense. Context even defines the framework of a virtual product.

> It's obvious really, but everything about us relates to context. Where we were born, where we live, how we talk. Our ambitions, desires and fears all relate back to context in some shape or form. It is embedded in the very DNA of our thought process. It can't be jettisoned simply because we can so easily communicate across borders.

Google developed because its founders had found a new and extremely powerful way of cracking the maths of context on the Internet. The operation of a free global service was ultimately paid for, and then some, by using the same core technology to provide a context for advertisers.

Contextual advertising gives a strong material incentive for vast amounts of money to get diverted away from print advertising and onto Internet advertising. This is what will make Google, and some of its competitors, into the flagship industries of the 21st century.

As long as Google keep tapping this seam, the banks cannot touch them. If Google is safe it is because its IPO made no concessions to short-term profit or speculation. If you wanted to back the strategic vision of the founders and their CEO, you could have bid for shares, otherwise you could naff off.

Company structure is a Delaware Delight: the dual formation allowed by the State of Delaware means that the founders and their CEO with B-type shares have ten times the voting power of other shareholders. They have almost complete control and they intend to keep almost complete control, for the foreseeable future, partly by trying to spread the sale of "A" shares as widely as possible through a Dutch auction. And they are paying no dividend.

Long-term only

Google will preserve its long-term goals by effectively remaining a privately-run company, even though its shares are publicly traded. This was spelt out by Larry in the SEC (Security and Exchange Commission) filing.

Since Larry uses first names for himself, Sergey Brin and Eric Schmidt, Google's CEO, in their IPO filing, at the risk of being over-familiar, this book will do the same. This is also the moment to apologize if through laziness I have sometimes attributed too much to Sergey and Larry, and not given enough credit to the perspiration and inspiration of the rest of the Google team. Although, like Microsoft, the founders' leadership remains critical to what Google is and will become, that future depends ultimately on the quality of work they inspire from the collective effort of the whole company.

"If opportunities arise that might cause us to sacrifice short term results but are in the long term interest of our shareholders, we will take those opportunities." Google said. "...As a private company, we have concentrated on the long term. This has served us well. As a public company, we will do the same."

The core message of the SEC filing is that Google's IPO is solely a long-term investment. There will be no quarterly massage of their figures and there are a dozen pages of good reasons why your initial purchase could decline in value in the short term and is subject to significant risk in the long term.

Over time, Google's founders have learnt how to rewrite their operating system from scratch until it works the way they want it to. It was natural for them to do the same thing with their IPO. Back on planet Earth this caused consternation, and the SEC's server was reported to have crashed with the demand to see Google's documentation.

Google and the Mission

The **FT** reported it fully, explained industry concerns and then, via its **Lex** column, came down firmly in favor. They must have been relieved that their world scoop in the Fall of 2003 predicting Google's IPO in April 2004 had come true, albeit on the last possible day. Two days later, after studying Larry's exhaustive summation of all the things that could possibly go wrong (...earthquakes in California and Japan? - check) they were a little less confident.

Schizoid reactions

Meanwhile the Business and Media section of the Sunday **Observer** in London became quite schizoid. A page one splash complained that UK citizens were being discriminated against by not being allowed to buy shares. On page two readers were advised to:

> "Avoid (the IPO auction) like the plague" (because it is) "a throwback to the inglorious days of the dot.com bubble" (which) "could end up massively over-pricing the shares or perversely, selling them at a huge discount" with a "mind-blowingly hip prospectus - which could have been written by the re-incarnation of Mother Theresa".

Shares in US IPOs are rarely sold outside North America, because they are primarily subject to state not federal law. So **Observer** readers faced the Groucho-like paradox of being refused shares in a bubble company run by Mother Theresa in iPod earbuds and bitch jeans. The **Observer**'s usual well-informed sanity had returned by page 3 for a full-page analysis of the IPO, culminating in veteran IT-watcher John Naughton taking an engineer's pleasure in their final joke [7].

> "The 'proposed maximum aggregate offering price' is $2,718,281,828...It's e - the base of natural logarithm. With the possible exception of pi, e is the most important constant in mathematics since it appears in every calculation involving limits and derivatives."

Another wag suggested this meant the correct bidding price for Google shares was either $2.71 or $27.18. The more serious implication is that while Google can describe just about all the conceivable future threats to the company, they can only guess its current and ultimate value.

Blind bids as context

But then, nobody else knows any better. Revenue over three and a bit years of profitable trading in a new product is not going to predict values in another three, or thirty, years time. But Google already had another cunning plan in place: better maths for a healthier future.

At the heart of Google's technology is the experience that "democracy on the web works" because it creates part of a measurable context for web pages. By requiring blind bids, they did their best to create a similar grand consensus of what potential investors and their financial advisors really believe the company's finances and brand identity are worth.

Although take up by retail investors was disappointing, the auction did appear to work, because Google's core indexing technology was able to process the results properly, which is rare. In July 2004, Google opened a site to allocate bidders' IDs and suggested that they expect to sell their stock in mid-August for between $108 and $135 a share, valuing the whole company ultimately at up to $36 billion. Shortly before the IPO this dropped to $85 to $95, and on the first day of trading the shares closed at $100.34. Glitches aside, it is all good. Now they have to create the products that justify their $23.7 billion market valuation, 30% less than Yahoo!. Yahoo! is a huge success story, again, but may still be significantly over-valued in 2004.

If the company was broken up tomorrow, that sum might look ludicrous, but if they stick to their knitting and maintain their priorities, in ten years it could look quite modest. Twenty years ago nobody came close to guessing that Microsoft's revenue [8] in 2003 is "expected to be in the range of $8.9 billion and $9.0 billion" with operating income "in the range of $2.8 billion and $2.9 billion". This is not to imply that Google is 'the next Microsoft'; far from it, the creation of both companies was determined by variables that are now both historic and unique.

To be fair, the *Observer*'s completely contradictory response to Google's limits and derivatives, as manifested by an IPO through 'Dutch auction', exactly reflected what was going on in the global news media. Internet veterans were delighted by another enthralling chapter in the Google saga; bankers hoping for short-term gains (and devil take the pension funds) were appalled. Insider trading was made virtually impossible, banking behemoth Goldman Sachs was shown the door after 'playing politics' by arranging a

Google and the Mission

separate meeting with one of the original investors; the banks were being paid a miserly 3% for their services, a fraction of what they had expected. A number subsequently dropped out, complaining of too much work for too little money: clearly a shocking reversal of the proper order of things. However, the departure of Merrill Lynch, with the biggest retail client list, may have hit Google's retail sales volumes.

Dual ownership - Uses and abuses

Blaspheming against mammon makes powerful enemies, but Google, rather than striking out on their own with a mixture of innocence and arrogance as usually described, are actually following a path they have learnt from the real veterans at Intel, Microsoft, News International and Berkshire Hathaway. Although the founders are world-class developers, not MBAs, they are great learners and their close relationship with Eric Schmidt is based on taking his business experience with Sun and Novell, where he was CEO before moving to Google, very seriously indeed.

News International's parent company, News Corp is moving from Australia in mid-2004 to incorporation in Delaware, for similar reasons to Google, upsetting the Australian stock exchange in the process. Split voting rights for shares is not unusual, but the tiny state of Delaware has a legal framework that is recognized to be amongst the fairest, fastest and most intelligent, almost anywhere in the world. A recent example, reported [9] by Geoffrey Colvin of *Fortune* suggests: "A Delaware ruling could make directors personally liable for pay suits" as a response to the revelations of the kind of perks that Kozlowski enjoyed at Tyco.

A dual ownership structure lends itself to long-term focus but is clearly also open to corruption and abuse. The Australian version enabled Rupert Murdoch to maintain his corporate and dynastic strategy when News International's resulting debts made his bankers change their pants. Similar Canadian law enabled 'Lord' Conrad Black to siphon off large sums from the company that owned the *Chicago Sun*, the UK's *Daily Telegraph* and the *Jerusalem Post* groups, according to depositions by the A-group shareholders. When Black subsequently attempted to sell some of these titles, a Delaware court under Vice-Chancellor Leo Strine forced him to hand them back.

Dutch auction apart, Google's IPO strategy imitates closely that of Microsoft, twenty years ago. Their SEC filing makes it clear that they have listened, and listened good, to Warren Buffet and learned a great deal from Microsoft's strategic history since its IPO. Both share the conviction that the long-term value of the company is everything; nobody and nothing is going to interfere with that. Speculation is death.

The IPO death march

Like Gates and Ballmer, who led an IPO which was "a Bataan death march" according to their bankers, Google's IPO attempted to prevent litigation and depress speculation by taking the worst possible view of the company's prospects. Sergey even adopted a central Billism, that an IPO is an inevitable but unwanted "distraction" from the long-term goals of the company. This is the exact, dialectical opposite of what the dot.coms did, where hype was transmuted and spun, albeit briefly, into fairy gold.

By also using a blind auction it disperses ownership as widely as possible, making a future hostile take-over much more difficult.

Yahoo! already had 2.7 million shares of Class A stock as part of its settlement of the Overture suit on keyword auctions, and sold 2.3 million for $191 million. That was a mistake; if they had hung onto them for a month they would have made 40% more. AOL finally did something right by bringing 1.9 million shares for $22 million to parent Time Warner (at about $12 a share).

Sergey had even said that assimilation might be Google's ultimate destiny, resistance may be futile, but people said he was depressed by the problems of the forthcoming IPO. Takeover is a problem that Microsoft have never had to face.

Rather than simply brooding, Sergey was probably gestating ideas of the best way of coping with the intense local pressure within Google and the SEC rules which had made an IPO inevitable, when that IPO would be more than capable of destroying the company, and statistically was likely to do so. Larry has mentioned a similar mood in Y2k when Sergey was pondering on Google being a highly successful operation, which was fashionable enough also to be losing money, and what to do about it. The answer, contextual text advertising, is now worth billions and is definitely responsible for [95]% of Google's current income, well worth a dark mood.

Google and the Mission

The co-pilots

Perhaps the biggest small miracle of all is that the business friendship of CEO Eric Schmidt, Larry Page and Sergey Brin's has been declared to the SEC as a significant asset (another first) despite the G-forces that the IPO must have subjected their relationship to. Silicon Valley is paved with the bones of founders and CEOs who have fallen out with each other. (Steve Wozniak, co-founder of Apple, did not speak directly to Steve Jobs for years after a misunderstanding about some money).

This may be because Larry Page shares the philosophy of Intel, the Dutch, and his late father, Professor Carl Page, that violent controversy is the negative feedback on which friendship, business and science can flourish. When they first interviewed Eric for the job of CEO the founders started arguing with him and have been doing so ever since. Once they agree, if the maths runs and the engineering model actually works, then it flies like Cassini, as they have demonstrated.

If the prospect of an IPO made Sergey depressed, some of Google's oldest friends - people who had been watching the company professionally since it first exploded out of Stanford, were almost equally worried. They felt that if Google became overvalued in a wildly speculative IPO then it would go the same way as Netscape.

We knew that Google, unlike Netscape, have been making huge profits out of contextual advertising: the AdWord/AdSense programs. But if this was a temporary, windfall profit which the likes of Yahoo! and Microsoft would be quick to reclaim, then expectations of growth and profits would be a mirage, and the company itself would do a dot.com. A high valuation of Google means that it has to be capable of producing products in [7] years' time that people will still want to pay for. While Netscape never did get that, Microsoft never forgets it.

If history repeats the old deceits

Google's valuation problem is that it does not make better washing machines. Like the water supply in *Chinatown*, its business is perceived as "The future Mr Gittes. The future." In the short term this makes over-valuation of the company almost inevitable, as everybody wants a piece of the future. A dot.com-style over-valuation is what concerns Bambi Francisco [10], of CBS Marketwatch. At a valuation of $35 billion, Yahoo!'s current worth, Google:

> ... would be closing in on Walt Disney's $47 billion valuation and would stand at more than half of Viacom's $67.4 billion value.
>
> If history repeats itself, maybe Google will buy Viacom, Yahoo! will buy Disney and some starry-eyed analysts will begin slapping $400 price targets on both Google's post-IPO shares and Yahoo's.
>
> Yep. We've seen it before. Remember when Amazon.com got the infamous $400 price target back in 1998, or when Yahoo! received a $600 price target back in January 2000?
>
> Or, recall when AOL scooped up Time Warner just when AOL hit its peak valuation? ...Well, we all know what happened after that. Most of us went on sabbaticals, and some hid deep inside caves.

If the founders are ever pictured in the tabloids as having developed a taste for yachts, bimbos and cocaine, then dot.com investment idiocy is probable, but on their current track record? No chance.

All their acquisitions to date have been strategic, extremely cautious, and, apart from Google News Alerts, all have become profitable. Much-envied employee benefits aside, they have never wasted a penny and show no sign of ever losing track of what generates the bottom line.

The Netscape switch

There are good reasons in their backgrounds why this is likely to continue; both founders are only a generation away from hardship. Sergey was born in Moscow and Larry's father, the late Professor Carl Page, was the first person in his family to graduate from high school. The only sad note in this story is that Professor Page should have died in 1996 before Larry and Sergey published their breakthrough paper on hypertext search architecture. But by then Larry's brother Carl, was already on his way to becoming a multi-millionaire by selling his eGroups software to Yahoo!. Over-achievers? You betcha.

The real concern of experienced observers was not that the founders and the CEO would start developing delusions of corporate grandeur and were about to try and buy Sony or the Danish Royal Family, but that their market-share could prove temporary, and their ability to generate a range of profitable products over time was unproven.

Fred Vogelstein [11] of *Fortune* identified the problem after doing an extensive series of interviews inside the Googleplex company headquarters. In an article entitled "**Can Google Grow Up?** - **A talented company facing trouble**" he was concerned that the company culture was too spontaneous and chaotic to cope with organized competition, but even more worrying, Google's service was impersonal. It appeared to have no permanent user base.

Although the Internet Protocol (IP) number of every searcher, which (temporarily) identifies any machine connected to the Internet, is buried deep in Google's archive, there was nothing more to connect the user with the company. That would mean that if Yahoo! or Microsoft developed a better search technology, as they promised, users could switch from Google without penalty, just as they had switched from Netscape as soon as Explorer became a better browser.

The reply - Gmail

Studying the technology for several years had suggested to me that this view was overly pessimistic. Google's core technology looked highly transferable from Internet search to information management elsewhere, as in its 'Google in a Box' Enterprise Intranet Search servers. There was no actual proof that this was happening - plans and finances were confidential - but it certainly smelt right.

Second guessing Google's plans is like playing chess against a team of grandmasters; you will never have thought through as many of the possible options and combinations as they have. No one, as far as I could discover, saw the strategic significance of Google's apparently very modest acquisitions, whose cost was trivial compared to the billions of dollars worth of established search companies that Yahoo! was intent on buying up. It was also true, but little noticed, that Google also already had a strong user base not amongst its users but from its advertisers, who cannot as a rule switch their budgets easily and quickly.

The question of a floating user base was met on All Fools' Day 2004 with the release of the Beta (trial version) of Gmail, giving users up to a gigabyte of email storage, searchable using Google's technology, and funded by contextual advertising. This blew everybody's hats off. At a stroke Google had moved from an impersonal service to providing one of the most personal services on the planet.

The Gmail privacy storm

Nobody wants to change their email account and hence address once it is established, and email has proved the stickiest parts of Yahoo! and msn.com (through Hotmail). Email itself dates back to the early eighties, and was heavily used well before the Internet appeared, so the chances of a successful email business maintaining its broad customer base past 2010 is quite feasible.

So much for the problem of an impersonal service without strings or ties for the user. Email is so personal that the requirement for Gmail to search text automatically spooked up a storm on privacy. Liz Figueroa, the Californian state senator, introduced legislation to block indexed email services like Gmail. According to one UK magazine (which cannot be named for legal reasons):

> Apparently, this violates the assumption that emails are private. We don't know which is worse - interfering in something she appears not to fully understand, or the naivety displayed by that assumption...

Their veteran tail gun proposed a new service - BlackMail - based on the Monty Python TV gameshow. All emails would be searched for incriminating and/or embarrassing details and then, in return for an adequate payment, partners, parents or bosses would *not* b e informed of their contents.

It looked as if for once Google had failed to do their prep, one of their great strengths, and had delivered a crucial new product (albeit in Beta) without having thought through all the legal and security implications - or so I complained to Danny Sullivan's forum on Google's strategy at *Search Engine Watch* [12].

Controversy marketing

Wrong again, because this was to miss the bigger picture. Google's IPO, launched 29 days later, required full disclosure of company activities. Failing to release Gmail, the clearest indicator to date of Google's long-term product viability, would have made them vulnerable to legal actions on the grounds of hiding critical future assets. Ready or not (and the engineering was in much better shape than the public relations) it had to be released before the IPO.

Although the sheer scale of Gmail news coverage, and the size of the resulting privacy storm took Google, and everybody else, by surprise, scanning hundreds of Gmail stories using a Google newsfeed suggested that [65-70]% of coverage was positive.

Google have previously earned a Kim Song Il level [98]% of positive publicity, so adverse publicity must still be painful, particularly when most of it was so darned ignorant, but it also meant that without spending a penny more than the original press release Google had achieved saturation press coverage comparable with the launch of Windows, which had cost Microsoft millions of dollars. Like the golfer Gary Player, the more they practice, the luckier they get.

Embrace tiger?

Being praised by Bill Gates at the World Economic Forum in Davos was probably a bit like Shere Khan admiring your cubs at the *Jungle Book*'s [13] watering hole. (**"Damn - I knew I should not have missed that session**", said Sergey when asked about it afterwards). Google had already let it be known that they had refused to sell themselves to Microsoft, preferring to be offered for sale to everybody else either on Internet auction site eBay or in the "Dutch Auction [14] " which subsequently showed up better in the maths. In summer 2003, Google co-founder Sergey Brin had joked, "**I think there are a lot of liabilities in acquiring Microsoft.**"

Industry observers smiled and then shook their heads. 'Ah, remember the last company which humiliated Microsoft? Netscape? Bought by AOL for $9 billion in 1999, and now resting in pieces after final shutdown [15] in late 2003 by owners, poor Time Warner, whose total dot.com losses including AOL's other write-downs, hit another new record [16] of $99 billion. Google's been a great brand but now they have grown too fast and trodden on the tiger's tail. The fickle public will desert them in millions as soon as Microsoft starts to compete seriously, and then it will be tears before bedtime again'. Well, up to a point. Yahoo!'s CEO Terry Semel has pointed out that the Search field is not a zero-sum game and there is plenty of room for all three companies to prosper. More, if you include AskJeeves/Teoma or Baidu.com, which a Google-led consortium has bought into after it gained the majority share of the enormous, and exploding, Chinese mainland Search market.

Rather than attempting to crush each other, Google and probably Overture have enabled the diversion of vast funds flowing into classified advertising, worth up to 65% of *all* current newspaper and magazine income, to be diverted onto the Internet.

Simply put, this technology gives both classified advertiser and customer a better, faster, cheaper deal. That will spell the end of the golden age of printing enabled by digital publishing, although display advertising, which deals with image and aspiration rather than classified's hard product information, does not yet have, and is unlikely to get anytime soon, the quality it would need to migrate from print to the Internet. But it is still going to be a huge shift and Google are in the vanguard with a better indexing technology.

Microsoft plays catchup

This book will argue that there was something both new and very special about Google's breakthrough technology - context mapping. It has begun to unlock the capabilities of our machines to understand the context, and hence relevance of our documents, a major stumbling block for the whole industry for half a century.

Google represents the engineering of an idea or set of ideas about meaning, and whilst they can protect their engineering from illegal copying, ideas, of their nature, cannot be patented. Their technological breakthrough, unlike their engineering, is no longer exclusive.

Context mapping is a tad technical but it is worth understanding because it will be the beating heart, or so Bill Gates promises, of the computers you will be using in ten years time. It already concerns you every time you look for a new web page or lose a personal letter on your own pc.

Tony Perkins [17] of the ***AlwaysOn*** network reported from the Davos Economic Forum in early 2004 that:

> Mr. Gates admitted that Microsoft took an approach to search that he now realizes was wrong. "Our strategy was to do a good job on the 80 percent of common queries and ignore the other stuff," he said. He noted that Google was "way better" for people investigating a rare disease, exploring a hobby, or searching for a specific restaurant. "It's the remaining 20 percent that counts...because that's where the quality perception is," he said. "They kicked our butts," Mr. Gates said, as he took personal responsibility for losing out to Google.

> But as Gates also predicted that Microsoft search technology would soon outpace that of its rival, so he is really focused on the opportunity. "We will catch them," he said, smiling broadly.

Out of nowhere

Beware that Microsoft smile, but unlike Netscape, or even the Apple's desktop, Google employs a new logical method as its core, a different kind of maths application. You cannot really patent an idea, and the idea behind Google will probably inherit the earth, but there is a difference between understanding a fundamental theory, and being able to apply it in the very specific engineering context of four billion HTML web documents or the Windows desktop.

The mathematical engine that powers the Google Search program itself is its core technology, and it is new. It may be possible to reverse engineer the software, or reinvent it, but it cannot then simply be bolted on to established software, like email programs. Finding a solution to this problem is already requiring competitors, particularly Microsoft, to do a lot of real head-busting work to catch up and it is very hard to retrofit onto existing (legacy) software - Microsoft's most precious asset and greatest liability. Sergey refers to this as "integration challenges".

Microsoft CEO Steve Ballmer told *CNET* [18] that: "We did not commit serious research and development effort (to Internet Search) as soon as we probably ought have... We had a lot on our plate, and we did prioritize, for better or for worse. In a funny way, we made the same prioritization as our No. 1 competitor at the time, Yahoo!. I mean, as bad as I feel, I hope they feel even worse, because they actually had the lead in search, and they didn't invest, and Google came out of nowhere relative to both of us."

Windows needs Google technology

During the nineties, Microsoft had had little incentive to intervene in the crowded field of Internet Search. Free search was simply not a profitable arena. That has changed with the success of Google's AdWord. Initially I believed that the more targeted advertising Google pulls in, the greater the pressure on msn.com as an advertising-funded portal. That was wrong.

Partly as a result of Google's activities, Internet advertising has strengthened considerably overall, taking msn.com into its first profit (in February 2004) in nearly ten years of competition with AOL and Yahoo!. Ad sales are driving both growth and profits at msn.com. The $200 million in profits anticipated for the year ending June 30 contrasts with a $500 million loss the year before.

Google and the Mission

This is the reverse of the Netscape-effect which had forced Microsoft into strategic investments without any model of how to get that money back. But still, it must hurt Bill Gates's indomitable pride that Google Search has made most of Microsoft's search look sick, and the exceptions, on msn.com itself for example, have usually had their search functions bought in from outside Microsoft.

Google may now have given the same energizing shock to the heart of Microsoft that both Apple's desktop and Netscape's browser have delivered in the past. Painful for Microsoft's competitors and executives, no doubt, baby, no doubt, but a fit and fighting Microsoft is darn useful for the United States as a motor of the world's economy. Put bluntly, to stay on top Microsoft now have to adopt Google's core technology, by whatever means necessary, and apply it to Longhorn [19], the next generation of Windows.

Context mapping is possibly more important than Apple's desktop - the Mac's and then Windows' adoption of the Xerox Menlo PARC's desktop metaphor (Graphical User Interface) - now on almost every pc in the world. Applied maths is an acquired taste, so I will try to explain the general ideas in English rather than algebra, but understanding Google's triumph does require some thinking about the maths and engineering of some of the fundamental theories of how machine intelligence works as well as the blind clash of armies of software hacks in the night.

Permission requested from Dilbert.com

A user-centric brand

At the dawn of the 21st century, Google has been a phenomenon, no question, but not an anomaly, as co-founder Larry Page points out. It is one of very few really significant survivals of the dot.com bubble, when it picked up the seed capital that enabled commercial development. **"We missed both,"** says Larry with a certain relish: **"We did not launch during the boom and we did not crash during the bust".**

This book is mainly concerned with the how and why of the ideas which have made Google a phenomenon, but good ideas do not pay the rent, and it is the engineering of Sergey's "pretty maths" into a user-centric software and hardware under Larry Page's leadership which does.

Focus on the user and all else will follow: This user-centric, rather than profit or developer-centered design philosophy is still unusual. Apple and Sony are masters in the field, and the loyalty which their brand inspires has helped them through patches when their technology has faltered. Google will benefit from the same loyalty; although their brand identity is a lot more complex, it can be simplified as the general perception of a company led by a couple of brilliant nerds that you can trust.

Considerable as have been the achievements of Gates, Jobs and Ellison, this is probably not the accolade that they have sought. There is a better parallel here with the founders of Adobe, but luckily for them the closest that Adobe have ever had to confront the general public is in the legions of not-very technical designers who adore Adobe Photoshop. Google's relationship with the public is now much more intense.

Iconic

The fact is that almost everybody loves Google. Co-founder Sergey Brin knew how and why that had happened when some kids wrote to say that they had used Google to diagnose their father's heart attack - in real time. "**An iconic moment**" said Brin in an meeting with Danny Sullivan, editor of searchenginewatch.com [20]. No kidding. Equally iconic, if less serious, has to be an appearance with **Bart Simpson**.

When I searched Google for this picture, someone on the same thread pointed out that Springfield's main cinema in *The Simpsons* is called the Googleplex, the name of Google's headquarters in Mountain View (Calif). (So target readers can be Lisa Simpson and the Comic Shop Man - Matt Groening's portrait as an obese nerd obsessed with meticulous detail - and Tom Baker's Dr Who scarf.)

After Y2k

For those who like their consumption more conspicuous, the *Sex and the City* 'girls' started checking the status of their (phew, final) dates on Google. There were a lot of subsequent puns about the interest of bankers in Google's IPO and potential billions of dollars in commission. In an investment environment still blasted by their own greed and stupidity during the dot.com bubble, the fees the banks were promising themselves from Google's IPO were huge, but Google's founders had other ideas.

There was also a tremendous amount of internal pressure for an IPO from original investors and those already vested with stock options, or employees who want to be.

In 1999, the *New York Times* [21] had reported that:

"Google is not 'even on the radar screen' of most users and that it will be hard for the company to compete with sites like Yahoo! and Excite for advertising dollars".

So all this happened in the first three years of profitable trading, whilst Excite [22], and a great many other dot.coms went down the pan. Their first paid product, Adword, was released in 2001, because, as Larry Page [23] tells it, the girls of Palo Alto were not interested in Sergey the dot.com president if Google was not making any money. There was just too much competition from other virtual millionaire males, most of whom found buying a garage in Palo Alto in Y2k was a lot easier than impressing its savvy daughters.

Developing a new technology, which is centered on the needs of the user rather than market-share or profit, without ever neglecting the bottom line, has made Google into a world brand. In 2003, it became the most trusted brand in the world by leapfrogging over Coca-Cola and even Apple's notoriously fanatical fans. By the end of 2003 it had been "profitable since 2001:Q1, employed 700+ people, of whom 60+ have Ph.D.s, was available in 86 languages, had 14 offices, and delivered 150M searches/day", and was valued by the *Financial Times* [24] at $15 billion in October 2003, when a 2004 IPO was first mooted.

Optimizing it

The recipe is easy, but the ingredients are hard to get. Take an unfashionable area, which everybody uses and nobody is satisfied with: here, the messy, unprofitable and increasingly disappointing field of Internet search in 1997. Combine a brilliant mathematical breakthrough with some world-class engineering at a university - Stanford - with massive resources and a relaxed attitude to thesis completion (both co-founders are still 'on leave' from their PhDs). Adopt clear engineering targets and stick to them. Find a new way of generating (advertising) revenue. Then work on Optimizing it until it grows exponentially into one of the most widely loved, and useful, pieces of software on the planet. Simple really. Co-founder Larry Page listed the reasons "Why Google is still around" very modestly:

"We're lucky. We have a deep technical understanding of what we are doing, which is not true of many companies. Everybody searches. Copying does not cost anything. Distributing another copy costs basically zero because Google surveys the free part of the web."

Google's triple whammy started with a technological breakthrough triggered by the most advanced applied maths and computer thinking at Stanford, Michigan and Maryland universities. They declared a new open world standard for Internet Search on behalf of science and democracy and borrowed enough equipment, money and talent to give the world an enormously powerful, free, Internet search service before developing its technology to generate the Internet's version of classified (contextual) advertising: a 'river of gold', now worth squillions of dollars.

Google and the Mission

"An unhealthy influence"

Google's technological supremacy not only helped create the brand, it also gave them 70% + of the global Search market in early 2004, (before the divorce from Yahoo!). This makes Google's benchmark ideals of an unbiased, free public service, not controlled by commercial interests, increasingly important.

As the web continues to grow exponentially, it gets more and more technically difficult to achieve that standard both for Google and for its competitors, because the commercial and political incentives to screw up the Open Search advocated by Google and smaller rival AskJeeves(Teoma) increase daily.

But as Biggie Smalls remarked shortly before they shot him: "Jealousy comes with the territory. The more money, the more problems". Ironically, given Google's genesis, The *Times*'s technology columnist, David Rowan has attacked [25] Google's success as a threat to free speech in the *Times Online*, London.

"Google, the online world's dominant information provider, is now so powerful as to constitute a potential monopoly. If Yahoo! and Microsoft fail to squeeze Google's market share in the search engine wars now being fought, every internet user will be the poorer".

... "Any company that controls around 80 per cent of web search requests is starting to wield an unhealthy influence on our access to information. If your opinions fall foul of Google, who can stop it from dropping links to your web page? Already the Church of Scientology has used legal threats to have anti-Scientology pages removed from the search index, albeit temporarily. And when Google was negotiating with China to have access restored to the country's web-surfers, there were rumors of compromises, never confirmed, that had blocked sites that might embarrass Beijing."

Political opposition to Open Search is not always for bad reasons. The German government set the legal precedent by demanding that Google (Germany) conform to German federal law and ban the search of neo-Nazi and fascist regalia sites. That seemed acceptable, and Google had complied when the government of China objected to dissent sites appearing in Google and AltaVista searches.

China

But that note on China is a little odd coming from the *Times* - a paper owned by News International whose Harper Collins publishing division decided against publishing former Governor-General Chris Patten's account of the return of Hong Kong to China because it might have been offensive to the Chinese government. James Murdoch, chief executive of BskyB and son of founder Rupert, spelt it out when he said [26] :

"...Hong Kong's democracy advocates should accept the reality of life under a strong-willed "absolutist" government. Speaking at the Miliken Institute's annual business conference in Beverly Hills, Murdoch criticized the press for "portraying a falsely negative portrait of China" by focusing on "destabilizing" issues such as human rights and Taiwan.

Closer to home, that *Times* article accused Google of invading users' privacy. This proved prescient if a tad paranoid given the fears of privacy-invasion when Google proposed Gmail. The raw common sense that services have to be paid for, and if you find contextual advertising intrusive, then there are plenty of other (non-searchable) email services around, that you can pay for, seems to have eluded some people.

"All this should not, of course, prevent the ordinary web surfer from using Google in preference to some of its increasingly effective rivals, such as Teoma.com and Vivisimo.com. But if you do, you might like to know that Google stores for years a detailed note of everything you search for, and at what time of day, which it logs according to your computer's address. It may, it says, "release specific personal information about you" to the powers that be. You're not feeling quite so lucky now, are you?"

Open Search

Serious issues, but that last comment, a swipe at Google's much-liked 'I'm **Feeling Lucky**' button, verges on the malicious. If a user is making repeated searches on for example 'child sex pain' then maybe Google or Yahoo! *should* be asked to tell the police in his/her area. Privacy is important, but some issues, like child protection, matter even more. We Europeans sometimes like to duck responsibility. We can now start to set public standards of what we expect from the Internet in open, democratic debate or we can leave it to very large commercial companies and the US government to decide on our behalf, and then complain about it afterwards.

Out of scientific idealism more than anything, Google set the Internet benchmarks on honest information searching in 1997. Or as Brin put it: "**Basically, our goal is to organize the world's information and to make it universally accessible and useful. That's our mission.**" Since then Google has become a universal tool and a global media brand. Conflicts between public service and the need to grow profits are going to be inevitable. So maybe this is now a job for a W3C and/or a UN/International Atomic Energy Authority task force to work on.

This is not frivolous. IAEA experts showed that Niger's 'sale' of Yellow Cake (uranium ore) to Iraq was a forgery by getting comparable documents from Google. "**What? You Googled them?**" The BBC2 Newsnight presenter was almost incredulous. "**But, naturally.**" the expert replied. Google's idealism has been crucial, but we cannot rely on it forever. Time, maybe, for Google's founders to set up an Open Search research foundation, perhaps with Gloria Page or Professor Michael Brin as trustees.

Spam, spam, spam or spam

In commercial search, Google are still highly unusual in declaring their belief in open, unbiased standards, AskJeeves [27] is another more recent, exception. Google have been unique, perhaps, in publishing the methodology of some of their central ideas and core methods; (there's also now a fully open source alternative, but it is not very good yet). No good deed goes unpunished, and Google's core ideas, if not the actual maths and engineering, are almost invariably incorporated into the new generation software of spammers, competitors, clones and other developers.

Google's original open standards are now subject to a continuous war of attrition from link-farms - a form of spam designed to twist the technology until it breaks. To stay on top, Google have to continue to outwit and outthink the spammers, Microsoft and their commercial competitors.

Google's users finally only care about how well Search works and that quality is now subject to erosion, mostly malicious but also due to the exponential growth in the size of the web and its increasingly adept use of dynamic output. For Google, the serpent in the garden is currently not Microsoft but spam, spam, spam and spam. Not the unwanted emails which Bill Gates wrote [28] to the US Senate Commerce Committee about, because they currently constitute more than 50% of all email traffic, but link-farms which jack up a site's rating in a Google Search list by creating artificial, meaningless links to inflate the apparent popularity and hence relevance of a client's site.

One spammer even tried to cut out the middleman and extort $100,000 directly from Google in exchange for not releasing his Adsense-cheating software. Google got the police to record the calls and he was arrested. His lawyer will probably have a field day because it is clearly blackmail but even Californian law may not yet define it as such.

The politics of dancing

In order to counter the sheer, relentless scale of spam attacks as fast as possible, Google applied an arguably more erratic and unpredictable technology (Bayesian probabilities) as spam filters, beginning with the notorious Florida 'dance' (monthly index update) in November 2003. Sites claiming to be blameless and innocent subsequently disappeared from their most cherished search listings perhaps because this implementation of the Reverend Bayes's [29] theories was not quite up to the job.

Google can overcome this - they have the tools - but they do need the time and space to work the old magic, because their opponent is now hydra-headed and targeted at Google's methods, which the original data (Internet pages) was not - just very full of innocent mistakes. But Google's usefulness since 2000 has already built up a tremendous fund of goodwill amongst millions of ordinary users. This loyalty can cushion you if your technology goes through a bad patch, as Yahoo! also knows.

A long way to fall

Seasoned industry savants are still amazed by the loyalty that Google evokes from consumers and concerned that this might become a liability. "When you're God, you have quite a long way to fall

Google and the Mission

if you do something wrong. It's hard to think of a company that's been put on a pedestal as much as they have." According to Danny Sullivan, quoted in the *Washington Post* [30].

This status has been achieved by a combining a new mathematical solution to an ancient philosophical problem, developing an engineering distribution system with an unusual degree of speed, reliability and integrity, and then providing the results for free. That matters to most users a lot more than any mission statement even when Google's founders clearly believe every word of their 10-point credo.

10 things...

Ten things Google has found to be true [31]

1) Focus on the user and all else will follow.

2) It's best to do one thing really, really well.

3) Fast is better than slow.

4) Democracy on the web works.

5) You don't need to be at your desk to need an answer.

6) You can make money without doing evil.

7) There's always more information out there.

8) The need for information crosses all borders.

9) You can be serious without a suit.

10) Great just isn't good enough.

(But, of course, if you want really grand statements of the highest business ethics, those of both Enron and BCCI are most impressive: - It ain't what you do, it's the way that you sell it - that's what gets...)

A technology that began with Sir Tim Berners-Lee's free distribution of a common Web language (HTML) developed into the corruption of online fraudsters aided and abetted by the efforts of Wall Street's, and the City of London's, finest. Google is one of the very few companies to be seen by millions of users to have retained its integrity and its potential by not only promising, but actually delivering a new kind of free service only made possible by the new technology of the Internet.

Linux, php, the Open Directory Project, Wikipedia, eBay and Amazon have a similar cachet. The first four are some of the collective, voluntary manifestations of the Open Source movement, a strange new form of politics which tends to be understood only by techies and developers, whilst Amazon and eBay's achievements are obvious to any ordinary punter who buys books or wants to auction consumer goods. But both eBay and Amazon are primarily business successes, using established technology. Google's combination of sound business and revolutionary technical innovation has not been seen since the earliest days of Apple, when Microsoft was still called Traff-0-Data.

As a UK citizen, I was not entitled to participate in the IPO and, to avoid any conflict of interest, as long as I am writing about Search technology and Google I will not buy shares in them or any other technology company. This book's editors do not have any connection with Google, although we have asked, so far without a response, if the AdSense program can be added to this site; partly so that we can track how it responds to the text.

Google's competitors may complain that this book is the most-heavily annotated fan letter in history, and I admit that I am a fan, partly because I have been working with the ideas behind the technology for a long time and Google's technology has my unqualified professional respect; by raising the bar in Internet search they have made my own work much easier and more interesting. Five years ago I would have paid to subscribe to a Google service, and I believed that they would have to go that way. Keeping Search free by rethinking contextual advertising leaves me, and millions of what the French call *informaticiens* in their debt. That helps create a powerful brand loyalty.

The Big One

Google's technology is central to its present and potential success as a business but it is also part of a much wider and older story. Brin and Page have only made the most modest and realiztic claims for Google, but there is no doubt that what they are really after - and what Gates also wants most - is the Big One: a program that understands meaning.

Google and the Mission

Never settle for the best

"The perfect search engine," says Google co-founder Larry Page, "would understand exactly what you mean and give back exactly what you want." Given the state of search technology today, that's a far-reaching vision requiring research, development and innovation to realize. Google is committed to blazing that trail

Ok, it is visionary. Even with Google's significant contribution we are still a long way from the perfect search. Craig Silverstein, Google's head of technology thinks it could be two, or even three hundred years before our computers can understand the real meaning of a query. But bear in mind that Google was developed at Stanford, in what looks from London to be the best school of artificial intelligence in the world, led by Professor John McCarthy.

In 2004 Brin and Page were made Fellows of the Marconi Foundation at Columbia University, New York. Sir Tim Berners-Lee, who won the same prize in 2002, said in a statement: "**Google held a mirror up to us, reflecting the myriad little actions of linking as a set of concepts which society has discussed and sought.**" The meanings generated have been relevant enough to save lives and to move the whole Internet forward. Now there's Glory for you.

Footnotes

1: Form S-1
As filed with the Securities and Exchange Commission on April 29, 2004
2: An Owner's Manual For Google's Shareholders
Copyright 2004 Fran Finnegan & Company All Rights Reserved. www.secinfo.com - Mon, 2 Aug 2004
3: Cassini-Huygens Mission to Saturn and Titan
NASA Jet Propulsion Laboratory, California Institute of Technology Curator: Alice Wessen Webmaster: Lori Sears JPL Clearance:CL02-2452
4: Cassini Interplanetry Trajectory
NASA Jet Propulsion Laboratory, California Institute of Technology Curator: Alice Wessen Webmaster: Lori Sears JPL Clearance:CL02-2452
5: Burning Chrome
By William Gibson 1996-2004, Amazon.com, Inc. or its affiliates

2

Is Google a good investment?

Seriously sensible support

In August the world's largest mutual fund, Boston-based Fidelity, bought an estimated 26.6% of Google's A-shares for $549 million. Fidelity are regarded as conservative but with one of the best research teams going. Similarly, the really smart money - the venture capital companies that helped the company set up six years ago, were not selling much if any of their stake after the IPO. That is a significant vote of confidence in Google's technological leadership since 1997 and business acumen since 2000.

If buying shares in Google as a long-term investment is a good idea, and has done much better than expected in the short-term, the mid-term could be troubled. Although Google's IPO priced its shares at only about two-thirds of Yahoo!'s value, Yahoo! itself and the whole Internet sector looks historically over-valued. If there is a severe correction, then Google's share price will suffer, too.

Strangling speculation

Gambling runs deep in human nature, and it may be inevitable that people will attempt to speculate on future technology. If this book has an entirely negative view of speculation it is because speculation in the dot.coms killed off some very good companies, as well as some very bad ones, and put the whole industry into a severe recession. A few individuals benefitted from inflated sale values, but there was no other positive fallout.

The fact that Microsoft avoided speculation, and others such as RedHat, Amazon and Yahoo! managed to survive insane gambling on their share prices, was down to an essential core integrity, good management and the underlying value of their products. Mark Twain pointed out during the Silver Rush in Nevada in the 1860s that speculation and long-term success do not mix [1]:

"You must remember this"

Stocks went on rising; speculation went mad; bankers, merchants, lawyers, doctors, mechanics, laborers, even the very washerwomen and servant girls, were putting up their earnings on silver stocks, and every sun that rose in the morning went down on paupers enriched and rich men beggared. What a gambling carnival it was! Gould and Curry soared to six thousand three hundred dollars a foot! And then --all of a sudden, out went the bottom and everything and everybody went to ruin and destruction! The wreck was complete.

The bubble scarcely left a microscopic moisture behind it. I was an early beggar and a thorough one. My hoarded stocks were not worth the paper they were printed on. I threw them all away. I, the cheerful idiot that had been squandering money like water, and thought myself beyond the reach of misfortune, had not now as much as fifty dollars when I gathered together my various debts and paid them.

Diverting the river of gold

But Sam Clemens does point out that the wealth of Gould and Curry's Comstock mine was quite real, it was the speculative wildcats that it inspired which were valueless. The equivalent of Comstock today is contextual Internet advertising. The repercussions of using context to target advertising and move it away from print publishing and towards contextual search on the Internet will fundamentally change the future of both industries. We are also only at the beginning of what can be done with context mapping.

Until very recently, almost all the publishing on the Internet has had a parasitic relationship with older media in that it takes income generated from other areas of publishing without generating any profits itself or doing much more than promoting the parent brand. For msn.com it was not publishing that kept it going for almost a decade of good service and heavy losses, but the profits from Microsoft's Windows division.

That is about to change forever as the river of gold that is classified advertising is increasingly diverted away from print media and onto the Internet, where it can sell product more cheaply and more efficiently. But all that hinges on the current and future development of the technology of context and Google now has far more experience of that technology than even its closest competitors. That should enable it to stay out front.

The competition

Google's main market is in intelligent indexing and contextual advertising. They have no monopoly, and have never appeared to seek one, but they do have a big lead in the quality of their engineering, in a field which has no choice but to expand, as the public demand is currently growing exponentially. Google's main competitors: Yahoo! and Microsoft, are probably the best weathermen. Both have been investing squillions of dollars in catching up with Google. Both have some way to go.

Companies with a proven capability like AskJeeves are also worth watching, as is Baidu, where Google has joined a seven member consortium investing, terms unknown, in the Chinese baby giant. The global demand for Internet indexing (and contextual advertising) is enormous, but the supply of reliable technology is a trickle. China apart, this flow is not likely to increase by much because frankly, this is not 1997 and entry into the market for global Internet Search is too difficult and expensive for start-ups.

Yahoo! AND Microsoft

Yahoo!'s watchword is consolidation and they have characteristically bought almost every other established Internet search company, spending an estimated $2 billion by the summer of 2003, according to Michael S. Malone [2] in *ABCNEWS.com*.

> Last December the company bought Inktomi for $235 million. This week, it announced its purchase of Overture Services, a company that itself has been on a buying spree, having picked up search companies Fast Search & Transfer and the venerable AltaVista in the last eight months. Thus, with this week's acquisition announcement, Yahoo! effectively buys four of the major players in its market.

Google and the Mission

The resulting product looks quite strong but will not win any prizes for innovation. Microsoft went the opposite way and took the strategically courageous decision of rebuilding the entire Windows operating system in order to try to integrate Search on both the Windows desktop and the Internet around a relational database.

By Fall 2004, it was clear this was too ambitious, Longhorn's crucial WinFS filing system has been put off. Modules from Longhorn itself - presentation and some search functions - will be incorporated into Microsoft's current systems. An effective email search has also been bought in from another company.

A big loss of face, if only because Google promptly (October 15, 2004) released a free desktop search. Microsoft employees went public with "They kicked our asses" complaints on the Internet and that will probably make Microsoft even more determined to succeed in the long term.

Yahoo! and Microsoft both understand the Internet market, and both take Google seriously enough to bet the farm, or at least the huge proportion of their strategic investment, on the future value of competing systems. As Brin put it in the interview [3] with Danny Sullivan:

"The whole industry is a little bit crazy right now. I personally prefer the previous generation, when we could go about building our search technology. But we are where we are. Unfortunately, there are companies out there with trigger fingers. There will be integration challenges for all of these companies."

Or will they do a Netscape?

And this is where the comparison with Netscape starts to cut in. If Microsoft and Yahoo! are apparently investing enough to cream you, then surely the happy dream of world-beating but ethical technology will have to end? A strong brand does not make you invulnerable or even safe, as Netscape proved.

The comparison between Google and Netscape was made as soon as an IPO was promised. It was actually a very bad comparison, but with Google's finances and strategic planning remaining an intra-company secret, it looked fair enough. In fact, Google is as dissimilar from what Netscape was, as any big Internet company could be. That's quite deliberate. Google's strategic priorities have always been the opposite of Netscape's, which were to grab market share with free product and half-finished engineering and keep their stockholders happy with temporarily ramped-up share values.

Google will never be another Netscape. After all the hype, their engineering is simply in a different class. The most obvious apparent difference is how well Google's software actually works. Their engineering reliability is remarkable and their last partial system crash was three years ago. Sadly the bigger they become, the more vulnerable they are to hack attacks, and they were taken out for some hours in June 2004, along with Yahoo! and msn.com and again by a new strain of the MyDoom-0 virus in late July 2004.

"Keeping Eric out of jail"

Being compared to Netscape made Google's founders take a very long, cold and sober look at the financial engineering of Netscape's IPO, which had spawned a swarm of even worse IPOs during the dot.com bubble and subsequent bankruptcies. Yahoo! itself had looked like a certain bankruptcy candidate in 2001.

Faced with this threat, the founders kept their sense of humor: meetings about the business launch of the IPO were codenamed "Keep Eric out of jail", according to Fred Vogelstein. (As the CEO, Eric Schmidt would become the prime subject to any post-Enron scrutiny by the Feds.)

Sergey told Esther Dyson - reported on Jeremy Allaire's personal Radio Blog [4] - and using the same word as Bill Gates had nearly 20 years earlier, that:

"an IPO is a 'distraction'... public markets are too short-term focused and he wants his team focused on the long-run. Whatever the case, he admits that ultimately their employees and investors want liquidity and that will have to happen through an IPO or acquisition of Google".

The Driver and the Grease

Although Microsoft's IPO was a huge success, more than two decades ago, it was never part of Bill's master plan for world domination, according to the rather splendid description in Mike O'Sullivan's [5] *Corporate Law Blog:*

'Bill Gates was reluctant to have Microsoft go public -- as reported in *Fortune*, he worried that it would be a 'pain',

"The whole process looked like a pain," [Gates] recalls, "and an ongoing pain once you're public. People get confused because the stock price doesn't reflect your financial performance. And to have a stock trader call up the chief executive and ask him questions is uneconomic -- the ball bearings shouldn't be asking the driver about the grease."

However, Microsoft had granted so many stock options to so many employees that it feared that by 1987 it would have 500 stockholders and be forced to register under Section 12 of the Exchange Act. Rather than let that happen to it, Microsoft decided to call its own shots and go public when and how it wanted.

Microsoft's position at the cutting-edge of the brand new and volatile personal computing business and its rich IPO price of almost 20 times expected earnings made it a high risk IPO. As a result, *Fortune* reported:

One of Microsoft's high priorities was making its prospectus "jury proof" -- so carefully phrased that no stockholder could hope to win a lawsuit by claiming he had been misled. . . . Steven Ballmer, 30, a vice president sometimes described as Gates's alter ego, came up with so many scenarios for Microsoft's demise that one banker cracked: "I'd hate to hear you on a bad day."

After a prospectus drafting process one banker likened to the Bataan death march, with Microsoft actually being more "conservative and pessimistic" than its underwriters, Microsoft produced a jury-proofed prospectus containing just seven risk factors...

Far from being scared away by these risk factors, investors clamoured to buy Microsoft's IPO shares. Microsoft's road show went so well it raised its pricing range from $16 to $19 to $20 to $22. The IPO ended up pricing at $21, opening at $25.75 and closing at $27.75. Pretty heady stuff in the pre-dot-com-bubble days.

Gates, far from being exultant, fretted that the successful IPO would harm Microsoft. As reported by *Fortune*:

In the wake of Microsoft's triumph, Gates still fears that being public will hurt the company. No longer able to offer stock at bargain prices, he finds it harder to lure talented programmers and managers aboard. . . . Constantly urging people to ignore the price of Microsoft's stock, he warns that it may become highly volatile. A few weeks after the offering, strolling through the software development area, he noticed a chart of Microsoft's stock price posted on the door to a programmer's office. Gates was bothered. "Is this a distraction?" he asked.

Money porn

Somehow, Microsoft managed to deal with these distractions over the next 17 years." Mike O'Sullivan adds: '...It's impossible to review the Microsoft IPO without wallowing in money porn. If you bought one share at the $21.00 IPO price, today you'd have 288 shares worth $8,208. Collectively, the shares sold in Microsoft's IPO cost investors $58.7 million and, even at today's drastically reduced post-bubble prices, are worth $22.9 billion."

The potentially disastrous impact of IPO speculation on Google led to the creation of the Dutch Auction, the insistence on honest quarterly reports, and the refusal to pay dividends. All serve to make it very difficult to beat the market's consensus of Google's value, by selling short or long by speculating over blips in the price.

Dutch Auction

This is inherently complex, but one of the best simple explanations is from Shannon Buggs [6] in the *Houston Chronicle*, May 2004:

Known as a Dutch auction, the sales strategy gets its name from the days when it was used in the Netherlands to sell tulip bulbs in flower markets.

In a classic version, a seller says how many identical items are for sale and sets a bid price. Buyers say how many they want and at what price. The seller sets the price at which all the items can be sold, the market clearing price.

Everyone who bids above the clearing price may buy as many of the items as they bid on at the new price. Those who bid at the clearing price divide what's left. Those who bid below the clearing price get nothing.

That contrasts with traditional IPOs, where the shares are sold at a set price that's often much lower than what the shares go for on the first day of trading.

That difference in the two values gave IPOs the pop that in the 1990s made them a get-rich-quick strategy for Internet company executives and the lucky few investors who got the deals.

Google's founders want to lessen the incentive to flip its shares in the first few trading days.

In the Dutch-style auction, the company says it may sell shares for less than the clearing price and intends to set the per-share price high enough for winning bidders to get at least 80 percent of the shares they request.

Google also says it may limit the number of shares or percentage of an order any investor could buy to prevent bidders from placing extra high bids as a way to guarantee they get shares.

The upside to this unusual method of selling an IPO is that the small investor can compete for shares with big institutional investors and wealthy individuals.

Automatic - for the people

Like eBay and Amazon, Google use the consensus on value reached by the Web's users to create a better kind of service. Google's indexing and contextual advertising gives traders a better reason to use the net than print or tv, and assists the creation of public trust in the proven integrity of these services. Although often linked in the public's mind, Google and eBay have developed without needing the huge capital resources required by Amazon's physical storage and distribution system.

In their IPO, Google have moved their technology of relevance based on consensus closer to eBay's elegant model of the monetary value of assets being based on the consensus of those most interested in buying them. (In the UK, this new way of valuing assets efficiently, famously led to a student auctioning her virginity on eBay to finance her studies. This is now proscribed.)

Because of their very short commercial history, valuing Google's shares is extremely difficult, and Google themselves took their initial price range of $108 to $135 from a contextual index of all submissions. Gamers were excluded to prevent an over-valuation after sale followed by profit-taking. The plan was for there to be no real difference between the price posted for the auction and subsequent sales, because the posted price should represent a consensus of what everybody (who is seriously interested enough to invest money) believed it to be worth.

It worked, although a rip tide of negative publicity as described [7] by Jim Juback for moneycentral msn.com - **Why Wall Street wants Google to fail** - forced the shares down 20% before the first couple of days sale. It was nasty, but it did serve to prevent retail investors from doing a dot.com and over-valuing and over-investing without knowing what they were getting into, - a real worry before the IPO.

Google's income is split roughly 70% from US and 30% from international sales. Of that, at least 90% of income is advertising based. Growth like theirs is almost impossible to maintain, but there are too many variables in the competitive environment, and the company is too young, to say when we should expect growth to normalize. Couple of years probably.

North Americans aiming to bid for shares had to take advice from a qualified financial adviser, as the SEC filing insisted, but everybody, including the experts, was still guessing.

Google said that it generated revenues of $961.9 million in 2003 and reported a nett profit of $106.5 million. Sales rose 177 percent from a year ago although earnings increased by just 6 percent.

For the first quarter of 2004, Google reported sales of $389.6 million, an increase of 118 percent from a year ago. Net income was $64 million, up 148 percent from the first quarter of 2003. (Figures from CNNMoney [8])

The plan was that any silly behavior when the shares went on open sale days would have been bumped out statistically. This was not completely successful, but pretty good by recent standards. No wonder the banks were angry. Their influence with a media primed to look for disaster was much greater than Google's and one weekend saw just about every newspaper in the world declare that

Google's IPO would have to be postponed or cancelled because of infringements of SEC rules (mainly *Playboy* again). Nothing of the sort, of course, but it had the required effect on the initial selling price.

The subsequent jump of 18% in Google's share values on the first day and 40% over three weeks had probably not been part of the plan, but by comparison with Netscape's IPO, it fell into an acceptable margin of error. When Netscape launched its IPO in August 1995 things had quickly got very foolish according to Peter van der Linden's description [9] in his classic *Just Java*.

> "...investors could not buy (Netscape) fast enough. On the opening day demand was so high that the stock price doubled and doubled again. And kept on rising. This is almost unprecedented in the capital markets."

Gross != Nett

As a benchmark, Microsoft's IPO set their value at 20 times earnings. This was then regarded as nosebleed heights, because 14 is about the historical average. According to the Shawn McCarthy [10] of Toronto's *Globe and Mail*:

> eBay was trading (May 2004) at roughly 18 times expected revenue per share for 2004, while Yahoo! was trading at 13 times revenue. A similar valuation for Google would yield a market capitalization of about $12-billion to $14-billion -- comparable with the two more established companies.

The crunch comes with the difference between earnings and revenue, effectively nett and gross. In January 2004 Paul R. La Monica [11] of *CNNmoney* asked:

> If an Internet stock is ludicrously overvalued but nobody seems to care, will its stock keep going up?
>
> In the case of Yahoo!, the answer seems to be yes.
>
> Yahoo! surged 175 percent in 2003 and on Tuesday the stock briefly crossed the $50 barrier for the first time since November 2000. Shares now trade at 90 times 2004 earnings estimates.

By mid 2004, this had risen past 100, so heaven alone knows whether Yahoo! will continue to ignore the laws of market gravity.

It is certainly *possible* that IT technology companies will continue to command a much higher valuation than less sexy industries. The price of a barrel of oil is, as they say in Houston and Aberdeen, whatever people are prepared to pay for it, and the same could hold good for pure-play Internet companies that have demonstrated not only that they can create, but also that they can maintain, a global brand. One of the lies of the dot.com era was that this is easy from start-up. It ain't.

Pensioner(s) demand dividends

As always, the engineering model never quite fits the social reality. My mother (who as a Canadian citizen might have been entitled to bid for shares under the provisions of NAFTA - the North American Free Trade Agreement) wants to point out to Google that dividends are a significant part of her pension.

Whilst she supports the long-term investment strategy, she wonders whether Google would consider paying dividends to individual investors who are prepared to verify that they may not be around long enough to benefit personally from it? This could be a nuisance for Google to implement, but maybe not particularly difficult.

When demand exceeds supply

But does all this ambition to reform their not particularly small corner of modern capitalism, by taking out speculation and democratizing share ownership, make them a bad buy? A lot of sober bankers and commentators thought so, and if you read the SEC filings you can see why. Apart from minimizing the role of the financiers, they appear to be breaking the fundamental rule of Maximizing income as quickly as possible. Managing rapid growth is also notoriously difficult.

Everything depends on the timescale. Investing in Google could be like investing in the London property market. Those looking for short term gains almost invariably get burned. Those in for the long haul get one of the best legal returns on their money going, because the physical reality, in London's case for hundreds of years, is that demand always exceeds supply. Similarly, the near-universal need

Google and the Mission

to track information enormously exceeds the available technology that can do it. That's why Gates takes it quite so seriously as a challenge.

Google is not Gore-Tex, where the rain-wear fabric could be entirely protected by patents for decades. Cybernetic ideas can always be reversed engineered in principle, but if the business plan is strategically sound and the engineering quality is as good as it can be, then its future is no more threatened than any other market leader in a global economy where India and China are finally beginning to see the possibility of a level playing field.

Standard & Poor produced a report in early June 2004 which suggested that Google's market would atrophy as Internet Search became "commoditised". Well, when adding contextual search to a web site costs $30, then it will have been "commoditised" and the current Search market will be close to saturated. Currently it costs closer to $[50,000]. Go figure if that's a commodity where you come from, and why there is no quick fix for Microsoft to add contextual search to Windows without a complete rebuild of the core architecture of Longhorn. The cost of this is unknown but must be huge.

Back to the Old Skool

Once expansion made an IPO inevitable for Google, they needed to know why dot.coms like Netscape had gone out of control, and how twenty years earlier, Gates and Ballmer had retained control over Microsoft after its IPO. Different as they are, Google and Microsoft do share a couple of features, as Bill has pointed out, particularly in that their early success has made both companies more, rather than less, hungry.

In business terms, Google are certainly being radical, but this really signals a return to much older American values. Time was when an IPO was only used to raise additional funds for expansion, and that really remains its proper purpose. Microsoft was the first company forced into an IPO by the need to offer more stock options to employees than private companies are allowed by the SEC. (SAS is one of the very few software companies that still does not and it costs them a much higher benefits and wages package.)

Twenty years later, Google was faced with the same obligation and the same threat to the management of the company. They have responded by copying Microsoft's IPO very closely, and taking huge pains to avoid doing what Netscape did.

This is a return (garage-startup and all) to the great traditions of Hewlett and Packard, Moore and Grove at Intel, the two Steves at Apple, Warnock and Geschke at Adobe, Gates and Ballmer at Microsoft. Some of these companies were, and are, more ruthless towards their competition than others, but all have had a peculiarly American blend of visionary ideas, great engineering, personal leadership and a long-term commitment to the value of their products and the value of their companies. And almost all of them are thirty years old or more. Although Microsoft itself was barely affected, its IPO and subsequent trajectory had been so successful that IT became something for financiers, and ultimately everybody else, except Warren Buffet, to speculate on.

The truth behind the dot.con

Like all great lies, the great dot.com con had a kernel of truth. It was true that at some point a lot of traditional commerce would switch to using the Internet, when and if it was able to provide value more efficiently. The lie, repeated endlessly without checking ('I want to believe', indeed) was that the necessary technical infrastructure was in place for it to happen immediately. People like Henry Blodgett were paid to prime the pump not to check the water table.

Watching the banks then all but destroy the IT industry during the dot.com boom was like watching the breakup of the former USSR. No question that capitalism has beaten communism - centrally-directed economies simply cannot efficiently deliver the consumer products that people want - but that should not have to mean that cheats and thieves are allowed to take charge.

With a blind auction, Google are doing the exact opposite of what the oligarchs did in Russia. Both Sergey Brin and Roman Abramovich (who owns Chelsea football club and is now richer than the Queen of England) are Russian jews and near-contemporaries. While Roman hoovered up shares, quite legally, which had been distributed to the workers of the newly-privatized Russian oil industry, Google is distributing its shares to ordinary people as widely as possible (which legally means North America only) and insisting on informed consent. (Places like Singapore, with a highly-educated population, are now very interested by the auction IPO concept.)

Google and the Mission

Breakpoint

The critical moment, for the long-term prospects of the company, was bringing in Eric Schmidt as a third partner. Although they had once considered selling Google to Yahoo! for a million or so and then going on to other things, like finishing their Ph.Ds at Stanford, the inclusion of Eric with his distinguished management career at Sun and Novell showed that the founders were now serious about winning any business war.

Their relations with Eric are such that there is currently no chance of them retreating into figurehead positions and becoming Google's greatest living ancestors. Nor are they likely to find, like Steve Jobs at Apple in the eighties, that the CEO they appointed is being used to oust them.

After Sun and Novell, Google's CEO has had plenty of direct experience of Microsoft, who have made corporate ruthlessness into an art form. Ever since Stac [12] won their patent suit against Microsoft but lost their business, the conventional wisdom has been that if Microsoft moves in, then your only option is to sell up and move out. Netscape was disembowelled in public, but Microsoft had already done the same to CP/M, Lotus 1-2-3, WordPerfect and OS/2, and a number of others.

Microsoft itself has a much more serious problem than Google, whose threat is clear and visible; what Microsoft really fear is the Open Source attack below their waterline, out of sight of many journalists and the public, and described in the next chapter.

The comparison with Netscape was probably most useful for focussing Google's management triumvirate on their imminent danger, but it was otherwise misleading. Netscape was set up to crush the leading Internet browser, Mosaic, which was relatively easy. It then announced that it would take control of the desktop from Windows. The reality was that Netscape had laughable profits and only a couple of products, browsers and servers. The servers did not survive, and the engineering of the browsers was truly dreadful, created in haste and repented at leisure by millions of users, who swapped to Explorer without a backward glance.

Engineering assets

Unlike Netscape, Google have never tried to take over anybody's else's market, although producing a better technology did for poor

AltaVista and pretty much all the other search engines which preceded their launch (except Inktomi, maybe). Because their engineering is probably the best in the world, and they have such a strong brand, their profit strategy has already been spectacularly successful in the short term, and with the Beta of Gmail they have demonstrated a potentially huge and relatively stable userbase for innovative products.

That is worth a very great deal of any media company's money. The excitement is in (and most of this book is concerned with) the ideas that have made Google such an enviable success story, but ideas are fluid and, in this field at least, turbulent. The real investment in lasting value is in the level of engineering which the whole Google team have shown themselves capable of. High and holding, on the Edisonian principle of 1% inspiration and 99% perspiration.

That means that even if, let us say, Microsoft cracks it and starts to compete effectively in Internet search, Google's physical engineering assets are still going to be worth mega to its competitors and thence its own shareholders. This puts them in sharp contrast to most of the dot.coms, who were reminiscent of one of sf writer's Stephen Baxter's creations, the Qax, an alien mud whose complex turbulence has created sentience - consciousness and intelligence, but whose transient nature means it is only interested in one thing - short term profit (and like Internet portals, the Qax can only trade by proxy).

Things went very differently for Netscape, because once they had lost the market initiative, they did not really have any assets except a badly-engineered bit of free software which their owners, AOL, never used, preferring - like everybody else - to use Microsoft's Explorer.

Permission requested from Dilbert.com

Google and the Mission

Of all the crazy corporate decisions taken during the dot.boom, one of the most bizarre has to be the decision of the then AOL and Time Warner to spend a fortune buying Netscape and then to give their captive market of AOL subscribers the continued use of MS Explorer instead of Netscape.

Some fear, but mainly loathing

Gates's loathing of Netscape was very different from his attitude towards Google, which he clearly likes and respects. This will not stop Microsoft competing and if Google stumble, they will get trampled on, but that's purely business, nothing personal.

Netscape was personal, if only because they tried to replace Microsoft with hype, speculation and a badly-made product that nobody ever paid for. (The main advantage of Netscape was that they showed how much better Microsoft could be.)

Of course Gates was angry. By his mentor Warren Buffet's standards, companies like Netscape had no integrity whatsoever, because in the classic definition of a bubble company, their only real customers were their own stockholders.

There may be an inverse proportion law of IPOs: the more important the IPO in a new company's strategy, the less chance they have of surviving or making shareholders any profit. The real difference between Google and Netscape is the quality of technology, engineering and revenue generation. The similarity is the tremendous growth velocity of both which the infrastructure of universal personal computing and the Internet have made possible.

Selling the hype

Netscape ushered in the dot.com boom by divorcing its IPO from actual revenues. By the end of the boom, companies were being brought into existence with no purpose other than to try to cash in on an IPO. The belief that the business only needed to appear to work in order to be sold at a vast profit seemed characteristic of many of the dot.coms.

Permission requested from Doonesbury.com

Netscape made two mistakes, they inflated a badly-built, but free and timely product, the Netscape 1 browser, with an absurd valuation on Wall Street and then announced that they, in the personable shape of chief executive Marc Andreessen, were about to become the next Microsoft, so buy now while stocks last...

Bad mistake, guys. Fatal, as it goes. The ceiling must have melted [12] when Gates was reading those interviews with Andreessen. Big money showing disrespect to Microsoft's achievements and Gate's leadership? By giving away product? By having no sales and no profits? Planet Capitalism calling? "**Intelligent life? Sorry sir, no sign of it**", as Eminem observed. A contemporary logo for Netscape Navigator is alive with St Elmo's fire, fairy lights and fairy dust that lighted fools the way...

Mister Gates was forced to invest millions providing a better browser than Netscape - MS Explorer, and then giving it away to Windows and Mac users. No wonder he was miffed and introduced Netscape and its investors to a few of the capitalist realities he had grasped in high school. Hard to blame him when you read the appalling guff that was written about Netscape in its early days:

Try this on Dilbert

"You do it in a different way and a different time -- you do it in Netscape Time", according to FastCompany [13].

> Netscape Time is only partly about speed, although it is most certainly about that. It's also a genetic endowment, an operating system cooked into the DNA of hungry young programmers going about their work. It is as much a mind-set as a business model. Part paranoid, part predator, it shapes everything Netscape does. It's hardwired into how a company in overdrive -- a company

whose headcount, in 15 months, has gone from 2 to 330 with little sign of slowing down -- recruits and evaluates talent. It shapes its uniquely interactive relationship with customers. And it explains its co-evolutionary relationship with the technology itself -- how Netscape uses the Web to win control of the Web.

In this bifurcated economy, where tired, sclerotic organizations struggle against long odds to cross the gap between those who get it and those who don't, Netscape Time is the defining birthright of a company born on the right side of the Great Divide. Indeed, in an economy where even breakthrough technologies become obsolete within a few years, where even the deadliest competitors must change their game in the face of changing circumstances, Netscape Time may be the company's most enduring invention.

Well, they nearly got that last bit right, but really what they left behind was Yahoo!, whom they helped establish, the Open Directory Project, which Netscape also initially hosted, and the Open Source Mozilla Firefox browser which started to make an impact in 2004. The industry joke, which may be true, is that Netscape founder Jim Clark is now selling condominiums in Florida.

Google's symbiotic relationship with Stanford contrasts well with Netscape's predatory relationship with the University of Illinois, National Center for Supercomputing Applications, where all the initial, and conceptually most difficult, development work was done on the Mosaic browser.

> "Soon after they created their company, Clark and Andreessen had assembled ten programmers, nearly all of them in their twenties, six of them friends of Andreessen from college. To these young programmers, Clark and Andreessen presented a life-or-death challenge: obliterate (NCSA's) Mosaic, the very product that brought the two founders together in the first place."

Netscape was never particularly innovative; most of the ideas even in Netscape 1 had already been successfully developed at the University of Illinois by 1994. It gained total market dominance because the public was well ready for it, and although it was licensed up to 1998, I have never met anyone who ever actually paid for it, so it was, effectively, a stand-alone free product. They also sold some servers.

Netscape's legacy

Netscape's IPO was determined by greed rather than sense, or even brand loyalty. Like most free products, Netscape was remarkably shoddy, it included what may be the worst programming (scripting) language ever conceived: JavaScript - where the test for 'true' is 'not equal to minus one'.

While this probably made perfect sense at 3am during those crazy, young, mad, happy days of early development - it is, trust me on this - utter baloney in terms of logic. (Sorry to sound bitter but I was one of the Dilberts who spent all those millions of work hours trying to get Netscape to show HTML consistently, or, for the real masochists, programming Netscape in JavaScript.)

JavaScript is HTML's dark, occult twin. (Occult, because no properly trained developer ever wants to dirty their hands with its wretched syntax deviations, when they could be working in a nice clean, utterly consistent language like Java, which shares the name - nothing else.) JavaScript, the remnant of Netscape's fast-forward dreams, is such a mess that few but Australians and Kiwis, who like extreme sports, seem to fully master it (apart from Danny Goodman and Michael Morrison, who wrote the *Javascript Bible*) so Google have good reason to be wary of it. Microsoft's jScript is not much better, but that's not really their fault; Explorer had to be broadly compatible with Netscape, so they had no choice at the time.

Once Gates was on the case, Explorer became a much more robust alternative, and the public, a fickle beast as any pop star will tell you, forgot any loyalties they may ever have had to Netscape and moved en masse to Explorer.

The tiger's smile

Netscape's development centre was closed down in December 2003, with the bitter-almonds smelling suggestion from Time Warner that they might name an ISP after it. Time Warner's new wave of top executives did not simply dislike AOL's fancy financial footwork with Netscape, they clearly loathed it. They were brought up to sell honest media properties, in film and print, not the nonsense the company had got talked into - ultimately, that $100 billion write down.

That was a lot of false promises from former wonder-boys like AOL's Steve Case. Microsoft paid $750 million to settle the suit for un-competitive practices brought on behalf of Netscape and will continue to license Explorer to AOL for the foreseeable future.

Andreessen himself never makes comments about Microsoft any more. They are an important client of his current venture Opsware Inc. [14] (formerly known as Loudcloud Inc.) which is a provider of data centre automation software with headquarters in Sunnyvale "running 10,000 servers, probably 5,000 of those are Microsoft servers". With the smile on the face of the tiger.

Permission requested from Doonesbury.com

Much more like Adobe

As well as Netscape, Google are also compared with Yahoo!, who have already succeeded in competing directly against Microsoft's msn.com. Their origins at Stanford were similar, but there the resemblance stops. In 2001, as Google was beginning to see the first fruits of contextual advertising, Yahoo! went into meltdown on its trading results, and its shares had to be suspended. But as Mike S. Malone reports (in the article quoted above):

> And yet, in a miracle of good management, good marketing and good products, Yahoo! has not only come back, but these days it is one of the most exciting companies in American industry.

Yahoo!'s resurrection has been remarkable, and some observers are hoping that CEO Terry Semel will be able to work the same magic on his previous company, Disney. But rather than the Yahoo! phoenix, a better comparison is with Adobe.

Like Google, Adobe was started by a couple of brilliant research engineers (from the legendary Xerox Menlo PARC) who stayed in charge of a company which has earned such strategic power that they have maintained a healthy relationship with Microsoft, seen off the competition (including Microsoft) and currently seem to have finally lost patience with Apple whose video software benefits from access to the core operating system. But unlike Google, Adobe are not a pure play Internet company; instead they have made the difficult transition, like Microsoft and Apple, of incorporating the Internet into their software, rather than the other way round.

The comparison with Yahoo! must have left Google's founders feeling distinctly jumpy. Google's relationship with Yahoo! is complex and unstable; within a year they have moved from close partnership to close competition and then legal action through Overture, whose settlement cost them a quarter's profits in shares paid to Yahoo!. When Google was developing, Yahoo! helped and hosted, much as Netscape had done for them. "They were really kind to us", Larry Page remembered (rather wistfully, it sounds like).

Disposable heroes of the Webocracy

The real problem with becoming like Yahoo! for Brin and Page was that Yahoo!'s founders appear to have been quietly sidelined by the company years ago. Another Stanford graduate with a lot of experience, Tim Koogle, had become CEO to the unanimous applause of Wall Street who did not want Yahoo!'s profitability to be compromised by its founders' lack of business experience. If founders Filo and Yang minded, they did not make it public.

As Bambi Franciso pointed out in the first chapter: Yahoo! then received a $600 a share price target back in January 2000, before reality set in and Koogle and most of the senior managers were purged. Filo and Yang now appear, rarely, at Yahoo! presentations.

According to a regulatory filing in May 29, 2004, Yahoo! co-founder Jerry Yang planned to sell 8 million company shares, worth $245 million, over the next year. Yang also used blind trusts to sell 3 million Yahoo! shares in 2002 and another 3 million company shares in 2003. (Those sales were made before the company's two-for-one stock split in May.) These sales are regarded as nothing more sinister than a routine release of liquidity, but as part of their due diligence responsibilities, Yang's blind trust will doubtless have had to consider participating in Google's IPO auction.

This is not the future that Brin and Page have chosen for themselves. People tend to say: "Why don't they just take the money and retire?" Because it is not in their nature. As Gibson's Molly Kolodny has it, "If you are really good at what you do, that's what you *are*, right? You gotta jack, I gotta tussle". You have little or no choice, when you are that good and care that much about your own work. Initially their music was the technology of Internet search, but after profits became an issue in Y2k, it became the business as a whole and a big chunk of the future direction of the Internet itself.

The more money...

Late in 2003, when an IPO looked inevitable, "*Fortune* magazine conducted more than two dozen interviews with employees, investors, business partners, and people exploring employment or business deals with Google, along with veterans of the search, online advertising, and computer business - and what it found was a talented company facing trouble.

"(Google) has grown so fast that employees and business partners are often confused about who does what," reports *Fortune* writer Fred Vogelstein [17]. Stock- and option-stoked greed is creating rifts within the company, and heated questions continue about whom is really in charge: CEO Eric Schmidt or co-founders Brin and Page.

As one CEO puts it, "My take is that they are crumbling under the weight of their own success." Says an investor, "Google has a lot of momentum, but its current position is probably not defensible."

The bottom line? Google's numbers are strong and revenues continue to soar. But with competitors gearing up for a search-engine battle and turmoil within, Google could be worth much less by the time investors in the IPO are able to cash out."

Some of the tension between temporary contractors and full-time staff, which Fred Vogelstein described, may look rather worse than it really is. Fred Moody's book: *I Sing the Body Electronic* [16]: A Year With Microsoft on the Multimedia Frontier, describes very similar problems within the Microsoft team working on the children's version of Encarta - contractors treading water and complaining bitterly once they realize they are not in line for full-time jobs and stock options, confused lines of command, unrealiztic deadlines, political feuding and continual reorganization.

Moody tells of two Microsoft managers who were so mad at each other that they had stopped talking, but still spent most of their days flaming (hostile emailing) each other from next-door offices. Accustomed to the relative stability and well-defined management of newspaper publishing, it looked almost absurdly chaotic and wasteful. Yet Microsoft itself has hardly suffered since. Gates would almost certainly regard this as a necessary price to keep Microsoft on its toes. Both Gates and Page regard complacency, rather than particular competitors, as the biggest threat to their creations.

SWOT

A brief Strengths, Weaknesses, Opportunities and Threats analysis suggests that Google's strengths are in its technological leadership of an extremely profitable field, the unusually high build-quality of its engineering and distribution systems, and a warm relationship between brand values and many millions of happy users in [86] languages.

Google's main weakness is that its commercial history is very short, and the future product chain necessary to justify its valuation cannot be developed overnight. This makes it more difficult to manage their rate of growth, and failure to manage growth has usually proved fatal for Internet companies, particularly when mistakes and slippage cause enormous changes in share values.

The big opportunity is contextual advertising, which will continue to expand exponentially for some time, to the benefit of possibly all the major and some more minor players, and at the cost of the equal and opposite contraction of the print publishing industry for magazines and newspaper. For Google this is an essential extension of the much more interesting problem of how information, despite its huge growth, can be specifically accessed more efficiently and more cheaply.

The main threat to Google comes from Microsoft and Yahoo!. Both are determined to reclaim market share and both have a formidable business record for getting what they want. Neither should ever be underestimated, but each has very different and quite fundamental problems, likely to make their offensives a lot less lethal, as the next chapter explains.

Google and the Mission

And will an IPO steal Google's soul?

When it looked as though their IPO would be postponed, the working title of this Chapter was: "Will an IPO steal Google's soul?". Companies do not have souls, of course, but corporations are treated legally as a single individual and they usually develop a personality to match that identity. **"The company has a high capacity to disappoint if it undercuts principles for profits,"** according to Danny Sullivan.

There is a Peanuts cartoon where Schroeder tells Charlie Brown that when he grows up he is going to be very famous, very rich and very successful, but is going to retain his humility, honesty and integrity. Beat - one frame, then **"Lots of luck"**, says Charlie Brown.

In **Google vs Evil** [17] : *Wired* magazine's Josh McHugh provides a perceptive review of all the problems, mistakes and compromises which global success had already brought by 2003. He also joshes that an NDA (non-disclosure agreement) is now required to get into Google's canteen.

Growing up and keeping schtum

Research, and the free exchange of ideas, is part of Google's soul, as it once was part of Apple's, but sadly, there is an irreconcilable difference between business research and academic research. It is a career imperative for scientists at university to publish as widely as possible, but scientists who work for business cannot usually publish much more than is necessary to apply for a patent. That now applies to Google.

So it goes, business and science have different objectives. One widely-circulated complaint in the Open Source community was that Google had 'ceased to be a Search company and become an ad-agency'. Which is true if you believe that *Time* magazine or the *Financial Times* are ad-agencies. They are certainly almost entirely dependent on advertising, but their value extends a long way beyond that. (The revenue from a magazine and newspaper's cover price is often relatively quite small, although many journalists prefer to believe otherwise because they do not like the idea of being beholden to advertisers or salespeople).

Commercial secrecy often has to be ruthless. After howls of pain followed changes to the search rankings in Google's late 2003 data 'dance' (system update), according to Kate Kaye's analysis [18] in mediapost.com:

> "Google has remained tight-lipped about the modifications it made in November (2003) and thereafter. A company spokesman was unable to comment specifically about Google's recent re-indexing updates, but did acknowledge that Google's goal is to improve the search experience for its users."

In business, you simply cannot afford to give your competitors, as well as everybody else, the fruits of your own expensive and hard-won research. Sony have made remarkable progress in a parallel field with their research-level Aibo robot dog, but they do not give away that research cost by making public many of their very significant science and engineering findings. The interest of the company and its stockholders has to come first and it is rarely to their advantage to let competitors and the wider world know very much about your technical plans.

The Intellectual Commons

That means that often most of the really significant progress on the Internet has come from the new intellectual commons created by academics who have donated their work into the public domain. Sir Tim Berners-Lee is the prime example, but he is not alone. Google are unusual because they are a commercial company that began with a belief that the publication of open standards was politically essential. They also continue to discuss publicly, if necessarily cautiously, some of their most important methods.

This has made it possible to write most of this book without resorting to educated guesswork, but it inevitably gives their competitors a significant advantage. As professors' sons, doubtless brought up to believe that scientific publication and subsequent peer acclaim is the highest achievement, the most difficult part of Google's path into industrial adulthood for the founders was probably the necessity for commercial secrecy.

56   *Is Google a good investment?*

Footnotes

1: **Roughing It**
By Mark Twain, Alan Eliasen for the Mark Twain Library
2: **Yahoo! Renewed**
By Michael S. Malone: Special to ABCNEWS.com Internet Ventures
July 17 2004
3: **Danny Sullivan interviews Sergey Brin**
By Greg Jarboe: Search Engine Watch Jupitermedia Corporation
October 16, 2003
4: **Interview with Sergey Brin, Google Co-Founder**
Jeremy Allaire's Radio 1/6/2004
5: **MS IPO: money porn**
By Mike O'Sullivan Corp Law Blog
6: **Google's populist IPO mixes upsides with pitfalls**
By Shannon Buggs: Houston Chronicle May 31, 2004
7: **Why Wall Street wants Google to fail**
By Jim Juback, moneycentral.msn.com, Microsoft 2004
8: **Google files for $2.7 billion IPO**
By Paul R. La Monica: CNNmoney Cable News Network April 29, 2004
9: **Just Java**
Peter van der Linden, Sunsoft Press, Prentice Hall 1996
10: **Investors frothing over massive Google IPO**
By Shawn Mccarthy: Toronto Globe and Mail, April 30, 2004
11: **Nothing compares to Yahoo!**
By Paul R. La Monica: CNNmoney January 13, 2004
12: **Internet Killed the Video Star,**
By Mark Cohn and Ken Martin, Atom Films, AtomShockwave Corp.
13: **Can You Work in Netscape Time?**
By Tom Steinert-Threlkeld: Gruner + Jahr November 1995
14: **OPSWARE INC. On the record: Marc Andreessen**
San Francisco Chronicle December 7, 2003
15: **Can Google Grow Up?**
By Fred Vogelstein: Fortune Time Inc Dec. 8, 2003
16: **I Sing the Body Electronic: A Year With Microsoft on the Multimedia Frontier**
By Fred Moody, Amazon.com, Inc
17: **Google vs. Evil**
By Josh McHugh: Wired Digital, Inc. The Conde Nast Publications Inc. January 2003
18: **After Florida, Search Marketers Have More To Handle Than Hanging Chads**
By Kate Kaye: MediaPost Communications March 03, 2004

Electric Book

3

Could Microsoft (or Yahoo!) total Google?

And Ol' Captain Ahab
He ain't got nothin' on me.

Tom Waits

Unlikely

Unless Google lose their luck and the initiative, the scenario is probably that 'they would if they could, but they can't so they won't'. Both Microsoft and Yahoo! have some significant structural limitations to overcome first.

Microsoft, after launching their own robot, or spider, to search the Internet (MSNBot), in 2003, still have a good way to go. Humiliatingly, they have had to postpone Longhorn, the next generation of Windows, having promised that it would have a new file structure that enabled integrated desktop and Internet Search.

Steve Ballmer was in full Gates' maxi-me mode when he suggested that Yahoo! had sacrificed their lead in Internet Search (quoted in the first chapter). Without their alliance with Google, terminated in early 2004, Yahoo! have never had a lead in Search. Their strength was in directory technology (which is very different and is described in a later chapter).

Yahoo!'s initial alliance with the Inktomi search spider, which predated Google, was markedly unsuccessful. It was their subsequent joint venture with Google that managed to combine Yahoo!'s own resources with Google's to provide probably the best Search then available.

This success story was terminated early in 2004 as Yahoo! moved to replace Google with acquired technology, including virtually all the other commercial Search engines except AskJeeves and Teoma. These acquisitions included the Norwegian FAST (aka All the Web) and Inktomi, which Yahoo! have combined with Overture's Paid Inclusion program.

Google and the Mission

Yahoo! - consolidation not innovation

Yahoo!'s current strategy appears technically sound and commercially successful. Early reports suggested that while Google's share of tech and business queries is growing significantly, Yahoo! are increasingly used by consumers, presumably people already using other facilities on the Yahoo! site.

Yahoo! is continuing to consolidate and build on its strengths, particularly localization around the user, but there appears to be so little other innovation going on there that it is hard to see a real challenge emerging. This challenge could actually have come from Microsoft's traditional rival, Apple, which back in 1998 introduced Sherlock as: 'a search engine that works as well on your local hard drive, a server volume, or the internet itself' a phrase which Gates would love to be able to use about Windows/Longhorn six years later. Not all IT business moves at the speed of thought.

Sherlock works on Apples by kicking in at midnight to index the hard disc. This was impressive six years ago, but now looks distinctly shabby and is scheduled for a major update as Spotlight, but Windows has no equivalent so Sherlock could still probably give the Longhorn team some useful ideas.

Apple drops the ball

By Y2k, Apple aficionados often used Sherlock rather than Google to search the Internet. By mid-2004 the UK's *MacUser*'s review of OsX features found that: **'Sherlock has in most respects been supplanted by services such as Google...'**. Since its introduction, Sherlock has had very little subsequent investment, and has barely improved since it was introduced.

So how did Apple manage to drop the ball, when it was worth so much revenue to Google and so much subsequent investment for Microsoft? That's the point: Google did not succeed simply because of its technical brilliance, it was the fact that they saw the business value of using the context available from Open Search to generate targeted advertising, when nobody else had seen it.

For Apple, Search represented an activity that was very expensive in terms of its call on their best developers but contributed nothing to the bottom line; the same problem that had prevented Microsoft from investing. By 2004 Apple returned with a neglected Search technology that they had developed for the Copland operating system in the mid-Nineties. At the 2004 World Wide Developers Conference: thinksecret.com reported [1]:

> Jobs is showing off what he is calling a revolutionary feature for Tiger [the next version of Apple's OsX], a search feature called "Spotlight" which enables very fast searching of files and metadata through an interface similar to the current search box for Finder windows. Queries can be saved into "Smart Folders" that act like smart playlists in iTunes and auto-update. Address Book and Mail also have their own smart folders.
>
> ... The Spotlight technology can be integrated into third-party applications; Tiger will have a menubar search that searches applications systemwide. It shows matching files and emails, etc., and draws upon a full content index. It can also find text within [Adobe Acrobat] PDFs.

Microsoft loses the plot

Like the rest of the industry, Microsoft was obsessed with the sticky portal, the web site with a high enough circulation to make decent returns from generic advertising. At the time it looked like the only realiztic way of getting (some of) their Internet investment back. Internet Search appeared to be a really good way of losing money, and there were a dozen or more Search companies doing exactly that, having failed to see the significance of context mapping or the impact that it could have by creating targeted advertising.

Steve Ballmer's public *mea culpa* ('no, *my* fault, Boss') suggests that while the USS Microsoft was being safely piloted into Japanese waters and the Xbox was being launched against Sony's all conquering PlayStation, Google appeared out of nowhere, like some kind of titanic iceberg.

But this does not quite cover it. A large bet says that the majority of Microsoft's developers have been using Google for four to five years. Somehow nobody got around to mentioning this to senior management, and nobody asked whether Google were the only IT company left on the planet still able to indulge in initial-investment cashburn or whether those innocent little text ads represented something rather more fundamental.

Google and the Mission

This was an obvious question to ask in London, so why not Seattle? Maybe because Microsoft was actually too close to see the action, or perhaps because, like Apple, and possibly Google in future, Microsoft depends very heavily on charismatic leadership and seems to lack initiative if that leadership is busy elsewhere. In this case Bill was working with Nelson Mandela and Jobs was turning Pixar into Disney's nemesis and iTunes into the music industry's saviour.

...Back on the case

If Google was Microsoft's main problem, their days might well be numbered, but Google are only part of the much bigger threat posed by Open Source. Google represents a technical challenge, which both Bill and Microsoft relish. MS may not win, they have been technologically bettered and outsold by both Adobe and Macromedia at their best, but it raises their game and improves the overall value of their product, which is what they really care about.

Google's success is more limited than Microsoft's problem, which has been developing over time: keeping track of work requires better search (indexing) than Microsoft or Windows applications can provide. PCs, like their users, are much better at creating new work than remembering where it is or what it contains.

By making it so easy to find documents on the web, Google have raised expectations generally, but Microsoft can point out that searching HTML documents, because of their structure, is a great deal easier than searching documents created by software like Word. Like many other major pieces of software, Word was built before the Internet was thought of, and consequently it uses a file structure, which is now a major obstacle to global Search. Google's SEC filing warns that Word documents could become opaque to a Google Search.

Bill Gates has identified the central issue as: can future computers adapt to the user's needs? (instead of second-guessing them beforehand) but he has not succeeded in pitchforking any working products out of Microsoft and into public view, and he may grow impatient. That's when things usually get exciting. The idea was that the next edition of Windows, Longhorn, would bring a Google-level of functionality to the desktop. Instead Google brought Google Desktop Search to the Windows and Linux desktop.

The MSNBot strategy

In a piece in June 2003 entitled 'Microsoft, Google may go head-to-head' Jim Hu and Mike Ricciuti of *CNET News.com* pointed out [2] that Microsoft had:

'...quietly launched a new search program called MSNBot, which scours the Web to build an index of HTML links and documents. The homegrown system--which performs robot functions previously left to Inktomi and other partners--may pose a significant threat to Google if Microsoft fulfills its promise to make the program a cornerstone of its overall PC and services strategies.

MSNBot is believed to be the first step in a multiyear plan to build new search technology that bridges Microsoft's home and business customers. Company executives hope the program will eventually prove to be the elusive technology that binds its various Web sites, applications and, of course, the dominant Windows operating system.

Microsoft could then connect the search engine of its MSN portal to new file technology planned for the next version of Windows, code-named Longhorn, which will make it easier to search email, spreadsheets and documents on PCs, corporate networks and the Web. The result would be a powerful technology reaching from the desktop to the greater Internet that could displace Google as the Web's leading search engine.

"What Google has done in terms of doing a great end-user experience has led us to basically go back and redouble our efforts," Microsoft Vice President Yusuf Mehdi, who oversees the MSN division, said at a conference held by investment bank Goldman Sachs (May 2003). "We are investing a lot to build what we expect and hope will be the best-in-class search service in the near future."'

The integration challenge

It's the 'if' that counts, as in "*IF* Microsoft fulfills its promise to make the program a cornerstone of its overall PC and services strategies". As Sergey suggested above, that conditional loop is one gazonga of an integration challenge for Microsoft and Windows developers.

Google and the Mission

Google's breakthrough had a lot to do with HTML and hypertext links, but these are still rare in MS Word, and unknown on much of the desktop. Without the neat and certain definitions of hypertext, finding, or creating a reliable, indexable context of relevance is extremely tough. The sheer size of the problem became clear too late to save Microsoft's dignity.

Microsoft had also gone back to rewrite its file structure from scratch for Longhorn. Although Windows NT finally buried QDOS with a robust, reliable and well-constructed system (which has run the hectic weekly production schedule of the *New Statesman* magazine with hardly a whimper since we installed it in the mid-nineties) its internal file structure was still not good enough to handle context. No wonder even Gates said that 'Longhorn is a bit scary'.

Twenty years a-growing

On the Internet itself, Microsoft will try to compete head-to-head with Google, and will probably make a good fist of it, eventually, as they did with Acrobat's text print/display system: PostScript. Its competitor to Adobe's PostScript - MS TrueType - is of very good quality now, and MS Trebuchet (great name - it's a medieval siege catapult) is the typeface used in this book because it works as well on screen as it does in print.

This in itself is a real technical achievement, but fortunately for Adobe, getting to that point took almost twenty years while Adobe continued to build their market for PostScript into pdfs for both the Internet and print production. It is still their valuable friend, their legacy code that could stop Microsoft overtaking too quickly for Google to survive. To prosper, Google has to continue to do for Search what Adobe has done for images and text. That requires the kind of timescale, which the SEC filing insists on.

The argument, here, is that although Microsoft has some of the best software brains on the planet, they may have to relearn their craft or sullen art in order to be able to understand how and why context makes Google work so well, and, much more difficult, how it can be deployed without hypertext. While the proposed market for artificial intelligence for business rapidly spirals into uncountable (Cantorian) billions of dollars, it has taken fifty years of huge investment to produce very little, and Google's success and limitations can help show why. As Microsoft Chairman and Chief Software Architect Bill Gates told [3] Joris Evers, (*IDG News Service*, July 24, 2003).

Longhorn

"Longhorn, the next version of Microsoft Corp.'s Windows desktop operating system, will be so different from its predecessors that users may not like it right away".

"Longhorn is a bit scary... We have been willing to change things, ... It (Longhorn) should drive a whole range of upgrades, but that could be sort of delayed," Gates said. Because of differences with the previous versions of Windows, it could be a year or two after its release before computer users really pick up Longhorn", he said.

Gates appeared to distance himself from a commitment the company made at its Windows Engineering Hardware Conference (WinHEC) in May (2003) to deliver Longhorn in 2005. At lunch Thursday, he would not comment on the release date.

"Longhorn is innovative ... there is a lot of work to be done in terms of what has to go in and what has not," Gates said. Asked if Microsoft would consider dropping some of the innovations it has planned so the product can come out sooner, Gates said no: "If you split it up, then you delay one of the really great pieces," he said.

"We need a big bang release to drive excitement,". A beta of Longhorn is planned for next year.

Search Beyond Google

Wade Roush reported Microsoft's thinking for his in-depth investigation of **Search Beyond Google** [4] for MIT's TechNewsWorld, which generated so much interest that it is well worth quoting at length:

Another Microsoft Research effort is less concerned with how search engines work than with how and when users need information. "Right now, when you want to search for information, you basically stop everything you're doing, pull up a separate application, run the search, then try to integrate the search result into whatever you were doing before," says Microsoft information retrieval expert Susan Dumais. "We are trying to think about how search can be much more a part of the ongoing computing experience."

Toward that end, Dumais is developing a program called Stuff I've seen that's designed to give computer users quick, easy access to everything they have viewed on their computers. The interface to the experimental program, which will influence the search capabilities in Longhorn, is an always available search box inside the Windows taskbar. Enter a query into the box, and Stuff I've seen will display an organized list of links to related email messages, calendar appointments, address book contacts, office documents, or Web pages in a single, unified window. One emerging feature of Stuff I've seen, called Implicit Query, would work in the background to retrieve information related to whatever the user is working on.

If you're reading an email message, for example, Implicit Query might display a box with links to the titles and email addresses of all the people whom the message mentions, and to all of your previous email from the sender. To make the software even more useful, Dumais is working on adding an item to the two-button mouse's standard Windows right click menu that would be labeled "Find me stuff like this" and would search both personal and Web data for information related to a highlighted name or phrase.

WinFS-the heart of Longhorn

AskMSR, Stuff I've Seen, and related projects are all part of a larger shift in technology strategy at Microsoft, one that could position the company to convert hundreds of millions of Windows users around the world to its own search technology, much as it wrested the Web browser market from Netscape back in the 1990s. The crux of this transformation is the new Windows File System, or WinFS-the very heart of Longhorn.

Under the current Windows file system; each software application partitions its allotted storage space into its own peculiar hierarchy of folders. This makes it nearly impossible, for example, to link a chunk of information such as the name of the author of a Word document with the same person's address or phone number in Outlook. WinFS, by contrast, has at its core a relational database: an orderly set of tables stored on your hard drive where all the data on your computer can be searched and modified by all applications using a standard set of commands.

The single search box

If Longhorn includes tools based on Stuff I've seen and allows them to communicate directly with a Web search engine, it could create the "single search box" dreamed of by software makers-the gateway to all the information you need, whether inside your PC or out on the network. Gartner's Whit Andrews, for one, is looking forward to Microsoft's new software.

"Bring it on!" he says. "I am sitting here looking at my email. If I want to look you up, I've got to remember to go Google you. But what I really want is to find out if I have talked with you in the past. So I want to right-click and search globally, search my email and contact folders, search U.S. Search.com [which sells access to information stored in public records]. Who has that advantage? Microsoft is there, and for the low-price stuff that consumers aren't going to throw a whole lot of money at, they are in a terrific position."

Optimism and FUD

Some of this will work and some may not. Users will almost certainly benefit from the rivalry, as Gates told [5] an audience in Sydney in July 2004.

Calling the current search industry remarkably "low-tech," he hinted at a future of search where the engines actually understand the documents they index. Microsoft has already been researching linguistics in preparation for their upcoming transition into the competitive search industry, he said, and by doing this, Microsoft strives to make search "ten times better than it is today."

Google and the Mission

Over the years Microsoft have been known to announce 'vaporware' - the promise of a highly developed technology which sows fear, uncertainty and doubt in competitors and their investors, but never actually appears. This is probably not the case here, but like almost every other developer on the planet; Microsoft can have high expectations, when they begin development, which are then defeated by the complexity of reality.

This has probably happened more often with government-sponsored, commercial software intended to extract meaning from natural language text, than almost any other area of coding endeavor. Huge projects were funded by the US Department of Defense without producing any usable results, before BT, Autonomy and a number of others believed that they were close to cracking it in the mid-nineties.

Microsoft responded with AutoSummarize, which is probably the least effective and least used feature of MS Word. The reason for this is investigated below but generally Gates' genius, like Jobs', relates to understanding how a new and peripheral technology can be introduced into the mainstream. Pure innovation, and anything relating to meaning requires considerable innovation, has not been Microsoft's forte, and they should be judged on results not promises.

The battle with Google is about the quality of technology in general use and will probably be conducted in the same fierce but fair fashion in which Microsoft and Adobe compete. The battle with Open Source is very different; it goes to the heart of Microsoft as a company.

Linux and Open Source

Microsoft, with its enormous global power and huge cash mountain hardly looks like a company in trouble, but all is far from relaxed in Richmond, Washington. If Microsoft executives wake sweating in the night, it is not Google they are dreaming about, but Linux. Their nightmare probably includes a Dell brochure dropping out of their newspaper offering Linux-driven pcs - "100% Windows software compatible" at a price, which, because much of Linux development is often done voluntarily, and without charge, Microsoft cannot match.

The history of where they got their technology from continues to haunt them, but it would be wrong to suggest that Microsoft is only about ruthless business methods. The brand comes with the consistent promise that it will give the personal computer user as much functional power as possible, as cheaply as possible, even if that means low initial quality assurance. Apple's brand promise was as much power as possible, as well-engineered as possible, and never mind the cost. Over time the two companies (which developed out of the same Home-Brew teenage computer club led by Steve Wozniak) have become more like each other. Microsoft design has improved by imitation, and their prices have had to go up as Apple's have come down to sensible levels.

Nobody is forced to buy Microsoft at gunpoint, and both Gates and Jobs see themselves as revolutionaries who created the personal computer to give power to the ordinary user, rather than to the corporations who could afford to own mainframes and midis. We can all be grateful that they succeeded, but Microsoft did this so efficiently that they have also succeeded in uniting everybody else against them. The result is the Open Source movement, an anarchic, academic way of sharing code so that it can be developed collaboratively with standards agreed by self-selecting discussion groups or task forces.

Anarchists and suits

The technology of the Internet makes this level of organization cheap and easy, and IBM and Novell, their software markets devastated by the ubiquity of Microsoft and Windows, have joined up. The suits and the anarchists are now making common cause, but only a predator as large and effective as Microsoft could possibly cause them to unite in a common endeavor.

With Linux, the Open Source movement has a robust kernel; a central operating system capable of running software in the same way that the Apple operating system (which has moved over to UNIX, the Open Source language family) and Windows does. Linux only have about 6% of the world market, and Apple have 4%, but that fragment still represents 250 million machines, many of them strategically placed in publishing, advertising, design and the music industry. It's a niche market, certes, but what a niche.

At the heart of the open source movement is Linux, which Microsoft regards, quite rightly, as its biggest long-term threat. This is the submerged mass of the iceberg whose bulk is now large enough, and well hidden enough, to penetrate Microsoft's hull, and it is a threat, which has been building for a dozen years or longer.

Google's CEO Eric Schmidt was reported [6] by the *New York Times*, in early 2004 as believing that

> "Based upon [Microsoft's] visceral reactions to any discussions about 'open source,' they are obsessed with open source as a business model."

Networked software competition?

A couple of major commentators, led by Danny Sullivan, have been debating whether Google can now start to compete directly with Microsoft's Office software suite, by offering networked, indexed software services over the Internet for occasional rather than continuous use.

This is part of a 'distributed services' model where the user starts with the document and then brings in software to work on it rather than starting with, typically, MS Word and then bringing in the document. The idea of doing this over the Internet, using Linux applications rather than buying 'shrink-wrapped' software, is feasible.

Gmail makes a good model of distributed services, but Google's Spellchecker makes an even better example. Much of the spelling for this book has been checked using Google because for interesting technical reasons discussed below, it is a lot better than the ones that come with MS Word or similar programs.

One rumor circulating in 2004 suggested that Google was about to launch a new browser. This might be a rather dramatic response to complaints from non-Explorer users that Toolbar, Deskbar, and Picassa only work with MS Explorer 5.5 and not Apple or Linux desktops, or Firefox, OmniWeb, Safari or Opera browsers. When Google Desktop Search came in, it also worked with Linux, but not Apple, if only because Steve Jobs had promised something similar from Spotlight in the next (10.4 – Tiger) upgrade to the Mac operating system.

Eric would probably prefer it if Google were merely neutral observers in Microsoft's next war, but any neutrality is prevented by their engineering, which is all developed from RedHat open-source code, as Sergey told [7] the *Linux Gazette* in late 2000.

'Actually, we currently run over 6,000 RedHat servers. Linux is used everywhere... on the 6,000+ servers themselves, as well as desktop machines for all of our technical employees. We chose Linux because if offers us the price for performance ratio. It's so nice to be able to customize any part of the operating system that we like, at anytime. We have a large degree of in-house Linux expertise, too."

Linux's best ad

Google code is not itself Open Source. You certainly cannot borrow their central algorithms, which map context; that could see them replaced by Yahoo! and Microsoft next week. But the code they use to build the whole of their system is Open Source until Google starts to customize it, whereupon it becomes commercially confidential. Sergey has agreed, in principle, to release some specific parts of the code if there is a genuine public demand inside the Linux community, although he thought most of their code is too specialized for general usage.

But Google make an extremely powerful advert for Linux. It is generally so clean, fast and robust that it could convince senior managements that Linux is a viable alternative to Windows, and that really does worry the heck out of Microsoft. Having Google's Linux code originally written and then supervised by some of America's best young engineers and applied mathematicians also helps, of course, but Linux certainly benefits from being associated with a company that even the most technically illiterate manager, of which we in the UK have considerable numbers, has heard of. By 2004, according to Tony Perkins [8] of *alwayson.com*:

> "Google is, of course, the shining example of a business built on Linux and open source, so to applaud Google, is to cheer for a world that doesn't need Microsoft. The Google service is run on more than 100,000 servers in 12 data centers around the world, and the company is rumored to be building the largest data center in the world."

Tony Perkins is very well informed, but that figure of 100,000 which several observers including myself have previously quoted, may be a typing error because Google itself only specifies 'more than 10,000 servers'.

Google and the Mission

The attack on Microsoft

The big thing about Linux is that the great bulk of it is written by collective, free collaboration between anyone who has the interest and the technical skill to join in - hence the term Open Source. This has enabled everybody else to gang up on Microsoft in an attempt to wrest back control of both operating system and the industry's standards.

Linux is also an operating system that competes directly against Microsoft because it uses the same Intel-compatible chips that run in 'Windows' machines. (Apple uses different chips, Motorola or IBM). The kernel, core software engine, of Linux is a 'flavor' of UNIX written in 1991 by Linus Torvalds, something of a Finnish genius, from a free student version.

Stallman started what Linus completed

The key algorithms (kernel) are licensed from Linus who has moved on to the configurable, low power-demands of the innovative Crusoe chip design. The rest is open and freely editable by anyone who knows what they are doing (and doubtless a few who don't).

The original work on producing an open source version of UNIX - GNU - was done by Richard Stallman at MIT, who has defined Open Source 'free software' as akin to **'free speech, not free beer'**. Stallman became bogged down and his contract at MIT came to an end before he was able to complete the operating system itself. Linus just picked up the ball and ran with it.

Not for the novice

It would be dangerous for Microsoft to treat it as such but Linux may be more of a psychological than a business threat to Windows as a consumer product. In its commonest manifestation, RedHat is a code geeks' wonderland with endless choices of settings and changes to configure and play with. This is an awfully long way from the ordinary user's desktop, perfected by Apple and reverse engineered, quite legally as it turned out, into Windows. Normal consumers do not want complex interfaces, and by its very nature Linux has to be complex. That does give RedHat a problem because its IPO valuation was not tied to its revenues.

The non-geek beware! aspect of systems like RedHat only affects consumers, of course, who do not usually want to replace all their expensive software or have to learn complex methods of installing new ones, but IT departments often love Linux for opposite reasons. Consequently Microsoft have been fighting like fury to prevent at least one of the German state governments and an Israeli government department from adopting it.

Only the Paranoid Survive

Just because you are paranoid does not mean that they are not out to get you, and Microsoft have become absolute masters of creative paranoia. Microsoft's founding ethos, that old *Hill Street Blues* tag - **"Do it to them before they do it to you"** remains as fresh for them as the day they were founded.

They are not alone. Netscape were extremely paranoid and Google probably have their moments, although the founders' sense of humor rarely seems to desert them and that must help keep things in proportion. But the ecology of IT is that of businesses where *Only the Paranoid Survive* [9] according to Andy Grove, Intel CEO and a holocaust-survivor from Hungary. Grove wrote this book as part of a teaching course he was doing for the Graduate Business School at Stanford (again!).

Grove has enormous and deserved respect from the generation between Gates and the Google guys. Apart from anything else, Intel has not only survived but also prospered against the heaviest guns thrown at them by the Japanese and US shoguns like IBM. In his primer:

> Grove reveals his strategy of focusing on a new way of measuring the nightmare moment every leader dreads--when massive change occurs and a company must, virtually overnight, adapt or fall by the wayside.

Strategic Inflection Point

> Grove calls such a moment a Strategic Inflection Point, which can be set off by almost anything: mega-competition, a change in regulations, or a seemingly modest change in technology.

Google and the Mission

The application of context mapping by Google was just such a modest change in technology. Microsoft has previously experienced two: the Apple desktop and the Netscape Internet browser.

Regarding Strategic Inflection Points at Intel, Grove describes the loss of the DRAM (memory) chip market to Japan, which was unexpected and traumatic since Intel had pretty much created the DRAM industry and it was central to the company. The realization that the competing Japanese technology was likely to remain cheaper and more powerful came very slowly, because as Grove points out, senior management have a vested interest in not seeing a sea-change in an industry they dominate and are liable to discount early warnings coming in from the marketing side, if only because, in my experience at least, most sales people are always complaining in the hopes of increasing their territory and commissions.

For Intel, ceding the DRAM market to Japan was almost equivalent to Microsoft moving out of operating systems or Google dropping Internet search. The whole nature and culture of Intel had to change or risk seeing the company join the list of those honorable dead which this book, and any other dealing with the recent IT industry, is spattered with. Only a painfully honest analysis and decisive leadership from Grove, and Intel's top brass, saved the company. This has probably been one of the most important lessons from business history for Bill Gates and every other IT enterprise.

An almost invisible $475 million flaw

Grove describes a Strategic Inflection Point as ultimately the gut feeling that something irrevocable has changed, but it may only be years later that it becomes clear exactly *what* has happened. Grove's other major examples were the threat of Apple, IBM's shift from CISC to RISC chips {which helped Apple but ultimately made little difference to Intel), and the recall of half a billion dollars worth of perfectly serviceable but 'flawed' Pentium 2 chips with an error which would appear under normal usage about twice every millennium.

This was particularly hard for a cutting-edge engineering company to understand. Following an 'exposé' by CNNMoney the error in the chips caused public hysteria which seemed entirely absurd to the engineers that Intel normally dealt with, given the accepted and usually much more serious errors of many products rushed out to beat a rapidly changing market.

Branding beyond the buyer

The event was reminiscent of Google's Gmail privacy storm, but was much more serious, because while Gmail was a Beta version and only on trial; the cost of even the worst-case outcome of withdrawing it and changing its design would have been relatively trivial compared to recalling tens of thousands of motherboards in order to replace their Pentium 2 chips.

What Grove realized was that by becoming a brand, Intel had set up a relationship with the public which was entirely different from its usual relationships with its actual customers, the engineers and OEMs (Original Equipment Manufacturers) who actually specified and bought the chips. **"We found ourselves dealing with people who bought nothing directly from us yet were very angry with us."**

Intel inside

Intel's reason for creating a global brand in the minds of consumers was strategic. Although Mac-orientated commentators referred for years to Wintel, assuming that Microsoft and Intel's interests were so closely linked that they were effectively a single company, this was nonsense. Intel was a major force long before Microsoft even existed, and its relation with MS was highly profitable, but when dining with Microsoft, Intel always brought a long spoon. In the Open Source war, Intel, which ostensibly has no interest in the argument since both sides depend on its hardware, has joined the Linux legal defense fund.

In order to establish in the mind of the public and investment fund managers that Intel chips were not simply a disposable component of a Windows computer, Intel began the long-running **Intel Inside** campaign. This was a highly effective piece of marketing which culminated in Stephen Hawking declaring, **"Now I really am Intel inside"** when his Hawking mobile was upgraded.

Downside of a global brand

Intel's branding set up public expectations, and thence a fear of being disappointed; this helped create the conviction, fueled by a press happy to see a giant humbled, that Intel were deliberately unloading defective gear. This was untrue, which is why Grove and his colleagues found it so difficult to grasp the problem, but that was the public perception and once it was established, rational argument was almost useless.

For similar reasons, Google during the Gmail release found themselves the target for all the understandable but largely misplaced public concern about privacy and personal information on the Net. It was not what Google was actually doing; the more educated blogging community had quickly accepted the same techniques with gratitude, rather than disquiet, because they understood that it provided the commercial security, which would ensure the survival of their beloved medium.

Grove's analysis of the need for **"creative paranoia"** had a huge impact partly because Grove was writing from direct experience of successful crisis management at the most senior level. This is something that few journalists and commentators, including this one, have had to cope with. He also understood the specific local conditions of the IT industry, such as the rate of technological change defined by Grove's colleague at Intel, Gordon Moore ("processing power roughly doubles every two years"), but it also resonated with Microsoft because of the company's own early history.

Hindsight is always 20:20

With hindsight Microsoft's success looks inevitable, but it did not appear that way at the time. As Intel founder Gordon Moore told [10] *Fortune*:

> After the fact, we've been criticized for not developing the first personal computer - after all, we had the chips, but we didn't really see that it was going to go anyplace. The engineer who suggested the idea to me - the only application he could think of was having housewives' recipes on it. Even when Steve Jobs came around with the early Apples, it wasn't obvious.

Of all the computer companies in Seattle when Microsoft was founded, only one, a small computer repair shop, has also survived. World domination or annihilation seems to have been the only choice. While Google's founders had the support of Stanford, to which they could always have returned if their project had failed, Harvard gave no such support to Bill.

The tree grows as the twig is bent

It has been observed that Microsoft, despite its size and power, still has the corporate mentality of seven guys running a start-up in a damp garage with an unsympathetic landlord. This outlook is not unique to Microsoft and may be characteristic of all successful start-ups. As Grove recalled about the Pentium 2 disaster:

> **What was hardest to take was the outside world's image of us. I still thought of us a creative, dynamic start-up that had just grown a bit bigger than the other creative, dynamic start-ups. We could still turn on a dime. Our people still put the interests of the company ahead of their own interests and, when problems arose, employees would still rally around and put in incredible hours without anyone ordering them to do so. Yet now the world seemed to treat us like some typical mammoth corporation. And in the public view, this corporation was giving people the run-around (over Pentium 2). That outside image didn't jibe with my view of us.**

This seems a strange reaction from the CEO of one of the most powerful corporations on the planet but it is still a good picture of how both Gates and Brin and Page view their own operations. In Bill's eyes, Microsoft is still the diminutive David fighting for the people against the Goliath of IBM.

If individuals can be shaped by their earliest experiences, then the same is probably true of companies. Gates knows that Microsoft's huge early success was based not on its real technical innovations, including MS Basic, but on the colossal structure and resulting weakness and lethargy of IBM: "**weak as a kitten, dumb as a sack of hammers**" as the tee-shirts in Douglas Coupland's ***Microserfs*** [1] put it. This was almost matched by Apple's subsequent greed, complacency and arrogance, after the success of the Mac.

Google and the Mission

Big Blue's big mistake

Content with their then complete domination of corporate mainframes, IBM did not see personal computers coming. This mistake very nearly destroyed one of the most powerful companies in the world, and two decades later it is still hard to say that they have fully recovered, even if their revenues are still greater than Microsoft's.

If IBM had devoted even a tiny research budget to understanding micro development, they would have seen that the micro represented a quite fundamental change in the public availability of technology, and hence the scope of their industry and market. Instead they persisted in the belief spouted by every salesman (and they were all men in those days) that these were toys, which kids might buy to play Pong, but any serious business would ignore in favor of the 'mini' computers, which often cost many tens of thousands of dollars.

By the early eighties, personal computing had reached critical mass, but IBM had failed to develop their own operating system for micros that could compete with Apple or even Commodore. Instead they let Microsoft sell them a non-exclusive license to the well-named QDOS (Quick and Dirty Operating System). Gates and partner Paul Allen had bought the rights to QDOS only a few days before the critical meeting with IBM.

The end of CP/M

QDOS was based on (or in the opinion [12] of Digital Research's legal estate was "an unauthorized clone of") the then dominant operating system CP/M, which was written by Gary A. Kildall for Intel. Intel wanted to stick to hardware and firmware - chip design - so they let Kildall take it away and set up his own company, originally called Intergalactic Digital Research, to sell it. According to *The Online Software Museum* [13]:

> By 1978, CP/M 2.2 had been ported to nearly every 8080 and Z80 based microcomputer built. In the end, more that 500,000 computers would be sold with CP/M as their operating system. It so dominated the microcomputer world by 1980 that it seemed hardly conceivable that any other operating system would ever be used on Intel-based computers.

...As the now-famous story goes, Gary Kildall was not there to open that door when IBM came calling -- an avid amateur pilot, he was flying his private plane on a business trip to the Bay area. His wife and business partner, confronted with IBM's imposing code of secrecy and non-disclosure agreements, refused to sign even enough for talks to begin. Rebuffed by what they considered arrogance, the IBMer's went elsewhere -- to Seattle and another small young software firm called Microsoft. A deal was struck there, and as they say, the rest is history."

CP/M certainly was. Gates had doubtless noted that complacency had set in quickly at Digital Research. Gary said later that he was really only interested in funding his "gadget-habit" and let it go. After Kildall's sudden, early, death, CP/M (now called DR-DOS) was sold to Novell, who in turn sold it to Caldera Inc. According to Digital Research successor, Maxframe Corporation:

"...on July 24, 1996, Caldera Inc. filed a private Federal Antitrust Lawsuit against Microsoft Corp. for alleged illegal activities and unfair practices in the marketing of MS-DOS and its successors, including Windows 95 and Windows 98, both of which are still Digital Research CP/M at their essential core. The lawsuit was settled out of court in January 2000 at which time Microsoft Corporation agreed to certain terms and paid certain funds to Caldera Inc."

Microsoft are currently beginning to dominate video software, to the intense fury of the European Commission who can see the (European) investments of video players Real Player and Apple QuickTime going down the Swannee River, where pioneering innovations have now led to first-mover disadvantage. As a tribute perhaps to the lobbying powers of the Apple group in Paris, the EC has hit Microsoft with a 497 million Euro (330 million) fine and demanded that Windows Media Player (WMP) be separated from the Windows operating system.

Precedents

Still, Microsoft can always take a legal precedent from the German and French governments who have also been trying to avoid paying enormous fines from the European Commission for breaking its rules. This is a particularly good example of why government is a poor arbitrator of business, because the reality is that WMP, thanks to Microsoft's stamina, is now a better product than either Apple QuickTime or Real Player.

This was clear when I set up a comparison of all three and the Macromedia Flash player (which has the best, Sorenson codecs - compression algorithms) on the Mac platform, since Windows could contain a built-in bias. As a result of a side-by-side comparison a friend who works in video exclusively with Mac equipment decided to switch from QuickTime to WMP. That means that consumers, or rather the OEMs they buy from, will continue to install WMP rather than its competition and the net effect of the EC's intervention is to reduce functionality, which benefits nobody.

If the EC want to intervene usefully in Microsoft's competitive practices, they should take a close look at the recent history and financial relations of Caldera.

Caldera - a curious company

After losing to Caldera in court, Microsoft agreed to license Caldera's version of UNIX, thus effectively backing the company with a secure profit stream. Sounds too easy and maybe it was. Curious company, Caldera; it was originally funded by a Novell CEO after he paid top-whack for WordPerfect and then watched Microsoft liquidate it with Word for Office. Caldera's two founders were also from Utah (Novell is mainly owned by members of the Mormon Church in Utah) and have now moved into other areas of Linux (one of them to Lineo - embedded Linux systems, including Hitachi vacuum cleaners - where he can innovate in peace.)

Caldera meanwhile bought out, and changed their name to, SCO, an old Linux vendor and IBM's partner on the Monterey open-source project. There are certainly people at IBM who are still sore about OS/2, IBM's attempt to compete with Windows, which had sadly died, soon after birth; "and who's that, sneaking, round the corner?" as Kurt Weil once asked of MacHeath. By early 2004, desktop Linux systems had already overtaken Apple's market share. It would now make IBM very happy if Linux ever overtook Microsoft, but it is hard to see IBM or Novell as long-term friends of the volunteer global army who make Open Source happen.

SCO had bought all the original Bell Labs code from which UNIX originated. An amusing historical gesture was the general view, until SCO subsequently sued Novell for breaking the Bell copyrights. Once that was underway, they sued IBM and RedHat for breaking SCO's copyrights in the Monterey code. The Open Source Initiative was furious and recruited Intel and Novell to their legal defense fund.

The most prolific virus unleashed by early 2004 was the mydoom virus, which attacked both Microsoft (a little bit) after shutting down SCO, whose response to the attack seasoned anti-virus expert Mary Landesman regarded as distinctly odd. Open Source forums talked of dirty deeds done in deepest darkness, of a virus writer being hired by someone to smear them. It has certainly cast Fear, Uncertainty and Doubt on the rest-of-the-world's use of Linux to attack Windows directly, and the brand value of Linux as whole.

Permission requested from Doonesbury.com

Microsoft's vision

Microsoft's integrity - that will be a short chapter, said a neighbor - is not so much an oxymoron, a contradiction in terms, as a Googlewhack waiting to happen. Researching this book I was surprised at the degree of hostility to Microsoft expressed by people generally, particularly since Microsoft had just won top place as the company that treats its customers best.

This hostility is to be expected from Apple users, partly because there was a time when there was a huge difference in design

Google and the Mission

quality, reliability and usability, and partly because the price difference has been so extreme in the not-so-distant past that Apple users (like me), feel a need to justify spending all that extra money. But now according to Jef Raskin, credited with inventing the original Mac concept (without a mouse), and interviewed in the UK's *MacUser* magazine:

> What used to be a night-and-day difference in usability has become a small increment in Apple's favor.

Unlike Apple, Microsoft's promotion and advertising has until recently lacked flair. It has failed to convey a central truth about Microsoft which is that, however badly it may treat third parties, its interests and its customers' interests (and since its IPO, those of its stockholders) are pretty much identical. Microsoft's mission is defined (at least according to *Microserfs*) inside an indestructible Lucite plaque awarded to MS developers who get their software ready on time:

> 'EVERY TIME A PRODUCT SHIPS, IT TAKES US ONE STEP CLOSER TO THE VISION. A COMPUTER ON EVERY DESK AND IN EVERY HOME'

Apple's monopoly

Both Apple and Microsoft reacted to IBM's authoritarian strategies, whose very dark side is described in the next chapter, with a power-to-the-people ethos of delivering a previously inconceivable amount of power (greater than that available to NASA for the Apollo moonshot) to the desktop of ordinary users.

While Apple delivered this message with huge panache and style, particularly in its recently revived *1984* Ridley Scott ad, Macs were so over-priced that this really meant power to the people of Marin County. Early adopters in the UK had to remortgage, some of them literally. As Steve Jobs told Steve Levy *Newsweek* [14] in February 2004:

> "The Mac user interface was a 10-year monopoly," says Jobs. "Who ended up running the company? Sales guys. At the critical juncture in the late '80s, when they should have gone for market share, they went for profits. They made *obscene* profits for several years. And their products became mediocre. And then

their monopoly ended with Windows 95. They behaved like a monopoly, and it came back to bite them, which always happens."

Microsoft's stamina

By divorcing its operating system from specific hardware (apart from the central Intel chip) Microsoft introduced competition into hardware, which reduced prices to an almost ridiculous level, keeping its own prices very low, and making very little effort to prevent piracy. The other way of keeping prices down was to let customers, particularly early-adopters, do a lot of the quality-assurance.

The aspect of MS, which is often missed, is the enormous stamina it displays. Early versions of its software are often awful, but the company keeps hammering away until they are better than the competition. Twenty years after Apple's GUI, Microsoft introduced XP whose quality now matches Apple's.

"This aint rock'n'roll, this is genocide"

Microsoft's quality control has sometimes been, ahem, questionable but their ability to provide something that people want, at a price they can afford has earned them enough power over the market to squeeze to death any competitor smaller than MacroMedia that seriously troubles them. They have also sometimes been a bit over-enthusiastic about learning from others.

Permission requested from Doonesbury.com

According to angelfire.com from an MSNBC report [15]:

> " Microsoft has been named a defendant in at least 35 patent-infringement cases, compared with seven suits in the prior 22 years. Twenty-one are currently active..."

> But some inventors and their lawyers say they turned to litigation as a last resort, after being strung along by Microsoft in fruitless patent-licensing negotiations that gave it time to design competing products. Richard Lang, chief executive officer of Burst.com, says it showed its video-transmission technology to Microsoft, rejecting a Microsoft offer of $1 million for rights to its patents. The 14-year-old company, whose investors include the rock group U2, sued Microsoft in federal court in Baltimore over patent and antitrust violations after Microsoft announced plans for a version of its Windows Media product, code-named Corona. Burst.com once employed about 100 but now has just two employees.

Microsoft is gradually reaching the end of the current wave of lawsuits and in September 2004 settled with the UK's Sendo, a small mobile phone maker. Sendo's lawsuit accused Microsoft of a **"secret plan"** to: **"plunder the small company of its proprietary information, technical expertise, market knowledge, customers and prospective customers"**, according to Sendo's lawsuit which claimed that Microsoft then handed the information to low-cost handset makers in Asia.

Permission requested from Doonesbury.com

A saturated market

Google has six or seven years' lead with both its distributed engineering and its Search technology. Everybody has the right to compete in an open market place but Microsoft will always fight to the death for their own market share (90%+) of the consumer desktop and it is unwise to underestimate them.

Underestimating Microsoft, as Netscape once did and some sections of Linux (particularly Linspire/Lindows) have done by claiming to be about to wrest control of the desktop from them, almost invariably involves a very long walk off a very short plank. The Linux attack on Windows effectively makes Google into honorable enemy #2 and this is a much more defensible position than being Microsoft's prime target.

The Open Source challenge may require a complete change of company culture and direction at Microsoft. The physical reality is that most of the pc market, in the West at least, is saturated. Unless they have specialized needs, like professional video editing, most people have more power and more functionality in their machines than they have the time to use. In the developed world the demand for new equipment and software is returning to a more normal [3] year churn or replacement cycle. Most of the new growth is in China and the developing world where piracy is rampant.

Apple with a much smaller share of the market, have moved towards a subscription model. They offer annual updates to their operating software together with video-editing software, which is unique to their platform, competing with Adobe who have dropped some of their video-editing software for Macs, because the cost of developing for the Mac as well as Windows is prohibitive if Apple is building its own competing software. (Microsoft have dropped development of Explorer for the Mac for the same reason, which is a pity.)

Microsoft's image

Microsoft's policy of embrace and extend has meant meeting competition by working away until it has a matching or better technology. If its historic relationship with consumers is starting to atrophy because the market is saturated, it can beat Open Source by using the same methods to create fora and voluntary groups developing Microsoft code amongst IT managers and third-party developers.

It is not that Microsoft does not already spend millions doing this, what is required is a change of company image and attitude. Writing this book it was natural to send the code for Googly software to Google. Doing the same thing for Microsoft would never have occurred to me. That's perception not logic, since either would be equally useful to other developers. Microsoft is now moving both fast and hard to change that perception by creating a different image of the company amongst third-party developers.

Two straws in the wind indicate Microsoft are moving in this direction. In mid-2004 Microsoft sent one of its senior managers into the lion's den of the UK Open Source conference to argue the two philosophies of development in public. Then when it released the Beta of its new Internet Search engine with the specific request that experts in the field send in their comments and complaints.

Whether this is the beginning of a profound move in the company away from its traditional role as predator and towards a model of voluntary co-operation that powers the Open Source movement, only time will tell. Personally, the mellowing of Gates looks real enough, and it is possible that the character of his company is changing. It would still take a while to add trust to the respect and fear that the company already enjoys, but one thing that Microsoft can never be accused of is failing to learn from its competitors.

Footnotes

1: WWDC: Live Steve Jobs keynote coverage
By Nick dePlume, Think Secret The dePlume Organization LLC. June 28 2004
2: Microsoft, Google may go head-to-head
By Jim Hu and Mike Ricciuti CNET News.com June 25, 2003
3: Gates: Longhorn is 'a bit scary'
By Joris Evers: infoworld.com IDG News Service July 24, 2003
4: Search Beyond Google
By Wade Roush, TechNewsWorld MIT Technology Review March 2, 2004
5: Microsoft Promises 'Ten Times Better' Search
By Brittany Thompson Google Community (unaffiliated to Google.inc) Jun 29, 2004
6: NYT: The Valley v. MSFT, Round 2
John Battelle's Searchblog February 01, 2004
7: Interview with Google's Sergey Brin
By Fernando Ribeiro Corra: Issue 59 of Linux Gazette, November 2000

8: Gates on Google: Davos Dispatch
By Tony Perkins: AlwaysOn 02.03.04
9: Only the Paranoid Survive: How to Exploit the Crisis Points That Challenge Every Company
By Andrew S. Grove, Amazon.com
10: How We Got Started: Gordon Moore, Intel
Fortune Small Business Time Inc. September 13, 2003
11: Microserfs By Douglas Coupland
amazon.com
12: CP/M The First PC Operating System
MaxFrame Corporation
13: CP/M History
The Online Software Museum
14: OK, Mac, Make a Wish
By Steven Levy Newsweek Feb. 2 2004
15: Microsoft faces host of patent suits
angelfire.com MSNBC 2002-Oct

4

Open Search - It's a political thing...

Search beyond advertising

When Google's founders developed contextual mapping, they delivered an immensely powerful tool into the hands of the public. The intention was to free Internet Search from the deliberate and cynical bias of commercial search and in this they succeeded beyond any reasonable expectation.

This combination of political and scientific integrity is very unusual for successful Internet or IT companies and has helped establish the power of the Google brand, but would probably not have been possible without the support of Stanford and the unusual investment conditions of the dot.com boom.

Internet Search in the mid-nineties had two major problems: the technology was being rendered increasingly inadequate both by the size of the Internet and by the ease with which it could be manipulated to make money for advertisers. The incentive was that general, generic advertising simply did not cover costs and licensing search technology provided very small amounts of revenue.

The reasons why Search had hit its technical limits are described in later chapters, and is still only partially understood. Commercial bias was much simpler. The oldest trick in print publishing is to make an advert look like the magazine's or newspaper's independent recommendation, so the product is sold on the credibility of the publication, not on its own merits. It makes a fast buck and then helps destroy the magazine or newspaper; readers do not like being misled, and will stop paying for it.

A new way to cheat

The 'New Economy' alternative was to apply the same idea to web searches so that paid entries were presented as genuine search results. That this was happening, and still is, was easy to see but hard to prove and impossible (most of us believed) to do anything about. After all, Search was a free service and had to get income from somewhere, however dubious. By 1997 there was plenty of evidence that searching the net was commercially biased. Fortunately Larry and Sergey thought it could and should be otherwise. In their crucial *The Anatomy of a Large-Scale Hypertextual Web Search Engine* [1] in 1997 they noted:

"...there is virtually no control over what people can put on the web. Couple this flexibility to publish anything with the enormous influence of search engines to route traffic and companies which deliberately manipulate search engines for profit become a serious problem... There are even numerous companies which specialize in manipulating search engines for profit."

Sadly, and despite Google's best efforts, there still are. Spam mail promises to get your site listed in Google's top 10, but if the Google spam filter catches or even suspects you of cheating, you will be 'damped' into the outer darkness of the 100,000th most relevant result.

When Brin and Page published the central formula for PageRank they also showed its 'damping factor' d - usually set at 85%. This is the mechanism for changing a search result. Google use it to can the spam rather than to boost an advertiser up the ranks.

The probability that the random surfer visits a page is its PageRank. And, the d damping factor is the probability at each page the "random surfer" will get bored and request another random page. One important variation is to only add the damping factor d to a single page, or a group of pages. This allows for Personalization and can make it nearly impossible to deliberately mislead the system in order to get a higher ranking.

That turned out to be a bit optimistic.

"Advertising and Mixed Motives"

Currently, the predominant business model for commercial search engines is advertising. The goals of the advertising business model do not always correspond to providing quality search to users. For example, in our prototype search engine one of the top results for cellular phone is "The Effect of Cellular Phone Use Upon Driver Attention", a study which explains in great detail the distractions and risk associated with conversing on a cell phone

Google and the Mission

while driving. This search result came up first because of its high importance as judged by the PageRank algorithm, an approximation of citation importance on the web [Page, 98]. It is clear that a search engine which was taking money for showing cellular phone ads would have difficulty justifying the page that our system returned to its paying advertisers. For this type of reason and historical experience with other media [Bagdikian 83], we expect that advertising funded search engines will be inherently biased towards the advertisers and away from the needs of the consumers.

Since it is very difficult even for experts to evaluate search engines, search engine bias is particularly insidious. A good example was OpenText, which was reported to be selling companies the right to be listed at the top of the search results for particular queries [Marchiori 97]. This type of bias is much more insidious than advertising, because it is not clear who "deserves" to be there, and who is willing to pay money to be listed. This business model resulted in an uproar, and OpenText has ceased to be a viable search engine. But less blatant bias are likely to be tolerated by the market. For example, a search engine could add a small factor to search results from "friendly" companies, and subtract a factor from results from competitors. This type of bias is very difficult to detect but could still have a significant effect on the market. Furthermore, advertising income often provides an incentive to provide poor quality search results.

...In general, it could be argued from the consumer point of view that the better the search engine is, the fewer advertisements will be needed for the consumer to find what they want. This of course erodes the advertising supported business model of the existing search engines. However, there will always be money from advertisers who want a customer to switch products, or have something that is genuinely new. But we believe the issue of advertising causes enough mixed incentives that it is crucial to have a competitive search engine that is transparent and in the academic realm.

First and last public description

Which they succeeded in doing with PageRank and BackRub. Indexing is an arcane art, but Brin and Page published the outline of their indexing system, after pointing out that academic studies were rare (and in cases like the proposed Harvester system, conceptually grand but not very practical) and projects that had begun as academic research had become commercial secrets. In 1997 Google could claim that their "in-depth description of our large-scale web search engine - (is) the first such detailed public description we know of to date."

It was also just about the last, although AltaVista subsequently published a white paper when their (now defunct) Raging Search product attempted to out-google Google. Page and Brin's argument in their breakthrough paper may now sound idealistic, naive even, and certainly entailed a huge future commitment, but, given their backgrounds, they were probably brought up to believe that extending science - public knowledge, not making money, is the highest ambition. Stanford's support meant that they could solve the problem of commercial bias, before they needed to find an alternative business model to fund it. This they developed four years later.

The FTC intervene

In 2001 the US Federal Trade Commission stepped in after a complaint from Portland, Oregon-based Commercial Alert. After an 11-month investigation, the FTC told search-engine companies they needed to clearly mark paid listings on their sites. Companies named in the complaint were AltaVista, AOL Time Warner, Direct Hit Technologies, iWon, LookSmart, Microsoft and Terra Lycos. Almost all of them subsequently put paid listings at the top of search results, usually with a 'sponsored link' tag - which presumably sounds more webby (and ambiguous) than 'Advertisement'.

AskJeeves/Teoma dropped Paid Inclusion because it screwed up their results, and Microsoft planned to join them in 2004 by dropping its 'featured' results which mixed paid inclusion with non-paying sites.

Google and the Mission

The UK's Advertising Standards Authority catches on

In June 2004, Europe finally began to wake up to the problem as the UK's Advertising Standards Authority responded to a complaint from 2-Minute-Website.com by ruling against the very large ISP Freeserve/Wanadoo use of sponsored links. As Heather Tomlinson of the *Guardian* reported [2]:

> Regular users of Freeserve - which has been rebranded under parent company Wanadoo's name - might have noticed a small grey link beside the first few search results that says "overture": blink and you would miss it. This has been the only signal that the link comes from a paying advertiser - but in future the ASA will force the company to make that relationship much clearer.

> "Consumers were unlikely to realize that the Overture hyperlink indicated that results were sponsored, and [the ASA] concluded that consumers could be misled," the ASA ruling said.

> With further complaints being investigated against the *Daily Mail's* UK Plus, AOL Europe, Microsoft's MSN and about 10 other web sites, the ASA is considering setting up formal rules on how search engines should behave along the lines of the strict rules that exist in the United States, set up by its no-nonsense regulator, the federal trade commission.

> "I am surprised that it has taken so long", said Danny Sullivan, editor of searchenginewatch.com.

Standards need to be international

The Open Search foundation advocated in the first chapter could begin by promoting a voluntary code of conduct and a logo that indicates adherence to a common international standard. If that does not work, then legislation should be considered. But the best legal efforts of governments are necessarily limited by national jurisdiction. Legislation has not been necessary for print publishing; as pointed out above, disguising advertising as editorial kills the credibility, and ultimately the sales, of a publication.

But the desire to control information can be political as well as commercial. Even though it started as an innocent research project, once Google had come up with a new way of finding information on the Internet, things got very commercial and very political.

Information is crucial to both business and the state, and collecting, editing, publishing and distributing information is very expensive. So control of published information is determined, generally, by a dialogue between large companies and national governments.

Sometimes this is in democratic agreement with the people whose data they hold. The UK's venerable Data Protection Act works on the principle that you should be able to see what information commercial companies hold on you and challenge it if it is incorrect. In the US, the Freedom of Information Act also makes provision for disclosure of other information held by the government. Unfortunately, despite promising similar legislation whilst in opposition, the UK's Labour government saw no urgency in the issue once they actually held power.

Technocracy and thought crimes

A great deal of information held by a government on its citizens is as generally harmless as the national census: useful for demographic predictions of housing, tax revenues or social services. Since information flows like water, it is often a question of who owns the reservoirs. Until Jobs and Gates came along with the personal computer and a philosophy of empowering the people in the eighties, that meant mostly IBM.

Most state information outside the Communist blocs was held on enormous mainframes built by IBM, whose chief executive judged famously that there would probably only ever be a need for six or seven computers worldwide. Hence Apple's famous, *Bladerunner*-style 1984 ad by Ridley Scott, showing a female athlete destroying the Big Brother control system of legions of blue androids.

When Vannevar Bush, America's chief scientist in the Second World War, started the concept of a hypertext-linked information system in his seminal essay *As We May Think* [3], he described an innocent, technocratic version of the use of personal data:

"The personnel officer of a factory drops a stack of a few thousand employee cards into a selecting machine, sets a code in accordance with an established convention, and produces in a short time a list of all employees who live in Trenton and know Spanish."

Unfortunately this technology had already been put to other purposes; what Winston Churchill had called the "perverted science" of the Nazis.

In 2004, Nortel and others, including Microsoft, were accused by Amnesty International of selling systems to the Chinese government that enabled them to switch off dissidents, literally. More than 60 dissidents had been imprisoned for breaking Chinese laws on permitted levels of Internet access. The forbidden areas included sites concerned with democratic dissent in Hong Kong and religious dissent by the Falun Gong.

Microsoft replied that they only provided the best possible technology; what purchasers chose to do with it is up to them. Which has unfortunate echoes, because as Edwin Black points out [4] in his *Review of IBM and the Holocaust:* The Strategic Alliance between Nazi Germany and America's Most Powerful Corporation not *that* long ago...

The dark side of Big Blue

'...a key IBM technology, the Hollerith-based card tabulating machines, became available for the Nazi war and Holocaust efforts. Although the details are murky (and may remain so), it is fairly clear that the use of this technology was sustained during the war years in part by shipments of customized (for each end user) tabulating cards from IBM in neutral countries for everything from blitzkriegs to slave camp scheduling to transportation to the death camps. There was not enough paper capacity to make the cards in Europe (that the Nazi and IBM records show were used), and there is no evidence that Nazis created substitutes for these essential supplies.'

"...IBM founder Thomas Watson deserved the Merit Cross (Germany's second-highest honor) awarded him in 1937 by Hitler, his second-biggest customer on earth. "IBM, primarily through its German subsidiary, made Hitler's program of Jewish destruction a technologic mission the company pursued with chilling success.".

"The infamous Auschwitz tattoo began as an IBM number." Black wrote [5] in the *Village Voice* in 2002, after giant publisher Bertelsmann apologized for their complicity and subsequent cover-up in funding the Nazi party and the SS.

And now it's been revealed that IBM machines were actually based at the infamous concentration-camp complex.

...IBM spokesman Carol Makovich didn't respond to repeated telephone calls. In the past, when asked about IBM's Polish subsidiary's involvement with the Nazis, Makovich has said, "IBM does not have much information about this period." When a Reuters reporter asked about Poland, Makovich said, "We are a technology company, we are not historians."

It now appears that IBM was supplying its technology to Nazi Germany through the freedom-loving Swiss in Geneva. Everybody was doing it, so "It's a sensitive subject, try and just not mention it" as Eminem puts it, but Daddy Warbucks can have invested in few things that cost quite so many innocent lives. It does not need paranoia to fuel a democratic concern over who controls what information about whom.

Gmail privacy fears

There is, and should be, a fundamental concern about privacy on the Internet. Google unwittingly collided with the issue when they introduced Gmail - its system of indexed email. Given that Google effectively created Open Search by making it a central issue in 1997, the founders had a right to be hurt that their company was now being cast in the role of Big Brother and castigated by a Californian state senator, no less.

Much of this was bandwagon jumping, because of its implicit assumption that Gmail users would not be capable of reading the Terms and Conditions and make up their own minds whether they wanted to pay for privacy. But it also bears out Danny Sullivan's warning that Google's "god-like" status made it very vulnerable if it started making mistakes.

In fact there was an oversight in that Gmail was vulnerable to complaints or legal action that incoming mail from non-Gmail accounts would also be archived and indexed. Apart from the privacy rights of non-subscribers (who would need to be explicitly told that their mail would be indexed) this could also make Google a tempting target for hackers out to get passwords or financial details. (Passwords and account information are routinely confirmed by email. Deleting these from the server reduces any security risk to the negligible; archiving them permanently would not.)

Google themselves do seem to have been caught off balance by the storm around Gmail's privacy implications, silly as most of the complaints were, the need for assurances of a well-protected security system for the Google server network, and the significant detail that somebody at Google forgot to check on whether the name Gmail was an existing trademark. (It is). Google responded to this concern and amended their SEC filing to warn that security and privacy issues could hamper sales.

Higher expectations of Google

WebProNews has published [6] a comparison made by Google interface designer and blogger Kevin Fox of fury.com, who pointed out that:

> Yahoo! requires the members First Name, Last Name, Zip code, Gender, Industry, Job Title, Specialization, Birth Date, and a check box for special offers from selected Yahoo! partners that is checked by default.

> MSN/Hotmail requires First Name, Last Name, Language, Country, State, Zip Code, Time Zone, Gender, Birth Date, Occupation, which of 40 newsletters you want to receive in your inbox, and which of 55 topics interest you, so that 'featured offers' from Hotmail partners can be delivered into your inbox.

> That's a nice amount of information that these two ask for. Google asks for First Name and Last Name. That's all. Yahoo! states that they ask for this information to provide 3rd parties for targeted advertising.

> Google, on the other hand, has no intention of renting, selling, or sharing information about Gmail members. They intend to place contextually targeted ads in emails themselves.

> Gmail has been hammered relentlessly since they announced this practice, although, the difference between Gmail's ads and Yahoo! providing 3rd parties with member information is huge. While it's true that Google may scan and retain member emails, it will not resell any member information to any outside companies, AdSense/AdWords client or not. Yahoo, on the other hand, does.

The question should be asked: why does Google get negative press for their email practices, but Yahoo! does not? Maybe this is because Microsoft and Yahoo! have never proclaimed any ethical standards like Google's ten-point credo quoted above, but Google often does serve as a lightning conductor, and they do not spend much on a professional press office that could help spin the right headlines.

No simple answers

It would be wrong to suggest that any of these issues are black and white or that anybody has the panacea for the use and abuse of personal information. I was interested to know whether Eric Schmidt was a Mormon, because Novell, of which he was CEO before being recruited to Google, is generally owned and managed by members of the Church of Jesus Christ of Latter Day Saints. I started googling for this, and then realized that if there was no obvious statement then I really had no business invading his privacy. It is clear that he is good at handling senior managers with strong beliefs and that, really, is all I need to know for the purposes of analysing Google.

Even the issue of Chinese state censorship is far from cut and dried. The Chinese government argues that an authoritarian state has enabled almost all the citizens of the world's largest country to enjoy, for perhaps the first time in two thousand years, rising standards of prosperity, health and education, whilst exactly the reverse was happening to Russia's people as democracy and economic freedom were introduced.

For companies like News International or Canadian telecom giant Nortel, the issue is very simple. China is becoming the world's most important market as Japan and Europe's growth stagnates and the US faces a terrifying balance of payments deficit which had reached 25% of GDP by 2002. As far as they are concerned, this is not a customer that you can afford to offend.

Global consensus required

Google's conscience is part of its appeal to a (US) public grown increasingly angry with boardroom greed, so it is not surprising that

Google and the Mission

is equally a source of profound irritation to financiers and competitors. It is not unique, companies like the UK's John Lewis Partnership and many of the great businesses founded by Quakers have had very similar principles, but in the long battle between money and morality, principles that helped to build customers' trust in a business tend to get lost over time.

For issues as important as these, we probably need the global consensus of the UN to set international standards. It is not that the 'tribal talking shop' is efficient - the amount of hot air generated from New York, Geneva and Vienna has probably contributed significantly to global warming - it is simply that the alternative is usually very much worse.

Compulsory regulation by governments is unlikely to achieve anything useful, and could increases powers that they do not need. Setting international standards of what we should expect from Open Search probably would be effective, if only because a negative press damages the value of the brands concerned. Legal regulation may not achieve anything beyond the prevention of outright fraud.

The technology has usually moved on by the time the judicial caravan comes around, something which Microsoft has exploited strategically. Like Coca-Cola's secret recipe, but for real, Search companies will not allow anybody sight of their primary algorithms and the regulators would probably have extreme difficulty understanding them anyway.

The price of liberty

You do not need to see the algorithms to identify the results of corrupted Search, as Brin and Page pointed out in 1997, even if you probably cannot prove it. However, the signs are usually clear and bad publicity for a Search company can hit them where it hurts to the extent of putting them out of business; so get some international experts and make sure that they are properly resourced and their reports are well publicized. Journalists will be interested because Search is part of their daily toil. This applies to authoritarian governments as much as companies. Even Hitler hated a bad press.

International standards of how information technology can be used and sold should mean a level playing field where companies that behave in a principled fashion do not see their markets lost to competitors with fewer scruples and a con that the public do not recognize. We have all been lucky that the company with the best technology for tracking information on the Internet has also been one of the most honest and principled.

In the kind of universe invoked by Gilliam's film, *Brazil*, which imagines an Orwellian future controlled by analogue not digital computers, the government would run all Search Engines and they would return results three weeks after you had forgotten why you wanted to know in the first place.

This is not a plea that governments should control Search, quite the reverse, but if the price of liberty is eternal vigilance, then we must ask who will own Google's information in ten or twenty years' time and what system of protection for the founders' ethic of Open Search will still be in place for Google, or their competitors?

Footnotes

1: The Anatomy of a Large-Scale Hypertextual Web Search Engine
Sergey Brin and Lawrence Page Computer Science Department Stanford University
2: Watchdog forces Freeserve to clarify sponsorship
By Heather Tomlinson: Guardian Unlimited Guardian Newspapers Limited June 17, 2004
3: As We may Think - Section 6
By Vannevar Bush: The Atlantic Monthly, July 1945
4: The Strategic Alliance between Nazi Germany and America's Most Powerful Corporation By Edwin Black
amazon.com
5: The IBM Link to Auschwitz
By Edwin Black villagevoice.com Village Voice Media, Inc. October 9th, 2002
6: Gmail Requires The Least Personal Info
Kevin Fox (Google) fury.com in WebProNews 2004-04-09

Google and the Mission

5

Features and futures

The big conditional

Google's future is highly sensitive to its product strategy. If they continue to get it right, then they will be able to keep their promise about the long-term value of their company, else, end if.

Since Google's engineering is currently unmatched and its products are generally doing better than hoped, the source of any creative paranoia has to be the sudden, unexpected improvement in Search technology. In classic Andy Grove style, they might expect someone else to come "out of nowhere" with the sort of paradigm shifting technology that they generated at Stanford.

This kind of paranoia is probably both healthy and necessary for long-term survival, but there are no obvious current contenders. Whereas in 1997 or even 2001, nobody outside Google saw the commercial possibilities of Open Search and contextual advertising, now the whole wide world knows about it. A sneak attack or invisible growth is not impossible, but is almost as unlikely as someone creating a wildly successful new operating system without Microsoft noticing.

Reasons to be paranoid or not

A good paranoia list would have to include:

- Yahoo!'s lead in Personalization and localization of results,
- Microsoft's pursuit of meaning inside natural language Search
- Microsoft's strategy of merging (Windows) desktop search with Internet Search
- Search through related topics, led by Teoma
- The creation of a "Semantic Web" indexed through metatext
- The 'Invisible Web' of dynamic pages stored in databases - rather than HTML or flat (static) documents

Other alternatives to Google Search will surely emerge, but in 2004 they are not visible and would probably not be viable commercially if they were hiding in plain sight. As Larry told [1] a seminar at Stanford:

> Industry seems to largely ignore users and excitedly follow the technology trend bandwagon. This presents an enormous opportunity to build new and innovative products. Google has grown to be used by a 100 million people without any significant marketing expenditures; it has grown by meeting people's needs.

Booty calls

Google has now entered an advanced features beauty contest, where a stream of newsfeeds suggest that such and such a search feature by one of Google's competitors will take over the Search market. A superior technology is always possible, of course, but if this book's take on context and meaning is correct, it would still have to be built on a foundation of context-mapping for an index covering four billion pages. Of course, if Microsoft really does crack natural language search in Longhorn, for both the Internet and your hard disc, then that will be game set and match to MS and both this book and Google itself will be cold product. If.

Unless it collapses under the weight of spam farms, which is as unlikely as almost anything listed above, Google's technology would have to be replaced with something not only better and faster, but with an equally strong attraction to advertisers. A slightly cleverer take on Search is not going to cut it without an equivalently strong brand that can compete with the circulation not only of Google, but also msnSearch, Yahoo!, and gallant little AskJeeves/Teoma.

Sell the steak not the sizzle

Google did not buy their public image with advertising but by being honest about what they were trying to do, after rather than before they have done it. This makes the company "notoriously secretive" but what the heck. Promising software before a public Beta (trial) is something that Microsoft does for specific, not very neighborly, reasons. Most software companies do not do this, because unless the software is in Beta, you cannot tell if it is ultimately going to work; it is just too complex.

Since Google's brand depends almost entirely on what they have done and are doing, and has not been generated by image-makers, brand managers or advertising sales messages, replacing it in the public mind with anything less real, but with a larger marketing budget, is going to be almost impossible. This is a market where week by week the customers become more educated and more discerning.

All the best engineering is very simple in what it actually does, however complex its methods of doing it. Google has a simple primary vector, go wherever there is free, public information and make it easy to access and hence available to both the searcher and to a classified advertiser. This is freedom of information through better engineering, funded by non-intrusive, quality-controlled, contextual advertising always based on the results of a specific Search query rather than being paid to include adverts disguised as genuine search results. That was a strong enough model to generate nearly a billion dollars of earnings in 2003.

What you do on the Internet

The founders defined their initial premise by saying that what *they* mainly do on the Internet is to look for information. Is it different for you? That is what it is there for, and that is what it is mainly used for. By engineering their technology round this simple truth Google built both the business and the brand. It did what people wanted and did not cost them anything. It is only going to become redundant when people no longer use the Internet to find information, which might happen, but not any time soon.

You can only compete in this field if your engineering is better and faster. You would also need to have the same circulation, which ultimately means brand strength, so that you can compete on advertising revenue. A fundamentally new, better and different way of searching the Internet would still has an awfully long way to go in terms of public image and advertising revenue before it gets close to critical mass. Teoma, probably Google's most successfully innovative competitor, was established relatively early and is doing very nicely. Later entrants would have to be engineering and semantic prodigies to make much impact.

Basic search still central here

Writing this book involved creating a web page archive with thousands of entries and using Google Search many times more than that. Mainline search without undue spam or obvious bias was generally easy, and there was very rarely any real need to use another search engine. This intensive usage includes services like Define: or exact phrase, but mainly it is simple search on well-chosen keywords, which I suspect mirrors the great majority of users.

Spam is the real threat, but was still relatively trivial in 2004. It seemed to improve considerably during the year, but that is impressionistic, and it may be that I have been using Google in areas where Spam is unusual.

Time's arrow

One thing Google's competitors cannot do is put the clock back to 1998, since when Google has built itself into users' working lives. Simply because it has been better for longer, Google now have a brand which has won people's trust and 150,000+ advertisers have followed. This has entirely changed the landscape of commercial Search and Internet advertising. Google's quality of results will have to erode a lot faster, and provide results which are a lot weaker, before the power of the Google brand diminishes significantly in favor of the competition.

Google's ten thousand servers and an almost fault-free engineering system do not come cheap. Couple that with a massive circulation and they now have critical mass. Google could not have survived on licensing deals alone, and new competition - however clever - needs to generate a massive amount of ad revenue before they can begin to compete for profits.

It is now the old Catch22 of newspaper and print publishing, advertisers are only interested in the largest circulations, but media companies need to be as large as Bertelsmann or Time Warner to afford national promotions and high print-runs (or bandwidth) whilst waiting three years after launch for a return from matching ad revenues, or a write-off as a tax loss if it fails.

Sometimes sheer size matters most

Google are now big enough to retain circulation in the same way as Yahoo! has done, because the bulk of its audience like and trust the product and don't like learning new interfaces. Size matters enough for Yahoo! to continue to compete successfully against msn.com, which was launched at about the same time, even though since its TCP/IP directory development, its own search technology has long been outsourced - the original Yahoo! directory has been replaced by the ODP, and Yahoo! Search was bought in first from Inktomi, then Google, and now from Inktomi, FAST and Overture.

The oft-repeated lesson from Netscape, that users can switch from Google very quickly if other search engines show better results, is certainly worth remembering, but the difference comes in ad revenues. Advertisers like size and continuity, and unlike users, they take months to agree a budget and cannot switch suppliers quickly, simply by clicking on another link.

Contextual advertising

Ask a potential advertiser to choose between a search engine with less than 3% of the market or Google with, depending on country, [35-70]%+ or AskJeeves or Yahoo!, it's a no-brainer. Taking market share needs a better product AND deep enough pockets to sustain a price war, probably whilst promoting heavily. AltaVista spent $120mn on advertising in 1999-2000 when Google spent nothing, because AltaVista's word-frequency technology was no match for PageRank's context mapping and everybody who used both knew it.

Relevant context can matter as much in advertising as in Search. Internet ads are actually welcome in the right context, but wholly unwelcome in the wrong company. I really do not want generic slutchat turning up in my email, or any advertising aimed at the 0.1% of the readership who might respond, but when I recently typed 'motorhomes sales UK' into Google, the ads were as useful to me as the actual found pages. I then found that coincidentally, my brother had done exactly the same thing and like me, clicked through all the ads.

Providing context in advertising is relatively easy for Google to organize because AdWord auctions the keywords competitively (here 'motorhome') and they only appear if the user is actually interested in that word. That usually generates a useful context for the ad to appear in - advertisers get their business and come back - like eBay or newspaper and magazine classified ads. (Whether an advertiser's contents are worth a clickthrough is another matter, but the owner will lose that business if they are not.)

Suits you, sir

Admittedly, this can still be fairly crude. A google on 'Microsoft faces host of patent suits', looking for a specific article, offered ads on quality menswear, while the AdSense forum on webmaster.com found refrigerator ads turning up on a page devoted to poems suitable for funerals.

Presumably this is because funeral homes have a big requirement for fridges. This is insensitive but not as bad as the guestbook for the memorial to a dead friend, which was spammed with downloadable ringtones.

According to Mark Pilkington in the *Guardian*: Bell, Edison and Marconi all believed their respective inventions would eventually make radio communication with the dead possible. He wondered about when the first texting service for the dead would appear. Emails to be sent out after the death of the sender are already available.

Adsense revenues for almost anybody

Adsense goes one step beyond. Webmasters, even small ones, can add an Adsense panel to their pages which carries 'relevant' ads supplied and paid for monthly, by Google. The contextual aspect needs work and Google are moving away from the 'broad match' that can fail to distinguish between legal and woollen suits.

A much bigger problem is the manual filter, which should prevent competitors from advertising on your site. The *Guardian* was amused when Sky's Adsense panel was seen promoting ads for arch-rival, the BBC. Although it is relatively easy to block competitors' URLs (internet addresses) that does depend on knowing beforehand exactly what URL they are going to use. One small publisher dropped Adsense from their site because it required a daily check to prevent competitors from appearing in the AdSense panel.

Google and the Mission

Payment on results - now that's a revolution

Google's innovative method of charging for advertising by results - the number of clickthroughs rather than eyeballs (page impressions) was something that David Kirkpatrick of *Fortune* magazine found [2] very convincing in *How Google Is Revolutionizing the Ad Game* (March 17, 2004).

The search company's model, in which advertisers only pay for success, should make other media companies nervous.

Most advertisers seek to stimulate demand by reaching a certain group of people with their message. In order to do so, they figure out which demographic segments are likely to respond to their messages and craft the ads accordingly. Google throws this model out the door. For Google, the key to an ad's success is not reaching the right demographic, but understanding the attributes of the product itself. When you can properly identify those attributes, you can buy links to keywords that describe or relate to them. The "demographic" is self-selecting. Anyone who seeks information about those subjects will see that ad. If it appeals to their interest, they click on it, see a message on the advertiser's website, and Google gets paid.

In today's conventional advertising process, marketers do demographic analyses, media planners select appropriate media, media buyers place the ads, then the company and its ad agency analyse the results. That can take many months. But on Google an analogous process can take mere days. A shoe marketer like Nike might select 3000 keywords-"pronation," "distance running", "Michael Jordan," etc.-and write five messages, so-called "creative," for each keyword. Thus, it's not unheard of to have 15,000 pieces of creative for just one product. The messages for each keyword alternate, and the ones that result in the least hits are eliminated. Feedback can be almost instantaneous. "Even overnight you can see which ads work best and shut some off," Armstrong says. "And there's no penalty for trying every idea, because you only pay for what works." Unless they run out of a product, advertisers have no incentive ever to shut off a campaign, which flies in the face of typical industry practice, where so-called "flights" of ads are run for a given time period.

"Shockingly easy"

...With these multiple avenues for distributing its advertising inventory, Google reaches 80% of the U.S. online population every month, according to comScore Media Metrix. I suspect no other property in any media can make such an extraordinary claim. An advertiser can manage its use of all Google's offerings on one spot on the site. It's shockingly easy.

... I'm convinced that this new model, in which advertisers only pay for success, will influence - in unpredictable ways - how all advertisers think about every medium. But I don't yet see the other media businesses reacting sufficiently and adjusting their own strategies accordingly. Being in the magazine business myself, that kind of makes me nervous.

Fortune's writers very rarely get things wrong, which is why, along with *Search Engine Watch* its reports on Google and Microsoft's IPO have been used as a benchmark for this book. The impact of contextual advertising and Google's role in pioneering it is already, and will continue to be, huge on the Internet. But there are really two kinds of advertising, display and classified. Display usually features large color ads and 'sells the sizzle not the steak' because it contains little or no new product information; it serves to reinforce the brand by selling an aspiration, ideal, or impression.

Classified not display

Display advertising is very weak on the Internet, picture quality is relatively poor, video very expensive and still unavailable to the majority who use dialup not broadband. Compared to tv or print, the Internet is a narrowcast medium with very few sites, apart from Yahoo!, AOL, msn.com and Google themselves, getting the kind of exposure which *Fortune* or the *Economist* print magazines would regard as routine. Little of this has changed in the last ten years.

Classified advertising is much less glamorous than display ads - hire-purchase signet rings rather than Bulgari, but much more profitable. Overheads are very low because classified salespeople are rarely allowed out of the office, it can all be done by phone; display sales people are expected to be out there selling on an expense account. Information advertising is wider than classified because it also includes new products or sale prices, but both depend on the reader actually seeking information.

Classified advertising is so profitable that it was the mid-Sixties before it stopped being put on the whole front page of the London *Times*. Amongst professional advertising people it is almost heresy that there are no ads on Google's home page - 'one of the most valuable piece of real estate on the Internet', but then the White House and the Imperial palace in Tokyo do not display billboard advertising either.

Faster feedback= $$$$$$$$$$$$$$$

At the time Kirkpatrick wrote this, Google almost simultaneously launched a 'channel' system so that advertisers can see the different level of responses that they are getting from different types of ads. Because feedback is intrinsic to hypertext, information-based advertising on the Internet can provide feedback overnight.

All types of advertising depend on feedback, but in print or tv it usually takes months before it is clear whether an advertising campaign has been successful, and it is hard to see how that could change. Interactive tv advertising, unlike the print, can also provide instant feedback from consumers. Red button tv is increasingly successful but sales are restricted by the number of 'opportunities to view' rather than being always available, like Internet material, and are too expensive for products much below the scale of George Foreman's grill.

Contextual advertising on the Internet is becoming so much more efficient than classified print advertising that it is almost certain to take over. The main current constraint is how well potential advertisers understand the medium, according to one Search Engine industry roundtable (**"Danny Sullivan in discussion with a hundred of his closest friends"** as it was described).

If your business depends on small-scale print advertising, and millions do, moving to sell it on the Internet can look like a significant risk. (My brother's success in promoting his business entirely on the Internet after years of expensive print advertising is purely anecdotal, but still convinces me that a huge shift in the advertising industry is already underway).

Other money-making methods are rare

Competing systems of contextual advertising, such as that developed by quigo.com [3] were being launched by 2004, and attempts at catch-up are underway. But Google uses an enormous, continually updated index, and without access to an equivalent Internet index it is not entirely clear how competitive such systems are going to be. This applies to the new third-party desktop Search software led by Blinkx.com (described below). Good search results are only the beginning; they can only be maintained with an effective income generator. AskJeeves/Teoma have an excellent index, and the ninth most visited site in the US with 32 million unique visitors, but they still have a deal to carry AdSense/AdWords which was worth an estimated $100 million to them and has now been extended to 2007. Their competition with Google is real and very healthy, but it is technological rather than commercial.

World domination - the map

When Google launched their IPO, the 'Road Show' designed to sell the company to institutional investors went flat. There are probably a lot of reasons for this. Google's healthy aversion to hype and marketing, the founders lack of experience at presentation, and the fact that they had been so deeply involved in the project for so long probably meant that they were too far away from the knowledge level and mind-set of their audience. The *FT* complained that they should have explained the company strategy.

This probably came as a surprise to Page and Brin, who would have expected that if a commentator with very few resources, like this one, can see the strategy, pension funds could afford a lot more expensive research. Spelling it out in greater detail would mainly benefit competitors, like Microsoft.

Google's stated plan is to go *everywhere* there is free information on the Internet, and then index it for Open Search and contextual advertising; and when they say everywhere... Apart from search results from a squillion ordinary web pages, everywhere now includes email, newsfeeds, blogs, friendship networks, shopping comparisons, usegroups, picture management and possibly, Instant Messaging and a new Gbrowser to match any future restrictions on MS Explorer. Since that includes just about everything except

Google and the Mission

subscription services, strategically they have the world wide web covered. Not bad after six years existence as a company and three years' profit.

...and a few wrinkles

For images, Google has bought up an online image management company, to supplement its much-loved, much-used, but possibly not enormously profitable, Internet image Search function. (For the sake of millions of webpage designers it is probably best for this not to be too profitable or it might attract more attention from the kind of corporate copyright lawyers who are currently suing Google for misuse of trademarks.)

Google's Orkut friendship network has become very fashionable amongst the digerati but subsequently attracted a legal claim of code theft from another company.

The next step was rumored to be Google's entrance into Instant Messaging and the creation of a new HTML browser, not confirmed by Google themselves. Instant Messaging is potentially a bit problematic since all the other Internet sources that Google taps into are stored somewhere, usually at least semi-permanently. Instant Messaging information is not stored by default and disappears into the background hum of the information universe as each message is sent. That could make it tricky to index.

Already works for blogs...

The release of Gmail was stormy but clearly established this direction. Although Gmail's funding method looked quite new to the public, as mentioned above it had already been run successfully to finance the blogging community. Google had already transformed blogging - online diaries - by making the service pay for itself with contextual ads.

Seriously as the blogging community takes itself, after the initial shock of Google purchasing blogging supremos pyra.com and 500 million pages of usenet news groups published by deja.com (now Google Groups), nobody from either community seems to have subsequently complained much about ads invading their pages.

The bloggers knew that their beloved technology was so commercially inefficient that it had all but bankrupted the companies and individuals, like the hero-developer of blogging, Evan Williams, who had developed and provided these services for free in the vain hope of finding adequate generic banner ads to pay for them. Alas, Internet marketshare means nothing if nobody is paying for the product.

None of these services had a strong, native, search capacity which Google could provide. There was some unease by veterans of both well-beloved services, (ok, some purists were furious) but Google has subsequently managed its stewardship of both these two pillars of the Internet successfully and provided an elegant commercial solution, when nobody else had any working ideas beyond wanting to continue to blog without having to pay for it.

...but not newsfeeds

The one service which Sergey has complained is not profitable is Google's newsfeeds, also known as Google News or Google Alerts. Newsfeeds are an addictive service on which this book has partly been built, from its first paragraph up. Google sends me an email when any newspaper carries a story about Google, using a format called RSS [4] to track its contents. This is a very fast alternative to the old press cutting agencies, which send out newsprint cuttings, usually weekly.

Alas, this is a free service which costs money to provide - a problem as old as publishing itself. The first copyright law was instigated by the London artist William Hogarth, because the then new technology of print-making made his pictures so easy to copy, badly. In the episode of Matt Groening's *Futurama* when they clone Lucy Liu, the chief nerd of Nappster (sic) protests **"You can't close us down, the Internet exists for the free sale and exchange of other peoples' work"** - so no change there then.

Lack of income returns is always a bad sign for long-term survival - so one suggestion for making this service pay comes in a later discussion of the eternal royalty problem. The Google news-alert Beta was replaced in 2004 by a Google Alert, previously provided by a third-party company. There were slight teething problems; the format improved but with a lot more mistakes which have gradually disappeared.

Google and the Mission

Sergey did not explain why newsfeeds do not work with the current model of contextual advertising. Maybe this is because of the old email format of news summaries, which may not take ads even with additional HTML.

Ads are also rarely going to be appropriate to hard news stories - which almost always depend on the news being bad. They use XML metatext which may not contain enough of the keywords needed for non-offensive contextual advertising. So the problem may be, at least partly, the desire to be non-offensive and non-intrusive.

Competing strategies

Microsoft's aim of integrating natural language search into the desktop is still a distant prospect, particularly after Longhorn's delivery, and its mission-critical new WinFS architecture, had been delayed or postponed until 2006, probably. This is such a large part of Gates' strategy for Microsoft that it is galling for Bill to see it stumble in public; so do not expect him to forget about it and move onto other targets.

Google are after the same thing ultimately, but unlike Microsoft they had no plans, and almost certainly no need, to rebuild their entire file architecture around an objective that some major corporations and mighty minds have tried and failed to achieve over the last fifty years.

Before Teoma, AskJeeves was heavily promoted to Internet newcomers, on city billboards, as a natural language service which could answer questions. Their technique almost amounted to taking words they could not process in a user's question and simply disregarding them, rather than, as Google does, announcing that it cannot search for "who" or "the". These are traditionally known as 'stopwords' because they are so common, and have no usable meaning, so that you stop searching when you hit one.

It was almost a dodgy sell, but AskJeeves gradually got better at the technology and found ways of tracking and converting millions of similar questions into well targeted search enquiries. Teoma was adopted and then taken over by AskJeeves, whose index now provided a very nice fit with Teoma's clever development of part of Google's underlying method. They have also enthusiastically adopted Open Search, having found that paid inclusion screwed up the quality of their results.

Localization: Yahoo!'s ticket

If Google's golden ticket has been Open Search and contextual advertising, Yahoo!'s has been Personalization and Localization. It may not justify the size of Yahoo!'s p/e ratio, but in every other respect myYahoo! has been extremely successful. It is user-centric and it certainly does tie customers into the portal over time.

> "It's a key focus for Yahoo!," company spokeswoman Diana Lee told [5] Stefanie Olsen of *CNET News.com*. "Being able to bring a more personalized experience for visitors makes it better for them, for us and for advertisers."

Up close and personal

...The personalization of search tools entails matching results to user profiles. These profiles could include data such as zip code, birth date or individual search history. For example, the keyword "jaguar" might place car sites at the top of search results for someone who had recently visited automobile Web sites, but might lead off with Web sites about the cat for someone whose surfing history showed an interest in animals.

That's an old canard as Sergey has complained, since Jaguar also now means Apple's OsX v3, another mutually exclusive category. It's rather dubious, because someone can be interested in all three meanings at different times. I have no proof, but I suspect that most Google users have already made that mental jump and would search on 'jaguar cat', 'jaguar osx', or 'jaguar car'.

It is certainly an issue for contextual advertising, however. Amazon have been upgrading their search facility with a healthy mixture of cooperation and rivalry with Google. By coincidence, a search on Murray Gell-Mann's *The Quark and the Jaguar* produced ads in amazon.com for Jaguar cars, although sadly, none for Quark - the industry-standard desktop publishing program.

According to Stefanie Olsen:

> Many search engines already use some rudimentary personalization features. AltaVista (now part of Yahoo!) uses so-

called geotracking technology to detect visitors' Internet protocol (IP) addresses and guess their geographical location. That can provide useful context for some searches, for example, in returning soccer-related results for a query on "football" from a user based in the United Kingdom.

A single, universal search result

When Google's IPO looked inevitable, and its product chain plans were obscured, there was a lot of pressure for Google to adopt similar technologies of localization. Brin's target has been, since 1997, a single universal search result. Give or take advanced and non-English language Search, Sergey believes that anyone in the world should get exactly the same results from the same search words, as anybody else searching at the same time.

This obviously touches Google's brand-critical 'purity of search' ethos, because up until very recently the only reasons to skew results was for commercial advantage or political censorship. The first Google abhors, the second has apparently involved soul-searching compromises with both the German and Chinese governments. People like and use msn.com and Yahoo! for different reasons, but they probably do not really expect them to be pure. Google, partly by wearing its heart on its website, has created different expectations and will deviate from Open Search at its peril.

Personalization is useful but...

Personalization is probably something that people will want to switch on voluntarily, because it could be invaluable for some searches ('plumbers Hackney'), but a complete waste of time for others ('Kaltix purchase'). Its real future may depend partly on whether it is capable of learning changes in personal context as well as inferring basic rules of association from history or location. It also depends partly on whether Joanna and Joe Consumer object to losing any remaining privacy rights.

Google Local, in beta in early 2004, makes geographical search voluntary by asking the user to add the local area (or zip code) to their search query and thus avoids localizing a normal search enquiry. Google have also made inroads into some dynamic systems, particularly parcel and flight tracking. As Google's Businesswire press release explains [6]:

> Google Local search functionality is integrated into Google.com so relevant local information for specific keywords or locations is automatically presented to users at the top of search results pages. When these results are available, they are marked by a small compass icon which, when clicked, connects users to a Google Local search results page.

That old WAP promise: pizza anywhere, anytime

For example, users searching for a pizza restaurant in their neighborhood simply enter the keyword (pizza), and either a zip code or the name of a town or city (Palo Alto) into the search field to receive a comprehensive list of local pizza restaurants. Each result is accompanied by a phone number, street address, and a list of related websites such as those of local pizza restaurants, store reviews, and related information. Clicking on a business name delivers a new page featuring an easy-to-read map, directions, and more related web pages. If needed, users can limit or expand their results to include listings within a 1-mile, 5-mile, 15-mile, or 45-mile radius of a specific location.

Google searches its entire collection of web pages to pinpoint geographic information that is relevant to a user's query. Google combines this information with comprehensive local business, map, and service information drawn from a wide variety of U.S. databases such as the yellow pages and other sources. Today, Google Local connects users to U.S.-based local information. The company plans to include local information for international markets in the coming months.

Invading Bart Milner's privacy

Personalization works for Yahoo! but might be what Larry calls "a technology bandwagon" for Google. Whilst Yahoo! tie in users through individual services, Google retains users through the brand quality of a free product, it is their advertisers that they need to bind to themselves with hoops of steel. If visitors stop wanting or needing to use Google, then the advertising revenue will collapse with the circulation, but in the meantime it is the advertisers who are actually the customers and pay all the bills. They may need or want Personalization and localization but it would take another form than that needed for Open Search.

The other downside to localization and Personalization is that it not only provokes fears of intrusion, like Gmail, it is also a real threat to privacy which Gmail, at least in its current form, is not. At this point I have to apologize to Bart Milner for invading his privacy. This is not me, suffering from a multiple-personality disorder, but another Bart Milner. A 30 second search in Yahoo! from a Google link produced this:

PeopleData™ Find People Background Checks

Total Bart Milner Matches: 4

Summary of Results	Number of Matches	Location
BART MILNER	4	
B MILNER	Too Many. Click Here to Sort by Age, City or State.	
MILNER	Too Many. Click Here to Sort by Age, City or State.	
BART	Too Many. Click Here to Sort by Age, City or State.	

BART MILNER - 4 Matches

Name	Address	Telephone	Background Check	Satellite Photo	Birth Date	Location
BART MILNER	Address	Telephone	Background Check	Satellite Photo	Nov 1979	GA
BART A MILNER	Address	Telephone	Background Check	Satellite Photo		WA
BART A MILNER	Address		Background Check	Satellite Photo		WA
BART A MILNER	Address	Telephone	Background Check	Satellite Photo		WA

Returning Users Login here
$10 Reveals All Phone Numbers and Addresses for All 4 Matches Above!

If someone, like Bart Milner, agrees to background checks and can challenge the results, as in the UK's **Data Protection Act**, that is fair enough, but unknown checks of unknown information by unknown individuals, who may or may not have a criminal or hostile intent? I have a problem with this, and judging from the misdirected Gmail privacy storm, I may not be alone.

As mentioned earlier, Google restricts its personal information collection to first name and second name only, at least for Gmail. That means Google may do better to orientate and market their services as non-intrusive, impersonal and privacy-protecting. There will be a demand, the public Gmail debate demonstrated that.

Onfolio - the Allaire contribution

Personalization also invokes something else: the long hunt not just to find but subsequently to keep track of (index) personal collections of websites when they start to run into the hundreds or thousands and become impossible to find by Bookmark/Favorite or by Title, which is often generic and almost meaningless. Again that was part of the problem that both Yahoo!'s and Google's founders started with but never quite solved, as such.

JJ Allaire with brother Jeremy (technology director for Macromedia, but cited above in a personal Blog) created the pioneering Cold Fusion web database delivery system. JJ has now developed Onfolio which aims to solve the same problem, according to Tony Kontzer [7] of *informationweek.com*.

Onfolio's application is what JJ Allaire calls a search-information manager. Once installed, Onfolio embeds itself in the Web browser and lets the user collect, organize, and share search results and browsing activity so that information resources can be used repeatedly without performing duplicate searches. It combines one-click buttons on the browser address toolbar, tabs, and the Explorer-style file system familiar to Windows users to create a simple information-management interface. Browsing and search activities can be quickly captured with one of the one-click buttons, then organized and customized within the Onfolio file structure. A professional edition also allows for rapid publishing of collected information to a Web site or as RSS syndication feeds.

Allaire started working on the Onfolio technology soon after the sale of Allaire Corp. to Macromedia. While his brother, Jeremy, and other Allaire execs--including Adam Berrey, co-founder and president of Onfolio--stayed on at Macromedia, JJ Allaire took some time off, then got the idea for Onfolio while working on another project. "I was doing a ton of research using Google and was finding it to be an annoying experience to manage all this stuff," Allaire says. "It struck me that this is not something that's limited to savvy technical users."

Google and the Mission

Metatext - great if nobody cheats

HTML's solution to the problem of indexing the Web, more or less from its inception, was to allow web page authors to add invisible metatext which contained keywords and/or summaries of the documents contents. Spiders can read this text in the source code, so it can provide a guide to the most important words and themes without getting in the way of the text that the visitor sees.

This worked fine in the academic environment where Tim Berners-Lee built HTML for particle physicists and academics who had no reason to cheat on their articles and a lot of reasons not to. It was in the interests of those authors to make their metatext as comprehensive and useful as possible. Unfortunately, in the commercial world which HTML rapidly became part of, metatext was easy to manipulate because it cannot be policed outside closed business or university environments. It rapidly became used for an early form of spam, which Brin and Page went to war against in 1997.

Searching for 'Moby Dick' in the mid-nineties would find a porn star high on the ratings. This was because web page writers were only supposed to include a phrase once in their page description, and the pornographic pioneers of spam had found that you could jack up (or is that 'off') the search rating by repeating the same invisible keywords dozens of times.

But they do

In the early days of AltaVista, heavy reliance was placed on metatext. It was initially very useful, and still can be, but there is no way of making it trustworthy or reliable. This is part of the legacy of HTML (and its superclass SGML - Standard Generalised Markup Language).

It is not clear whether Google Search ignores metatext. Some observers thought that keywords were coming back because a new function in the Google toolbar uses keywords for simple search. If metatext is used, it certainly has a low significance compared to other parameters in Google; although some of their competitors still do pay a great deal of attention to it.

Although this book is clearly not a howto for Google or Search, there are several books that do that already, it is maybe worth pointing out that one of the best way of generating metatags is to index your site for unique words, using code, then throw away the stopwords, and add the results to metatext tags. This will list all the important words that the website is using. If significant words are missing from that list, they should be in the visible text anyway.

The Semantic web

Sergey and Urs Hoelzle (previously chief engineer and now in the first Google fellowship) are not in the least naive about commercial incentives to corrupt Search and simply refuse to take metatags seriously because there is no way of policing them if content is invisible to the user. Urs also points out that librarians take four years to train, and it is insulting to that profession to suggest that the untrained can produce equivalent results.

This does not make either of them very excited about the Semantic web, the efforts by Sir Tim Berners-Lee and colleagues at W3C. It's that old index the web problem, as one of the introductions explains [8]:

> What's the rationale for such a system? Data that is generally hidden away in HTML files is often useful in some contexts, but not in others. The problem with the majority of data on the Web that is in this form at the moment is that it is difficult to use on a large scale, because there is no global system for publishing data in such a way as it can be easily processed by anyone.

It is doubtless a good solution for self-policing networks, like the universities, but elsewhere it has the major drawback of being easy to circumvent and is very difficult to get any but the most competent webmasters to apply and even they might baulk at applying it retrospectively to the pages already up there. I've promised not to use code examples generally in this book but here's a flavor from the same introduction by Sean B. Palmer.

Non-trivial markup

> Once information is in RDF form, it becomes easy to process it, since RDF is a generic format, which already has many parsers. XML RDF is quite a verbose specification, and it can take some getting used to (for example, to learn XML RDF properly, you

need to understand a little about XML and namespaces beforehand...:-

rdf: RDF xmlns: rdf="http://www.w3.org/1999/02/22-rdf-syntax-ns#" xmlns :dc="http://purl.org/dc/elements/1.1/" xmlns: foaf= "http://xmlns.com/0.1/foaf/" rdf: Description rdf: about="" dc:creator rdf:parseType="Resource" foaf:name>Sean B. Palmer /foaf:name /dc:creator dc:title The Semantic Web: An Introduction /dc:title /rdf:Description /rdf:RDF>

DreamWeaver will save us - again

MacroMedia's wonderful web-authoring software, **DreamWeaver**, will probably come to our rescue as ever and provide an interface for this. The snag comes in that first line: "Once information is in RDF form, it becomes easy to process it...". *Any* information is a cinch to process once it has been imported into a database or has an index, it is getting it into an indexable form that is always the problem with natural language text.

It is not hard to get students competent and enthusiastic about building their own web sites, but getting them to implement this kind of indexing would border, from experience, on the impossible. Or as Sergey told the PC Forum 2003, in an "impressionistic transcript" [9] by Cory Doctorow:

> "The Semantic Web sounds really improbable. Asking everyone to write in a new language -- XML or RDF -- seems like an unreasonable burden on too many people, to make computer-readable info. We should use computers to understand humans, not humans to speak in computerese.

> We wouldn't ignore RDF or XML if it were present, but we don't expect it to be in great profusion. We'll go anywhere that there's lots of information."

Diversifying

One place that Google went was friendship networking, developing the Orkut friendship networking site, which is competing against AOL's universe.icq.com. Google's shopping comparison service, Froogle, has done quite well against the established services such as shopping.com, which was started by Hollinger Digital, the *Telegraph* company, whose former chairman and chief executive Richard Perle, was also a Director of Cambridge-based Autonomy.

Froogle has not attracted much comment, and apart from an early tendency to appear in a main Google Search, little or no criticism other than that it may be too far away from Google's core competency of Open Search. But it looks fast and efficient, localizes very smoothly to the UK even when being accessed through google.com rather than google.co.uk, and carries a healthy load of Adwords contextual advertising.

Google also produces an array of advanced search features, usually in Beta, often experimental and sometimes a bit flakey. This is really where Google employees can demonstrate the personal work they are allowed to do one day a week. Advanced features in Google, or its competitors, are worth tracking and Jack Schofield of the *Guardian* has provided [10] a list of some of Google's advanced techniques.

Teoma traces topics

The most interesting new services are finding more context within context by learning the way that searches tend to theme around certain 'nodal' topics. This is called topic-clustering. Rather long on promise, it was one of the great white hopes of Search technology which appeared amongst Google's predecesors, disappeared during the dot crash and has subsequently reappeared. It is an update of the Thesaurus concept: the idea is that when you do a search all the results from related subjects, and not just the searchterm itself, appear alongside.

Teoma is now generating very good results from related topics. According [11] to Wade Roush from *MIT's Technology Review*, March 2004, Teoma believe they are mining a deeper level of context than Google:

> Google "looks at the structure of the Web, but that method doesn't go down to the next level," says Paul Gardi, Teoma's senior vice president for search. "When you get down to the local level, you will find that links cluster around certain subjects or themes, very much like communities." For instance, pages on "home improvement" don't simply link upward to more popular

pages; they also tend to link to each other, forming circles around prominent sites like Hometime.com, Homeideas.com, and BobVila.com.

The Rutgers scientists designed Teoma (Gaelic for "expert") to find those subject-specific communities and exploit their wisdom. Before the Teoma engine presents the results for a given set of keywords, Gardi explains, it identifies the associated communities and looks for the "authorities" within them-that is, the pages that community members' Web sites point to most often. Teoma tries to verify the credibility of these authority pages by checking whether they're listed on resource pages created by subject experts or enthusiasts, which tend to link to the best pages within the community. It then ranks search results according to how often each page is cited by authority pages.

IBM and other organizations experimented with similar authority-based ranking systems in the late 1990s, but Gerasoulis says their approaches could take hours to slog through all the pages out there. Gerasoulis's proprietary technique does the same thing in about a fifth of a second. AskJeeves dumped its previous search provider and switched to Teoma's technology in 2001, and its query volumes jumped 30 percent per year in 2002 and 2003.

New engines with daffy names

Roush also describes Mooter, which produces a starburst of topics comparable to Teoma but whose results have been more interesting than useful, and Dipsie, which like Yahoo! aims to read the increasingly large number of web pages, which are dynamic - created 'on the fly' by a visitor's request to a database. (Search engines like Google are almost entirely dynamic, of course, because all pages are created by the searcher's request and then discarded).

Hard as it may be to believe when you're looking at a dozen pages of search results, today's search engines ignore most of what is out there on the Internet. Software spiders have difficulty indexing content that is protected behind sign-up forms or stored in databases such as product catalogues or legal and medical archives and only assembled into Web pages at the moment users request it. This so-called Deep Web may amount to as much as 92 petabytes (92 million gigabytes) worldwide, or nearly 500 times the volume of the surface Web, according to the School of Information Management and Systems at the University of California, Berkeley.

Mining the Deep Web is the mission of another fresh face in the search business-Chicago-based Dipsie. "Google and Teoma only index about 1 percent of the documents out there," says Jason Wiener, Dipsie's founder and chief technology officer. Wiener, a self-taught programmer who ran a San Francisco Web development company until the dot-com crash, has spent the last two years building a more nimble crawler, one that can get past forms and database interfaces. Say you're wondering about the standard equipment on a Mercedes 55SL convertible. At Cars.com, drilling down to the page with detailed product information will take about six steps. Dipsie, however, will have indexed the entire Cars.com database in advance, so it can send you to the same page with a single click. "We don't handle anything that requires authentication with a username and password, but we do almost everything else," Wiener says. He claims that by the time Dipsie's search site becomes publicly available this summer, its index will include 10 billion documents-triple the current size of Google's index.

The Deep Web

Urs was characteristically dismissive about the Deep Web, suggesting that since nobody could see it, they can make up any size for it that they like. One of his examples was the thousands of pages of historic meteorological data held by NOAA, which only have significance within a particular master page, and are meaningless on their own.

He also argues that dynamic data, as such, is "not that difficult to deal with". However, features like session cookies, which are included in URLs, make them unique and thus vastly increase the potential number of pages that have an identical content. The number of pages on the web, he says, depends on the way you count them (an old problem, as Professor Michael Brin had found with the economy of the former Soviet Union).

It is still not clear, and Google may have some solid commercial reasons for not enlightening us, how much dynamic data can be read by their Search spiders. The navigation and indexing for this book, for example, was done in JavaScript because, notwithstanding earlier complaints, JavaScript is installed on every browser after Netscape 4.0; it is free and can be extremely powerful because it works locally rather than having to make calls across the Web to a remote server.

How not to impress developers

Used on the browserbook version of this text, the automated index system means that data only has to be entered once but can be made available anywhere, and can be edited, moved or deleted without affecting any other links, which are self-organizing.

That simply is not possible with manual HTML. The bad news is that Google and probably all the commercial Search engines may be unable to read slightly complex, but standards-compliant, JavaScript. That would mean that its 600 references to web pages or books in Amazon make no contribution to PageRank, which as Tom Waits remarked: "is kinda tragic when you think about it".

Dipsie claimed that it was indexing ten billion pages of the Deep Web (Yahoo! was vaguer about its Deep Web targets). Although it was said to be undergoing private Beta trials in 2004, the cognoscenti of slashdot decided it was probably vaporware and amidst our nerdish chortles pointed to a page from the Dipsie site, which was labelled TECHNOLOGY but was completely blank apart from what appeared to be a shot inside a derelict railway carriage. It does not look as though Google needs to panic about Dipsie and the Deep Web yet

Language limits

By far the most important aspect of Advanced Search is the number of languages available. Some languages, particularly Chinese are bound to be more difficult. While Western language text can be broken down into its alphabetic characteristics, Chinese ideograms are relatively large and complex ideas and are inherently associative - 'pig getting trotters wet in stream' is one example of a basic Chinese character.

At the February 2004 World Economic Forum meeting in Davos, Google's CEO Eric Schmidt participated in a panel called Clearing the Data Smog, where the AlwaysOn network reported [12] that he said:

"...although the Google algorithms work quite well for Western languages, there are many languages for which the approaches we take do not solve the problem nearly as well. It has to do with the way language works and the differences in culture."

This is a little confusing, because Eric is supposed to be the hardheaded businessman keeping the wild technologists in line, and here he is concerned with a research issue some way from the company's profit streams. But he's not been led astray by wild techies; pure language questions today are bound to shape advertising capabilities tomorrow. And the Chinese, Japanese and Korean markets will almost certainly determine, for better and worse, the world economy in the 21st century. Research [13] reported by the *Guardian*'s science editor Tim Radford sheds a new light on some of the syntax versus semantics questions described in this book:

The music of Mandarin

The Chinese need both sides of the brain to grapple with challenges of Mandarin, but English speakers listen with only half their minds on the job.

Sophie Scott, a psychologist at the Wellcome Trust, and colleagues from hospitals in Oxford and London performed brain scans on volunteers as they listened to their native languages.

When English speakers heard the sound of Mockney, Mersey or Geordie, their left temporal lobes lit up on screen. When Mandarin Chinese speakers heard their native tongue, there was a buzz of action in both the right and left temporal lobes.

"We were very surprised to discover that people who speak different sorts of languages use their brains to decode speech in different ways, said Dr Scott. "It overturned some long-held theories."

The left temporal lobe is normally associated with piecing sounds together into words; the right with processing melody and intonation.

Google and the Mission

In Mandarin, a different intonation delivers a different meaning: the syllable "ma", for instance, can mean mother, scold, horse or hemp according to its musical sound.

"Speech really is a complex sound," said Dr Scott. "As well as understanding words, the brain uses the way in which words are spoken, such as intonation and melody, to turn spoken language into meaning. This system has to be robust and flexible enough to deal with variations in speech sounds such as regional accents. We think Mandarin speakers interpret intonation and melody in the right temporal lobe to give correct meaning to the spoken words."

The maths - the essential logic of external context and local proximity - should still hold, but the formations and frequencies will follow different patterns in both the spoken and the written text of the two kinds of language.

The magnificent gibberish of automatic translation

Google's automatic language translation does not seem to be generating much interest, but this kind of service does date back to AltaVista's glory days when they introduced the free Babelfish language translation service.

Google and other machine-translation services appear to be fairly basic and to make significant errors of meaning - hence the magnificent *Jabberwocky*-like gibberish generated by translating a Borges poem footnoted in the next chapter.

Translation agencies seem to be offering it as a free service, so it is probably a good starting point where Google does a lot of the gruntwork but then needs a linguist to judge ambiguous meanings by their, ahem, context. To advance further would require better contextual analysis to balance the deficiencies of current rule-based translation systems. But that could be expensive and difficult, and it remains a free service.

Deskbar and Toolbar

The Google Toolbar is the feature, which generates the most interest and anguish. Its central function is simple enough; it opens inside Explorer 5.5 in Windows and enables you to type in your search words without having to find the Google Search page first. It also suppresses pop-up advertising, a very popular move initiated by Opera, which was soon imitated by Hotmail and others.

Google Search boxes in browsers were pioneered by Opera, and followed by Apple's Safari for OsX. Google produced a mainstream version for Explorer in Windows that included some advanced features, including a message spot showing the PageRank of individual pages.

This tapped into a neurotic and obsessional minority who, particularly during the anti-spam 'dances' at the end of 2003, seemed to be checking their PageRank every hour and emailing or posting up horror at their site's (usually temporary) descent into oblivion.

Googly - Deskbar for the rest of us

Surprisingly for a "100% Linux" house, at least on the development side, Google had a tendency to provide consumer software only for Windows and Explorer. This is hardly unusual; Linux and Mac systems make up only about 10% of the market. It may also have been the result of a desire not to provoke Microsoft without good reason, but there have been public complaints that Google's image management system, picassa.com, only works in Windows and that most designers and most people in publishing have a strong brand loyalty to Apple.

I have found that Google, combined with an Apple iBook laptop, has been a superbly powerful combination, but there is no Deskbar for Apple, so I wrote one that launches a Google query response page from any default browser, Safari, Opera, Netscape, OmniWeb, rather than just Explorer in Windows (which it is equally happy with). It does not need the browser to be open already at Google's home page, saving RAM and screen real estate, which is particularly useful on a laptop.

I sent the code to Google because it interacts with their URL and while lawyers have already started arguing about what Google actually does own, this has to include their own URL.

I also wanted to show that it did not collect *any* personal data and should not be used in any Denial of Service attack because it can only be accessed through the user's mouse. This should prevent it being activated by a Visual Basic-savvy (or even Applescript-aware) virus or trojan.

That's the old skool to me

Google seemed happy and wrote a nice note, copied to my lawyer, so it was named Googly (a deceptive ball in Cricket) and posted on my site next to the opening chapter of this book.

This book is strictly Old Skool, arguing that web sites should be highly ranked in Search because they contain content that a significant number of other people want to link to voluntarily; anything else is either spam or delusional. Consequently, I have tried hard to prevent the explanations in this book making any contribution to 'tweaking the Google algorithm', which even when innocent is misconceived and misses the point about why Google works in the first place.

Footnotes

1: Google is not an anomaly:
By Larry Page, Google Seminar on People, Computers, and Design Stanford University January 11, 2001
2: How Google Is Revolutionizing the Ad Game
By David Kirkpatrick FORTUNE Wednesday, March 17, 2004
3: Quigo Launches Innovative New Content-Targeted Advertising Platform for Advertisers and Publishers
Quigo Technologies, Press Release, June 21, 2004
4: RSS - A Primer for Publishers & Content Providers
By M.Moffat, EEVL Development Officer, eevl.ac.uk, 20th August 2003
5: Searching for the personal touch
By Stefanie Olsen: CNET News.com August 11, 2003
6: Google Connects Searchers with Local Information
BUSINESS WIRE March 17, 2004
7: Allaire Founder Debuts Online Research Tool
By Tony Kontzer: Information Week TechWeb March 15, 2004
8: The Semantic Web: An Introduction
By Sean B. Palmer: informesh.net 2001-09

9: **Sergey Brin of Google at PC Forum 2003**
By Cory Doctorow
10: **Google -Search tips**
By Jack Schofield, The Guardian, Guardian Newspapers Limited
October 3, 2002
11: **Search Beyond Google**
By Wade Roush: TechNewsWorld MIT Technology Review March 2, 2004
12: **Google Is Searching for the Perfect Hit**
AlwaysOn February 26, 2004
13: **Brain buzz that proves Chinese is harder to learn than English**
By Tim Radford, Guardian, June 30, 2003

6

Roots

We are going to rebuild this whole shoosh,

From the underground up, citizens

Always remember that,

From the underground up!

Busta Rhymes (polite version)

Necessary and sufficient conditions

From Singapore to Bangalore, Moscow to Wapping, the question is being asked: "How do we create the conditions for the next Google to be created here?". Realiztically this does not mean the next Search engine, but the next generation of innovation.

Although "Google-killing" algorithms developed in garages are all the rage in 2004, those developing them do not have Google's advantages of engineering a new solution to an old problem, entering a huge field dominated by a moribund technology, or a Stanford-sized testbed to get the engineering right over a lengthy test period, Google's flair with distributed engineering at *all* levels, or indeed seed-investors with the attitudes of 1999.

Stanford can take considerable credit for the development of Google, literally in that they own the copyright to the PageRank algorithm, according to the SEC filing. This is in line with the usual arrangement whereby any university owns the copyright on anything developed using its resources.

Very few institutions would have had adequate resources or the flexibility to allow development on the scale required to develop Google from BackRub. Searches came into Stanford at the rate of one a second, used up half the university's bandwidth and generated enough heat to give the fire marshals a heart attack. (Heat dispersal is still one of Google's central engineering headaches.)

Centers of global excellence like Stanford are indispensable to developments of this magnitude, and it is no coincidence that much of the Apple Mac's innovation, particularly the now universal GUI (desktop interface) and mouse, was derived from Stanford's organization at Menlo PARC. Netscape rode on the wave of research that came out of the National Center for Supercomputing Applications at the University of Illinois and which, like Menlo PARC, was never organized to turn its mould-breaking research into commercial products.

Out of the rustbelt

Concentrating all resources on prestige institutions - Oxbridge in the UK or the Ecoles Normales in France for example - would be a mistake. Google is as much a vindication of the rustbelt, Michigan, Maryland and even Moscow, as of Silicon Valley. Brin and Page are not Orange County preppies or the children of IBM or Boeing employees; they came to Stanford with their degree-level education from the American heartland and obsessive, rustbelt hunger to work until they succeeded.

Their mindset of **Great just isn't good enough** was already set and in place before they started Google. That makes for a management style as driven, in its way, as Andy Grove's at Intel, and explains why although apparently so different, they reminded Bill Gates of the early dominate or disappear days of Microsoft.

The overwhelming superiority of the United States in IT is the product of this very American cando optimism of the intellect, a love of finding innovative solutions to physical problems. But America is also reaping the long-term reward of the huge investment in public (state) school education in science, mathematics and engineering begun by President Eisenhower's administration as a response to the Soviet threat, more particularly the early scientific lead that Russian science had demonstrated with the Sputnik satellite and R2 (Soyuz) rockets.

When the Brin family came to Maryland from Moscow, or Carl Page graduated from his Michigan high school, they were not yet part of President Bush's self-proclaimed "**base**" of the "**haves and the have mores**". The opportunities for education and careers in science, maths and engineering were there for the gifted and motivated to benefit from, making the American dream happen.

UK maths

In the UK, Chancellor Gordon Brown's prudent Treasury has agreed to Education Secretary Charles Clarke's, £5000 pa financial incentive for new maths teachers. Clarke is himself a mathematician (from the same college as Alan Turing) and wants algebra and grammar at the core of the UK curriculum. Traditionally maths is one of the weakest sectors in English education, despite the examples of Newton, Babbage, Boole or Turing.

Although teachers in the UK are resistant to any increase in an already over-loaded curriculum, it is worth considering making a module in IT, present, past and future, compulsory for university entrance, in the way that elementary maths was and, I trust, still is. The newly recruited maths teachers are probably also the people who should be teaching it, for reasons that I hope this book makes obvious.

The cost of over-runs and cancellations on UK government IT contracts, including the NHS (National Health Service) – the largest civil IT contract in the world - dwarf even the entire valuation of Google. The only way of stopping this is to educate a new generation of managers who are IT-literate beyond consumer electronics. The anti-trade snobbery of the English Public (private) schools means that this will need to be obligatory for all university entrance, or they will simply refuse to participate.

US education

It should concern Americans that foundation-level maths, science and engineering ("shop") is reported to be in very steep decline in much of the US school system. Good as they are, MIT, Stanford and their ilk require a strong domestic hinterland, as well as the ability to attract the best foreign students.

If they had never met, it is very likely that Larry and Sergey would both have had very distinguished careers in their respective fields, but like all great teams whether business, scientific or sporting, the whole is greater than the sum of the parts. There is a strong symmetry in the partnership of Sergey Brin, with his family's roots in the great intellectual heritage of Russian Jewish mathematics, and Larry Page whose background is very Michigan and part of the greatest tradition of American engineering.

Michigan mockery

Michigan, and particularly Detroit, seem to have a culture of mockery, which sets them apart from a prevailing American culture where optimism and positive thinking can often mean that uncomfortable realities are simply ignored. This jives with the saving grace of the English, an often-vicious sense of humor, which can confront serious social problems by joking about them. We like the kind of killing jokes told by Michigan's Michael Moore, Marshall M. Mathers and D12, MC5, Madonna and Lucy Liu, who are respected, apart from any other talents, for their wordplay and black humor.

Larry also likes to cloak with a joke, whilst putting across very serious points. Witness the unkind dig at Sergey's achievement in taking Google into profit when just about every other dot.com except eBay (and Amazon with a more difficult job) was cashburning into catastrophe, as blogged [1] by Brad DeLong.

"Google has been profitable since the first quarter of 2001. Why did we make becoming profitable such a priority? It's good that we did, because we might well be gone if we hadn't. The real reason is that we became profitable in the first quarter of 2001 because Sergey Brin made it a priority. You see, Sergey would try to go out on dates. He would call up women. And to impress them he would say, 'I'm the president of a money-losing dot-com.' But in Palo Alto in 2000, a huge number of people were presidents of money-losing dot-coms. And so they would not call him back. And he thought, 'If only I were president of a money-making dot-com, things would be very different...'"

Lucas Pereira: 'You idiots, you spelled [Googol] wrong!' But this was good, because google.com was available and googol.com was not. Now most people spell 'Googol' 'Google', so it worked out OK in the end."

First check users

Certainly did. That's Larry the Joker but do not be fooled. He is utterly serious about Google's first truth that everything hinges on the user. Like Apple at its best, you always get the impression that Google was designed by somebody who wanted to use it, rather than simply trying to shift x number of units by Christmas, whilst spiking the competition. This approach is still unusual in the West, although it has been quite dominant in Japanese design of consumer goods for companies as successful as Sony.

In 1997 Google's founders needed to be able to search the Internet and assumed, quite correctly, that their needs would be shared by just about every other serious Internet user. If you align design successfully with users' perceived needs before you calculate the profit margins, you can build up tremendous brand loyalty. Of course, the trick then is not to neglect the bottom line, and assume that (advertising) profits will inevitably follow a successful product, a mistake made by some of the better dot.coms, or like Apple before Windows, assume that user loyalty will entitle you to extract stratospheric margins indefinitely.

Lego legends

Maximizing bang per buck was an obsession of Larry's well before Google was created; his early fame at Stanford was gained "by building disc-drives and printers out of Lego". It's a nice foundation myth, and Douglas Coupland spun Lego into his haunting story of loss and hope (and object-orientated programming) in *Microserfs*; but Page says that Lego was not the point, the point was to use the cheapest Costco forms and clip-ons available to get the job done (presumably after you had recycled your own and your brother's Lego collection). The same thing is now true of Google's distributed servers: the base units may be Costco cheap, but Page and friends have engineered them to provide a combined punch equivalent to some of the most powerful, and expensive, equipment available anywhere.

Here's part of Larry's profile [2] from Michigan:

> ...His father, Carl, a professor at Michigan State University, was among the first to teach computer sciences. And his mother, Gloria, was a database consultant who holds a master's degree in computer science.

> Then there's his brother, Carl, also a graduate of Michigan, with a BSE in computer engineering (1986) and an MSE (1988). He's now travelling the world after selling his own Internet company-eGroups.com-to Yahoo! for $400 million.

Explained Page: "I never got pushed into it. I just really liked computers. I was probably the first student at my elementary school to turn in a word-processed homework assignment." His corporate biography notes that he first used a computer in 1979- in the era of punch cards-at the age of seven.

...and leadership

Following his graduation from high school in 1991, he headed to Ann Arbor to enter U-M's College of Engineering. While there, he received a number of leadership awards for his efforts to improve the environment for students within CoE. He also served as president of the U-M chapter of Eta Kappa Nu, the national honor society for electrical and computer engineering students.

... "I spent a lot of time in Engineering with the organizations in which I was involved, learning about leadership," Page recalls. "In particular, the 'LeaderShape' program was an amazing experience that helped me a lot when we started Google." (LeaderShape is a University-wide student leader development program that originated in the College of Engineering in 1992.)

"Always wear a helmet"

Sergey Brin came skating into Stanford from Maryland having received a B.S. in Mathematics and Computer Science from the University of Maryland in 1993, better prepared, he felt, than contemporaries from Yale or Harvard. (Recent advice to Maryland students: "Always wear a helmet".) Born in Moscow, his family emigrated to the US when he was five. His father, Michael Brin, is a Professor of Mathematics at Maryland, his mother a rocket-scientist with NASA (and her web page is too secret for anybody to look at, according to her husband).

He received an M.S. in Computer Science from Stanford University in 1995. Between 1995-1998 his academic work at Stanford involved co-developing and publishing some landmark ideas about data-mining under Terry Winograd, supervisor to the postgrad group that included Larry Page.

From Russia with...

Sergey's great-grandmother had left her degree in microbiology at the University of Chicago to return to Moscow in 1921 and help build Soviet Communism. Despite this, Sergey's family were refugees from another wave of anti-semitism in Russia in the Seventies.

His grandfather was a professor of mathematics in Moscow, and his father followed suit, earning a doctorate in maths. In Moscow, Professor Michael Brin's job had been, he jests, to prove that Soviet living standards were about to outstrip America's. It all depends how you count and what you count.

Recently Sergey has had to defend the high PageRank of an anti-semitic site in Google. Given his family's experience in Russia it must have been hard to take the resulting storm of criticism from Jewish interest groups. His position is that you do not doctor Search results however distasteful an individual site may be. It is the intellectual integrity of Brin and Page, not just the beauty of their technology, which makes Google such an attractive model.

Dimensionality

Together with Craig Silverstein and colleagues at Stanford and now Google, Brin has published more than a dozen publications in leading academic journals, including *"Extracting Patterns and Relations from the World Wide Web"*; *"Dynamic Data Mining: A New Architecture for Data with High Dimensionality,"* (which he published with Larry Page) *"Scalable Techniques for Mining Causal Structures"*; *"Dynamic Itemset Counting and Implication Rules for Market Basket Data"*; and *"Beyond Market Baskets: Generalizing Association Rules to Correlations."*

These yield insights into the ideas that became central to Google's core method and success, but are also a big help to potential competitors. If any of Google's competitors complain that this book downplays the technical achievements of others and credits Google with too much that is because Google have been exceptionally frank about how they were thinking. Where there is no published material available from the competition, Google can fairly be given the credit for having initiated that technology.

Version one point zero

Google's most obvious innovation, PageRank, has been adopted by others, simply because it was too obviously successful to ignore. If anyone was using a similar system before Brin and Page described PageRank, they were certainly not telling. Now every serious search engine has one; it is unthinkable not to.

The same thing is now happening with contextual advertising. If another company feels that they should be credited with creating what will almost certainly become the industry norm, they need to show that their logic was published before AdWord/Sense was operational. Unfortunately for Google, Overture did have the patents for auctioning the value of the keywords bought by advertisers. Not the same as contextual advertising, but a key to the commercial success of the process and it took Google a quarter's profits in 2004 to buy the perpetual license from Yahoo!

In Christmas 2003, the *Guardian* gave their now-traditional review of top Googles for the year. (The UK's first was Prince Charles, God save His Royal Highness). They then repeated the story that Google was started in a garage. Some garage. Although it's true that Google the company moved from a dorm room to a rented garage, Google the Internet Search engine was developed in the Gates Building, at Stanford University. Yes, that Gates; he paid for the premises where they built Google, the lousy ingrates.

Stanford v. Harvard

But why Stanford; didn't Gates go to Harvard? Indeed, and Harvard made the mistake of not remaining friends with him when he dropped - or should that be jumped - out. Although Stanford's name crops up close to all the major players in this saga, they could not refrain from gloating when Bill joined Hewlett and Packard (who also started in a garage) in setting up their new nerve centre: the Gates Computer Science Building. In a ceremony in January 1996 where it sounds like [3] the wine flowed as freely as the rain:

'President Gerhard Casper noted that the Gates Computer Science Building is "supported by two of our oldest and most dedicated friends (Hewlett and Packard), by other long-standing friends of Stanford, and by new friends, including Bill Gates, who did not even attend Stanford. Bill Gates, though, had at least enough good sense to drop out of Harvard."

..."The building is too new yet to have its own special history and patina, but it won't take the students too long to rectify that," James Gibbons, dean of the School of Engineering added. "So here is my prediction: within the next 18 months something will happen here, and there will be some place, some office, some corner, where people will point and say, 'Yeah, that's where they worked on the (blank) in 1996 and 1997.' And you will know it was a big deal. You will read about it."

Death or glory

And here we are, googling Google, but it was not the wildest of predictions. When the Yahoo! guys set Yahoo! up, they were asked how their supervisor at Stanford's Electrical Engineering school felt about it. "Oh, he does not know about it, yet. He's abroad on sabbatical, so we haven't told him" they replied, wide-eyed.

This is an environment that favors only the truly motivated; less gifted and less determined students would sink without trace if their allotted supervisor disappeared like that. Even Larry Page admits Stanford scared him initially; he told his old University that he thought he might be put on the bus back to Michigan.

Enter the godfather

Although both Yahoo! and Excite had also been developed out of Stanford, their explosive success caught everybody, including their developers, by surprise. But by the time Google started to happen, Stanford was able to provide pro-active support.

Stanford's ability to be at the forefront of almost all the most important developments in IT can be traced back to Vannevar Bush, who can also be credited with inventing the concept of a mechanical library, described in the next chapter. According to his biographer, G. Pascal Zachary, describing *"The Godfather"* [4] in *Wired* magazine:

> Bush was also among the first to see the importance of venture capital and the way risk-taking inventors, drawing on top-flight

universities, could spawn whole new industries - and, in the process, destroy the inefficient corporate oligarchies that ruled America from the turn of the century until the 1980s. At MIT, he began forging research partnerships with local companies and later cofounded Raytheon, then a radio-tube supplier, today a defense electronics giant.

And while laying the groundwork for the high tech Route 128 corridor around Boston, he made what may be an even more crucial contribution to the industrial history of this century: he helped create Silicon Valley by instilling in one of his graduate students, Frederick Terman, a belief that regional economies would someday depend on a strange brew of risk capital, hard-charging entrepreneurs, and dreamy academics. After World War II, Terman went off to Stanford - and played a pivotal role in engineering the academic-business partnerships that gave rise to what is now the greatest concentration of high tech power in the world.

"The Disgusting Mechanisms"

If it looks as though I exaggerate the paradigm shift between Google and its Search engine predecessors described in the next chapter, here are some views quoted by Zachary in the article quoted above in 1997, a few months before Brin and Page's paper on hypertextual search was published. (Andries van Dam was the originator of the first working system of hypertext.)

"Bush's vision is extremely relevant," says Andries van Dam, a professor of computer science at Brown University. "And the core of that vision hasn't been realized yet. So you can't just say, 'Been there, done that.'" Compared to Bush's ideal, van Dam points out, "the Web is embryonic. Its retrieval systems, for instance, are incredibly primitive. The mechanisms are disgusting. Bush talked about the amplification of the human mind. We don't have that today. Even the search engines on the Web do everything by brute force, rather than retrieving personalized links laid down by the user, which is why you get so much junk."

Finding useful information amid the junk is the great technical problem of the moment. "We are drowning in information," declared Interactions, the journal of the Association for Computing Machinery, in a tribute to Bush last year, "while precious little is in drinkable form. Bush knew a computer connected to a global information network could solve a problem that, in 1945, barely existed yet. We are just now learning how."

Bush's dream of a new class of professionals who would "find delight in the task of establishing useful trails through the enormous mass of the common record." describes Google with prescience. Since 20:20 hindsight is a wonderful thing, it may be better to deny any suggestion that Sergey and Larry started with a master plan. Larry again:

Serendipity strikes

"It wasn't that we intended to build a search engine. We built a ranking system to deal with annotations. We wanted to annotate the web--build a system so that after you'd viewed a page you could click and see what smart comments other people had about it. But how do you decide who gets to annotate Yahoo? We needed to figure out how to choose which annotations people should look at, which meant that we needed to figure out which other sites contained comments we should classify as authoritative. Hence PageRank. Only later did we realize that PageRank was much more useful for search than for annotation..."

These are from the notes on a talk given by Larry Page, from *The Semi-Daily Journal of Economist Brad DeLong:* **Fair and Balanced Almost Every Day** cited above. This blog is unedited to preserve the flavor, but quoted at length because it gives the best available picture of Google's genesis at Stanford. (William Gibson would recognize the image of India lighting up the matrix.)

At start interested in telepresence and all kinds of wacky things. Interested in link structure of web. A large graph. Big graphs are fun things. A large graph and the web might together make a doable dissertation. Interested in reversing the web structure to view annotations--transclusion.

Blagging the bandwidth

World Graph of where the searches are coming from (now)...
India pretty amazing... Lots more searches coming from India
than electric lights at night...

"Our original hardware acquisition strategy was non-standard. We
would go out and wait on the loading dock and beg for computers.
When new computers arrived at Stanford we would go up to the
people taking delivery and say, 'Surely you don't need all ten of
these computers. Surely you can give us one. We have a really
interesting research project...'"

"We used half the bandwidth of Stanford during our research
phase...Occasionally, we would shut down the nameservers at
Stanford, and nobody could log into anything... Pizza ovens:
roughly that size and that temperature. Heat still a huge problem.

Investment in 1999

The point at which it became too much was when we had so much
traffic coming to Google--10,000 searches per day, one per
second. At this point we decided to start a company. Andy
Bechtolsheim, "Who do I make out the check to?"

Stanford's Museum archive takes up the story [5].

"... After Google's lab inception, Brin and Page added their
promising infant search engine to the Stanford website. As
google.stanford.edu, first members of the Stanford community,
then increasingly others, began to enjoy the upstart assistant and
trust its ability to find what they wanted on the web.

Google soon overgrew the bounds of the lab of Page and Brin's
principal investigator. Aptly named after a googol -- a one
followed by 100 zeros -- Google began requiring expansive
memory and ever-increasing processing speed to keep up with
users' demand for search. Continually expanding, and drawing the
attention of an exponentially increasing number of searchers,
Google's commercial promise was becoming evident. In 1996, Brin
and Page disclosed the technology to Stanford's Office of
Technology Licensing (OTL), which contacted several Internet
companies to help identify industrial interest in Google.

Google and the Mission

A terabyte on the plastic

...Page turned his dorm room into Google's new home, importing computers to his bedside. And Google continued to grow. After overflowing from Page's dorm room, Brin's nearby room became the office, and Page's remained the data center. During Google's rapid growth, Brin recalls needing more computer memory: "We had to buy a terabyte [which cost about $15,000]... and put it on credit cards."

Brin and Page gathered money from family and close friends. Google's potential also attracted several notable investors, including Ram Shriram (past president of Junglee and VP of Business Development at Amazon.com) and Andy Bechtolsheim (co-founder of Sun Microsystems and current VP at Cisco Systems).

Bechtolsheim actually catalysed Google's incorporation. Meeting at the home of a common friend, David Cheriton (a professor of Computer System Design at Stanford and co-founder of Granite Systems), Page, Brin, and Bechtolsheim discussed Google. After meeting for less than thirty minutes, Bechtolsheim had heard enough and wrote out a check for $100,000, to "Google, Inc." Since Google didn't exist yet, Page and Brin promptly incorporated their newly discovered and partially financed company. (Later, in June 1999, Google's commercial promise was confirmed by its receipt of $25M in funding from investors including Sequoia Capital and Kleiner Perkins Caufield & Byers.)

And finally, the garage

In October 1998, searching for a new home for Google and their enlarging collection of Google-wares, Brin and Page convinced a friend to rent her garage and a spare room to them. Promptly running cords and "improving" her Menlo Park home, they added eight phone lines, a cable modem, and a DSL line. Soon they began hiring."

So it's no myth, Google really did the trad thing and got a garage, except that they had already swiped half of Stanford's bandwidth to develop their cunning stunts. Fair dues, Stanford's alumni seem to be making very good use of all those wonderful resources. After all, Netscape took the value of the work already done - and let's be brutal - paid for, by Illinois and competed directly against it. A one-way street. It is worth reporting that Google is still repaying its intellectual and financial debt to Stanford.

Stanford symbiosis

Stanford had a special version of Google, which was running version number 3.4.14. in early 2004 (with a bug report, hey, I said they were hot, not infallible). It's not meant for the public, but here are some of the aims [6]:

"Google is Stanford University's official search engine. Google represents a significant enhancement to the University's web environment, providing:

Better and quicker search results

Advanced search features, including searching for PDF, .doc and .ppt files, and displaying them as HTML

Easy and powerful search administration

Easy integration into web sites

Bringing the Google search appliance into the Stanford infrastructure allows us features that the commercial Google Stanford index cannot duplicate, such as:

control over our own crawling schedule

the on-site search appliance crawls the Stanford web weekly, with a daily incremental index for selected sites

the commercial Google service updates its university index approximately monthly"

Clearing the data smog over the White House

This is part of a wider project under Professor Hector Garcia-Molina, previously an adviser to President Clinton. Professor Michael Brin's own page joked that Bill Clinton was somehow involved with the genesis of Google. Perhaps in an idle moment he tapped 'Bill Clinton' into AltaVista and was not amused by the results: the Bill Clinton Joke of the Day and similar sites got high listings, the official White House pages was nowhere in sight. Maybe word was passed down via Professors Hector Garcia-Molina and Terry Winograd to get those clever post-grads to have a look at generating more representative results from Internet Search, something a little more dignified for the most powerful office in the world.

Certainly Brin and Page used 'Bill Clinton' as a benchmark search term for comparing their own results with existing search engines, which by 1997 had already been thoroughly spammed by some of the President's internet-savvy opponents. More recently, President Bush's enemies did the same with the phrase 'miserable failure' by 'Google-bombing' it (building links to boost its PageRank, as a non-commercial, joke form of spamming).

The Global InfoBase

Stanford's WebBase project has the following goals [7]:

Provide a storage infrastructure for Web-like content

Store a sizeable portion of the Web

Enable researchers to easily build indexes of page features across large sets of pages

Distribute WebBase content via multicast channels

Support structure and content-based querying over the stored collection

The WebBase Faculty includes: Hector Garcia-Molina, Chris Manning, Jeff Ullman and Jennifer Widom. It is part of an even grander schema:

"the vision of a Global InfoBase (GIB): a ubiquitous and universal information resource, simple to use, up to date, and comprehensive. The project consists of four interrelated thrusts:

(i) Combining Technologies: integrating technologies for information retrieval, database management, and hypertext navigation, to achieve a "universal" information model;

(ii) Personalization: developing tools for personalizing information management;

(iii) Semantics: Using natural-language processing and structural techniques for analysing the semantics of Web pages; and

(iv) Data Mining: designing new algorithms for mining information in order to synthesize new knowledge."

I was literally about to write 'watch this space' when I got a newsfeed (from Google News, natch) that Google had just bought Kaltix which had been spun out of the work done on context by the GIB(ii) Personalization team.

Bill's moral high ground

Unlike the early days of Google, Kaltix has been in 'stealth mode' since Stanford and little reliable information is available, beyond the above note. But because Personalization is Yahoo!'s great strengths, it is a critically important commercial issue.

Ironically this means that Google not Gates can now be accused of monopolizing relevant research from Stanford. Microsoft has earned its status as top predator, and that frightens people, particularly when they have (or had) money invested in Microsoft's competitors. But predators help keep the food chain moving; Gates is also generous in a way that benefits his Karma rather than his balance sheet.

His gift to Stanford has now generated an immediate problem for Microsoft but the intellectual achievements of the Gates building in Stanford have been shared, not provided to Microsoft on an exclusive basis. This is reassuring news for any Brits concerned lest Microsoft have bought the Computer Laboratory at Cambridge University by donating heavily to its foundation.

Footnotes

1: Google and Larry Page
j-bradford-delong.net Delong February 14, 2003
2: Alumni Profiles: Page By Page
Michigan Engineer Online Spring/Summer 2001

Google and the Mission

3: Bill Gates Stanford Dedication 1/30/96
microsoft.com Microsoft Corporation
4: The Godfather
By G. Pascal Zachary, Issue 5. Wired, The Conde Nast Publications Inc. 11 Nov 1997
5: Uniquely Google
By Rich Scholes: e-BRAINSTORM Stanford's Office of Technology Licensing (OTL) March 2000
6: Google Search Appliance
Information Technology systems and Services, Stanford Univesity December 12, 2003
7: The Stanford WebBase Project
Stanford University

7

Before Google there was...um, AltaVista

Lots of search engines

In 1997, when Sergey and Brin published their landmark paper on the architecture of a hypertext search engine, there were a dozen or more search engines around, the dominant one being AltaVista. Very few have survived; the strongest, such as Inktomi or FAST, are now part of Yahoo!.

It was not Sir Tim Berners-Lee fault, but by 1995 his invention, HTML, which made it easy for one web page to be read by millions, was so cheap and so fast that the Internet was out of control. Not the underlying network, which was coping magnificently, most of the time, but the sheer volume of pages had made it impossible to retrieve anything unless you knew exactly what you were looking for. Simple URL addresses (most famously sex.com) were valued in millions simply because they were easy to remember and find.

Babel and Ultima Thule

There were lots of indexes of the actual words that appeared on web pages, especially their invisible metatags, but these were becoming less and less useful as millions more new pages were added. The Internet soon came to resemble (what I remembered as) the lost library of Ultima Thule [1] - millions of documents in a completely random order, with no index of titles, many indeed with no titles, author, source, or dates.

But as Google's endearingly nonsensical translation of the Jorge Luis Borges poem suggests: "the forgetfulness, she is one of the forms of the memory". Right writer, wrong story. "Am I the only one who thought of Borges' *Library of Babel?*" [2] one poster [3] to Topix.net asked. Not quite. One of the editors, Geoff Williams, had already pointed it out and according to one reviewer on Amazon: "If Jorge Luis Borges had been a computer scientist, he probably would have invented hypertext and the World Wide Web".

Google and the Mission

The missing index

Phase Two of HTML was intended to be not graphics, but an agreed indexing system. Trouble was, that could take (and has taken in the form of XML) years to develop and before anybody knew it, HTML was already being used, unindexed, in tens, hundreds, and hundreds of thousands of new Internet domains.

Inktomi and AltaVista, Google's main competitors when it started out and now part of Yahoo!'s Greater Co-Prosperity Sphere, evolved from a small forest of earlier projects all intended to compensate for the lack of a master index for the World Wide Web (HTML). Google succeeded and became such a dominant force on the Net by using an aspect of its structure, which no one else had seen.

Netscape had a built-in Bookmarks system (soon to become Favorites in Explorer), so that the indexing is client-side - entirely private to the user's browser. At best you could move bookmarks between browsers, making it easier to migrate from Netscape to Explorer. The drive to make Bookmarks or Favorites available beyond a single user initiated both Yahoo! and BackRub (Google) at Stanford.

The Searching Graveyard:

Faganfinder.com [4] has surveyed the search engines developed in the last century:

> Even before the Internet bubble burst, great search tools have gone extinct. Other search tools still exist, but have changed. Here they are, organized approximately chronologically by inception (oldest is last):

Raging Search

Northern Light

WebTop

Inktomi

Infoseek & GO

Deja

MetaCrawler, HuskySearch & Grouper

Excite

Magellan

Snap & NBCi

Lycos

WebCrawler

World Wide Web Worm (WWWW)

Open Text Index

Harvest, NetGuide Live, JumpStation, AliWeb, Starting Point (no details known)

Not first amongst equals

The thrust of this argument is that Google was not *primus inter pares*, first amongst equals, all doing more-or-less the same thing but not as well. Google depends on a core technology - context-mapping - which differed significantly from the core technologies used by any of its competitors, few of whom survive. And it is context-mapping which makes Google work in the overwhelming majority of cases by using a different way of evaluating the significance or relative relevance of the words that you actually search with.

The authors of some of these search engines were fatally seduced by the mirage of untold wealth conjured up by the dot.com bubble, but nearly all of them suffered from the fact that their technology simply could not cope with the exponential growth of the web. The need to make money when advertising was generic, rather than targeted (contextual), sometimes led to them being enticed into commercially-biased searches or into becoming portals whose purpose was to deliver reliably large amounts of traffic for the benefit of advertisers, rather than users - as Brin and Page complained at the time.

It was not a lack of competition, which enabled Google to becomes so significant; it was the failure of competing technologies to provide adequate results. It looks so simple, now, almost obvious, explicable in a few paragraphs; but to see the secret heart of the matter, when some of the best minds in your field have seen nothing special, that is close to genius. To then take moral responsibility for the implications of your work, that is even more unusual.

AltaVista swamped

Younger readers (who may have been using the Internet that much longer) may remember when AltaVista was the dominant search engine before Google. In the early days of the web it was invaluable, by 1997 it was truly dreadful. It was eventually bought by Overture and then incorporated into Yahoo! As Brin and Page put it back then:

> "Junk results" often wash out any results that a user is interested in. In fact, as of November 1997, only one of the top four commercial search engines finds itself (returns its own search page in response to its name in the top ten results).

AltaVista relied on an index of the word/phrase frequency and whole-word search terms. This worked, even in a huge forest of results, if you could find exactly the words that would only appear in a document you wanted: searching on 'Zola Chelsea football club' might work, but searching for 'football' produced thousands of unsorted documents about American football. It was quite possible to get useful results, but a post-graduate qualification in research was a big help, because it required repeated honing of search terms based on knowing what you were looking for. It was skilled enough to be worth teaching as a class at Hackney College in the mid-nineties.

Before Brin and Page presented their architecture in 1997, the usual suggestion was that you just keep adding new keywords until your search produced results. They completely rejected this approach, on the solid ground that users should not have to learn to compensate for bad design. This is now part of Google's legacy; if you add too many keywords to your search in Google, it does not return thousands of partial matches, it returns a 'nothing found' screen.

By September 1999, AltaVista had an estimated 9.5 million unique visitors in a month compared to Yahoo's 32 million (Media Metrix figures). Microsoft had begun to bury Netscape, and was buying in services for msn.com to compete head-to-head with Yahoo!

This unkind timeline from searchengineworld.com shows [5] why AltaVista in particular and Search engines in general troubled Microsoft very little when msn.com was competing with Yahoo! for visitors.

AltaVista Timeline

April 1995 AltaVista is conceived by Digital Equipment Corp. engineers. The idea was to develop a software "spider" to crawl the Web, indexing and presenting the information it found.

December 1995 AltaVista launched altavista.digital.com. As it later turned out, this was a major blunder.

1996 AltaVista provides exclusive provider status for Yahoo.

1996 November Signs with DoubleClick advertising broker.

1997 Aborted attempt at an IPO by DEC (try 1).

1998 DEC is sold to Compaq. Many have speculated that Digital sold it to Compaq for a song ($1, dinner and a movie).

1999 Compaq plans an IPO for Alta (try 2).

1999 January, Alta became a wholly owned subsidiary of Compaq Computer Corporation. Compaq purchased Shopping.com in March and Zip2 Corporation in April of that year which are also heavily laced into the portal.

June 1999 Compaq pays a record $3.3million for the domain name. AltaVista.com.

Aug 1999 AltaVista is sold to CMGI announces IPO (try 3). All IPOs fail. In August of 1999, CMGI, Inc. acquired 83% of our outstanding stock from Compaq, and Shopping.com and Zip2 became wholly owned subsidiaries of AltaVista. Later in 1999, AltaVista acquired Raging Bull,

June 2000 Flat-fee internet service in England is announced as a Hoax. UK Head Andy Mitchell quits saying he wants to spend time with his family (ya right, he was fired).

Nov 2000, Alta goes through two rounds of job cutting.

Oct 2000 Alta chief Rod Schrock quits saying wants to spend time with family (ya right, he was fired).

It is easy to be rude about AltaVista in retrospect, but the project was intended as a research project at DEC's research laboratories in Palo Alto - a short-term demo of DEC's Alpha hardware. In the early days of the Internet, it provided an extremely useful free tool, which cost its developers DEC and thence Compaq a lot of development and bandwidth money.

While there certainly were some giddy management mistakes, AltaVista's problem was its technology. Word matches needed to be frequent to get a high listing for the page. The higher the frequency the higher the rank, because apart from using increasingly corrupt metatext, all it and its competitors could really do was to match the characters in a search query with the characters on its index of web pages.

Manual means very, very, slowly

Search results were so dismal that people began indexing the Internet manually, using human editors to sort the wheat from the chaff, pretty much as we have been doing ever since the Sumerians first kept records on clay tablets. Most successful was Yahoo! which in 2004 could claim to be the most popular site on the planet, but has long since abandoned its own manual indexing for reasons that Brin and Page outlined in 1997.

Yahoo!'s manual directory delivered a lot more of what people actually wanted than automated search, which languished, the technology was inadequate, ad revenues were hard to find. As Brin and Page described it in *The Anatomy of a Large-Scale Hypertextual Web Search Engine* [6]

People are likely to surf the web using its link graph, often starting with high quality human maintained indices such as Yahoo! or with search engines. Human maintained lists cover popular topics effectively but are subjective, expensive to build and maintain, slow to improve, and cannot cover all esoteric topics. Automated search engines that rely on keyword matching usually return too many low quality matches. To make matters worse, some advertisers attempt to gain people's attention by taking measures meant to mislead automated search engines.

Yahoo!'s genesis

Yahoo! had emerged out of Stanford a few years earlier than Google. At the heart of their initial success was an innovative development of TCP/IP (Internet connection protocol) to permit much higher levels of simultaneous access. But their directory depended on human editors to sift out the best sites and list them under specific categories.

Yahoo! itself had been put together for fun and then profit by two manic college students David Filo and Jerry Yang, Ph.D. candidates in Electrical Engineering at Stanford University, who started their guide by building it on their personal workstations at Stanford, whilst their supervisor was away.

They created an independent list of interesting sites, linked by their own hierarchy of manually edited categories. (Yahoo! initially did not include porn sites, not for moral reasons, but because they were too unreliable, the link could go dead without warning.) According [7] to co-Chief Yahoo! David Filo in 1995:

Stanford hosts again

We had a 10 Megabit connection to the Net at Stanford, which was connected directly to the Internet. So bandwidth was never a limit. Disk space was never a problem either. At Stanford, it ended up being that the machine could not handle enough requests. Limitations on the number of TCP/IP connections a single machine could handle was our bottleneck.

...We started Yahoo! in about April '94. It started out as a way for us to keep track of things that we were interested in. We began with a Mosaic hotlist, and we just added things to it. When our hotlist was about a hundred items or so, all you could do was scroll through it sequentially. Soon we couldn't find anything anymore because the list was so big and there was no way to search it.

So, we created some tools that allowed us to hierarchically categorize our links much the same way that many browsers like Mosaic and Netscape do today (May 1995). Once we did that, finding previously visited links and adding new links became much easier. We then made the list available via the Web to make it easier to browse and added the search capability to make it easier to find specific entries.

When there were only a few hundred thousand web sites, human indexing was useful and practical, but with 4 billion plus pages, and still rising exponentially, manual indexing was not commercially viable. According to laisha.com's history [8] of the Open Directory Project:

Scale ceiling hit in '98

> By mid-1998, "Poor Yahoo!, with anywhere from 85 to 200 (depending upon whose statistics you believe) professional editors on staff, was simply unable to keep up with the growth of the Web."

By 2000 Yahoo! were really struggling with their manual indexing and were using the Inktomi search spider to create an automated index for searches that fell through the gaps in their taxonomy. "With only an estimated 4% of all submitted sites entering the database, a great deal of bad PR has been building about Yahoo." as searchengineworld.com reported in early 2000.

Realizing that they were hitting the limits of scalability - they simply could not grow at the same speed as the Internet - Yahoo! have adapted, with no little skill, and became a portal which keeps track of personal information sources (tax, car prices, whatever). Clearly useful, and built both on the goodwill generated by Yahoo!'s early, and thoroughly altruistic service, courtesy of Stanford, again, and an existing database of useful results. Yahoo! have now transformed themselves into a very valuable media brand.

Yahoo! gets Google

Yahoo! subsequently switched to Google as their main search engine and merged its results with their own technology. (In late 2003, a Yahoo! search on "Angel of the North" homed in on the sculpture in the north of England, more effectively than any other search engine. Presumably this was because the phrase was well represented in Yahoo!'s own manual directories, which complemented Google in their joint results).

They then bought Inktomi and Overture and dropped Google. It will take some time before it is clear whether that has improved their Search results.

Yahoo! itself had started at Stanford as an open, collaborative project designed to let anybody else add their own categories, and Google had begun with Page asking Brin how he could create a working public index for his collection of Yahoo! Bookmarks. According to laisha.com, in June of 1998 a posse of early Yahoo! enthusiasts, disappointed by Yahoo!'s relatively poor showing, answered a call from Rich Skrenta, a California computer programmer and now a noted blogger. He was looking for unpaid help to develop a free, open-source alternative which became the Open Directory Project (ODP), initially developed using Netscape's resources.

"The Spirit of the Web"

Thus started the concept for GnuHoo, a directory similar to Yahoo, but edited by an unlimited number of volunteers. On June 5, 1998, the site went live. By June 18, there were 200 editors, 27,000 sites, 2,000 categories:

The Open Directory Project: The Spirit of the Web

The ODP was launched by a group of anarcho-idealists with a clear purpose - index web sites more effectively than Yahoo!. This was a manual directory scaled to the Internet by tens of thousands of volunteer editors, self-organized in the way that the development of Linux (and the Apache Web server software) had shown that the 'network of networks' could make possible.

Yahoo! subsequently abandoned its own manual indexing and, like Google, provided access to the ODP instead. Although most people have not heard of the ODP and do not use it, it still has a very influential role because of the significance of its links.

"Pissing contests"

"It's so crazy, it might just work", as Gene Wilder once remarked. You can see the results by clicking on the Directory tab in the Google, or just about any major search page or portal. GnuHoo mutated into the ODP, which is now mega. By the end of 2003 it was reporting 4,031,427 sites - 60,344 editors - 537,518 categories.

The thousands of volunteer editors are allowed to create their own rules of categorization, but cannot stop another editor from changing those rules. The chaff gets winnowed. **"Yes, we do have pissing contests between editors"** one justified ancient at ODP admitted, and people often join in order to boost the ranking of their own sites, but it all shakes down. The self-promoters either get bored or get caught up by the spirit, hive-mind if you will, of a hugely successful, collaborative project with the kind of built-in criticality (self-regulation) displayed by some of the maths of Per Bak at Murray Gell-Mann's Santa Fe Institute.

At the same time that ODP is indexing four million sites, Google reports - 'Searching 3,307,998,701 web pages' (December 2003). The two systems, machine indexing and manual taxonomies (categories descending in branches) are complementary. Some of the difference in those two figures comes from the difference between counting sites and counting pages. What is the average number of pages for a site? God (or maybe Jacob Nielsen, the guru of web usability and a Google board member) knows, but divide the Google figure by that amount and you would have a fair comparison of Internet coverage.

Dynamic text

Although it can now work with formats like pdf, Google's current technological envelope is mainly HTML with some specific text formats and dynamic data beginning to come in. It was no mean feat creating a system that works almost flawlessly in HTML. At the time, Brin and Page spoke plaintively of the acres of accidental garbage generated inside HTML tags, the online games that started interacting disastrously with the Google index (ro)bot and the daily requests from lonely site owners who demanded feedback on the contents of their site after failing to understand that it was a bot not a human being which was looking at so many of their pages.

Putting that lot under manners is a considerable engineering achievement; Bangalore, San Francisco and Shoreditch are full of people struggling with only a minute fraction of that canvas. So it is almost churlish to point out that HTML remains, even on the wilder shores of next-generation XML, solely a mark-up language for displaying text consistently on multiple platforms. Like context mapping, its functional strength and subsequent near-global adoption is the result of its simplicity. This enabled Google to crack the indexing problem globally - because HTML is a global language. More complex systems give much more complex problems, which Google and it competitors are now facing.

Desktop Search now

To get a good idea of how Google changed Internet Search, take a look at your own pc and try to find a document, any kind of document - Word file, email or saved web page - by its contents. Easy if you can remember its exact title, location or date or an exact phrase which is unique to that particular file. If not, it can border on the impossible unless you have Google Desktop Search (GDA) or one of its smaller competitors, or a specialist tool.

It does not matter if I have archived fifty good articles on something, if I cannot subsequently find them. That has been a problem for any pc user, including no doubt, Bill himself. For home users this was inconvenient, for business it is extremely expensive.

The only operating system with the tools to conduct a simple hard disc search based on a word list rather than an exact phrase: "Google value IPO" for example, was Apple's Sherlock (now Spotlight). This is so important that Gates has tried and, temporarily at least, failed to get Microsoft to rethink and to rebuild Windows itself around this central function. It's a setback, but when Gates sees something as critical as this, he seldom if ever lets it go.

Tracking work affects almost all business. As one of the editors of this book pointed out, finding specific emails in his legal practice, where one client can have dozens of related messages, is a major hassle. Gmail's indexing system looked like one solution, but the California legislature and users worldwide are still working through the privacy implications.

Privileged, confidential, legal or business documents almost certainly cannot be stored in a public system. Google "Search in a Box" intranet Search server for business may be able to do the job, but it may also be rather expensive for small to medium-sized companies.

Blinkx.com and Google Desktop Search (GDS)

One new system of desktop search, which has created a considerable stir, has been Blinkx.com. This was developed by a former software engineer from Autonomy. It works in the background and calculates likely search concerns from the user's current document.

Sadly, the print schedule of this book precluded testing it, or GDS, which appeared a month later, but users' reports swing from the wildly enthusiastic to the entirely disenchanted. It searches the net only by proxy, using other Search engines like Google and AskJeeves, and has no obvious financial model or access to advertising revenue.

If it is as significant as some adopters believe, it may be acquired by a large media property with secure revenue streams. The release of Google Desktop Search, working in the background in a similar way, with real, if privacy-careful, links to Google's advertising database will certainly overshadow little Blinkx.

Lost archives

The Webthreads buttons and footnotes for this book were created because the thousands of relevant web pages archived from my research are almost useless without a custom-built index; it was all but impossible to find a specific piece without remembering an exact phrase which is unique to that document. It was often quicker to find an archived page by searching online in Google than by trying to find it on my laptop.

As a developer I have better search tools than more casual users but finding things quickly from long lists of files is still a pig. Writing the (JavaScript) code for this delayed completing the book, but it was worth it because it makes accessing specific research sources very easy for me and, I hope, for the reader.

Internet Search then

Finding documents on the Internet, before Google emerged out of Stanford, was even worse than searching a pc's hard disc. Prior to Google, the technology of Search used locally on a pc or globally on the Net was substantially the same. There were differences, but their significance was limited. Google's breakthrough was to exploit the very specific nature of HTML - the common web language - to make Internet Search much more effective than local search.

The truth is that, before Google, consumer-level text Search - obviously crucial to almost any computer use - has made very little progress since about 1984. On your desktop, you can search for a matching word, or an exact phrase, and that's about it. Case sensitive searches are common ('IT' or 'it'); otherwise there is something called GREP, which allows partial pattern matching (show every word whose second letter is "X", for example). Extremely useful if you are trying to maintain a database, blaggerall use if you want to find useful information in documents containing text on your hard disc.

No usable theory of meaning

Because there is no usable theory of meaning for the binary logic of computers, we cannot search for meanings. Conventional search software, like AltaVista in the nineties, generally worked like the search on your hard disc. Their problem was that computers are extremely fast only at sorting structured information - information stored in the rigidly tidy and well-ordered sets of a database, where a single gap in structured data can be fatal. Exact matching of words or phrases ('strings') is relatively slow.

Natural language - even formatted as HTML text, is full of gaps, errors, repetitions, inconsistencies, irregularities and unknown information that make ordered sets almost impossible to impose. Computers have no other reliable way of knowing what the data is about - because they currently derive meaning only from its location - the place where the information is stored. Since we cannot search on meaning, outside of logical and symmetrical sets, we have to search on the patterns that the letters make when words are formed.

Search limits

If you search for the word 'cat', your pc has no prior knowledge of the word, and your software simply finds three letters "c", "a", and "t" next to each other in a document. This is extremely crude, and it will find 'category' or 'catastrophe' as well. So a more advanced search feature is 'whole word only' which allows 'cat' by putting a 'word boundary' around it.

That works, but knocks out 'cats' as well as 'cattle'. There is no simple rule for plurals: simply adding (or allowing) an 's' does not always work. More than one goose is geese - even if children and people learning English often follow the usual rule and talk about 'gooses'. More than one cow makes cows, ok, but what about cattle?

Another search refinement is to ignore a list of non-substantive 'stopwords' (typically 'of' and 'the'). The best text software (eg bbEdit on the Mac) lists passages found with the same searchterm in multiple documents. And that, outside of the realm of specialized business software, is pretty much that.

Searching for an email or Word file on your hard disc still relies on some of these techniques. Apple's Sherlock engine, which was probably the most advanced form of desktop search, at least before Blinkx, can also handle word lists rather than exact phrases, but not spectacularly well compared to what Google can do on the Internet.

Spiders and crawlers

Nobody searches the Internet in real time - that would have taken far too long, even in the early days. Instead, spiders - a series of robot software programs - roam the web looking for new or changed pages. They usually download copies of new or updated pages to the search engine's server - which is what you use if a site link has gone bad in Google and you find it in "cached pages" at the end of most entries. This is held inside Google's distributed storage archive, which it can also use to convert documents into HTML from Acrobat's proprietary pdf or MS Word formats, for example.

The primary purpose of spiders is to create an index which shows where a word appears anywhere on the Internet. This is very useful for unusual terms; but for common words or phrases, 'Bill Clinton', or 'football' for example, it became less and less useful as the size of the Internet grew exponentially.

Spider-generated indexes listed how often a given word appeared on each page and often listed whether a commercial page was an advertiser. Apart from advertisers (paid inclusion), they had no known way of finding relevance other than the frequency with which search words appeared on a given page, how closely they matched the search query, or whether the author had added invisible keywords as a metatext for each page. As the Internet grew, these indexes simply could not tell whether one page was likely to be more interesting, more significant, than another.

Frequencies

To search on word frequency means getting a list of pages where the search words fall most frequently. This needs a list of unique words, or Lexicon, with all of its locations (url and word count) listed for each word. But the index has to begin at the other end: each page has first to be mapped with its own word list. This is what the web spiders do, (Google originally called their web spider a crawler, to distinguish it from Inktomi's - Lakota for Spiderman - but crawl it does not - it is blindingly fast.) The spider downloads a complete index of all words for each web page, one page at a time, after checking to see whether the page is new or has been changed since it was last indexed.

This words per page index keeps a record of the words (and tags) as they fall on each page, but is no use for a search on those words. It has to be reversed so that the first sort is the word, not the page. The existing Lexicon then has to be searched, and where the word is already listed, its new location has to be added.

Within the index the relative locations of words within a given page are measured. The closer this distance is to the distance between words in the search term, the greater the internal relevance. But that figure can be identical for thousands of documents. What usually distinguishes the significance of a given page which matches a searchterm is the external context provided by PageRank's calculation of other people's interest in the links to that page.

Internal and external context

PageRank only works for a document if other documents have hypertext links to it or it contains hyperlinks. Google and any other respectable search engine also need to find documents which do not have hypertext links. It does this by plotting the internal context of the (directional) relationships of the words on a given page to each other.

If PageRank is the main measure of external context, relative proximity is probably Google's most important measure of context that is internal to the web page itself, even though there are scores of other directional signifiers, used, like relative font size. This is less simple than it might look to a developer, as MSN search is currently discovering, according [9] to Jack Schofield and others.

> To crack the search market, Microsoft will need to produce something that is clearly and obviously better than Google. That is, after all, what enabled Google to overtake established search engines such as AltaVista, Excite and Lycos. It is not impossible, but I can see no such advance on either of Microsoft's sites. At the moment, then, MSN is no threat to the search engine leaders, Google and Yahoo.

Two other critical aspects of web page context are the word patterns in the documents being searched and the search query itself. Word patterns had been heavily explored since well before Brin and Page hit Stanford, but not so the (relatively very simple) context of the search query itself. Google may well have been first in analysing the search query as part of their context mapping for the whole.

Their GDS desktop search relies heavily on this internal context, because hypertext is rare outside the Web's HTML, so stacking relevance probably has to depend fairly heavily on date of documents.

Shared meaning

One principle of common-sense semantics assumes that two substantive words close to each other, or within the same passage in a text will almost always share a common relationship with a shared meaning. The best match comes between a phrase whose words have exactly the same relative location in both the search query and the found document, but this is only one of the parameters used to rank results.

If you are looking for news stories using 'Google' and 'IPO', then the closer the words are to their relative location in the query, the more chance that its contents will be relevant. If the web page contains 'Google' and 'IPO' separated by [100] words, they may not be linked directly by shared meaning at all.

This is because the found page could consist of a selection of news stories where 'IPO' refers to another company entirely. Anyone who uses off-line Searches frequently will know just how common it is to find a query answered by an irrelevant usage, or a word that means something different because it is in a different context.

Larry Page Stanford = Lawrence Lessig

Without any equivalent method to PageRank's use of external context, AltaVista and other search engines struggled as the web grew. The upside was that using AltaVista could lead to acquiring a lot more, usually trivial and irrelevant, information about a different subject which had turned up in the Search accidentally, as Brin and Page pointed out in 1997. This can still happen in Google, but it is the exception. It used to be the rule.

A google on 'Larry Page Stanford' (not stalking, officer, - honestly, research) turned up a very high ranking for Lawrence Lessig, Professor of Law at Stanford. This looked like a Google/Stanford joke ("Touch our boy and know that we also have the best lawyers on the planet, who will have you in court so fast it will make your head spin round...").

Nothing of the sort of course, it's another of those semantic coincidences that bedevil natural language processing: Lawrence Lessig is a Professor of Law at Stanford and popular with searchers because of his blog and work on the Creative Commons - copyright law for the Internet. He is also known as Larry and on his ...Page... which is not case-sensitive... You're way ahead of me, I'm sure.

Reality being the enemy of mathematical models, Google's index is actually not quite as elegant as a map of all the context of the Internet. A large proportion of words on the Internet exist to modify other words, and have no substantive meaning themselves. Words like 'of', 'the', 'that', 'who' are known as "stopwords" which means traditionally that they are not indexed, because they do not contain enough meaning to justify the amount of processing time required.

Stopword lists have been used as part of complex search for almost as long as the technology has existed. But excluding stopwords can cause real problems. *The Guinness Book of Pop Records* had to write an entire, and expensive, sub-program for the band **The The**, because the definite article was built into its search stopword list and thus excluded from any search.

Stopwords in the real world

Google generally ignores any non-contextually mapped rules of meaning, except one, the logistical rule that searching for stopwords would generate too much work, need too much storage and too much processing, for too little useful semantic return. It seems like a harmless rule of meaning - users will not need or want to search on 'stopwords' like "that" or "whether", there are several billion 'that's on the Internet so they, and similar stopwords are probably not going to tell you anything useful.

But even a rule of meaning as simple as that falls over in the real world. If stopwords are not indexed, you cannot search for a perfect phrase match. To do that, you need to index all words on the web, including stopwords, separately.

Identical phrases

An identical phrase search using double quotes discounts PageRank and all its parameters of context and reverts to a single binary question: does any document in the index contain exactly this phrase, true or false? This apparently gave Google a problem in the early days according to Andrew Goodman at traffic.com:

> "As for technology, no question, Google has a great search engine. At the same time, they're not the only ones who do. And the serious shortcomings in its offerings in the not-so-distant past - such as the inability to properly search phrases - might have been enough to sink a less-charmed ship."

Eliminating the problem with double quotes doubtless also helped. It may seem surprising that Google ever lacked identical phrase search, because most programs begin with, and have always had it; very often it is all that the Search in programs like MS Explorer, does do. But although exact phrase search is important to people like me, I suspect that very few non-professional users know about or bother with it in Google, even if they have no other choice but to use exact phrase in, for example, MS Word.

Angel of the north

'Angel of the north' is my favorite Search test, but it is easy for Search engines to patch search results, so to test this you would do better to pick a similar, but different phrase. Angel of the North is a hugely popular English public sculpture - half man and half Spitfire. It makes a good search-engine check because the web contains millions of documents containing 'north' and 'angel' that are irrelevant.

The first problem is that "of" and "the" are not indexed and Google does not search them, as it informs you on the Search screen, unless you specifically enclose them in double quotes.

Relative location

What Google is doing in a full search is not matching an exact phrase ('string' in the jargon); it looks for relative location. When Google searches for "angel of the north", it cannot just knock out 'of' and 'the' or it would be looking for a best match on "angel north" (a bar in Sydney, Australia, if memory serves). So Google's Search treats 'of' and 'the' as positionals: words with relative location but without a relative meaning.

It is measuring the distance between 'Angel' and 'North' (2 words) and then checking its own index for pages that best match both 'Angel' and 'North' with a direction of two words between them. If you do not use double quotes, a search on "angel of the north" and "angel from the north" produces identical results. A bigger or smaller word distance between substantives (as in 'Angel of North') gets a lower ranking. Page Ranking then kicks in to sort the order of pages with similar scores. Pages which show only 'angel's or 'north's disappear off the end of the list.

A stopword like 'the' is obviously less freighted with meaning than 'elephant' or 'uncle'. Nevertheless, it is a modifier, which means something beyond the repetition and redundancy (the 'noise' that Benoit Mandelbrot identified at IBM), which helps, to ensure that the whole message is received and understood. What such modifiers actually do mean, and how that differs from a substantive word, has yet to be adequately defined, but within Google's contextual mapping a modifier is given no context beyond being a unit of space created by an 'empty' word. 'From' and 'of' are interchangeable in a full Google Search (rather than a double quoted exact phrase) because they have no context, or rather; it is impracticable to give them a context.

You want speed?

That is the sacrifice required for a super fast engineering of results. Treating stopwords as having more than one dimension (relative location) would give more accurate results but would vastly slow down getting those results back because of the enormous additional processing required.

Normalizing stopword data, and thus losing much of it, is the difference between a purely mathematical or academic approach to the problem, and a successful engineering one. If a search engine included stopwords and gave higher accuracy, but slowed search to a couple of minutes, few would use it.

Fast results through the minimum disc searches (10ms each in Page's '97 benchmark) was one of Google's initial, critical targets. The fact that they have kept meeting it reflects on the quality of an engineering whose real-world demands can never be quite as pure and elegant as ideas behind the maths which powers it.

Footnotes

1: **Psychoanalysis in the Web**
Jorge Luis Borges automatically translated from the Spanish - Google
2: **Labyrinths**
By Jorge Luis Borges, James E. Irby, Donald A. Yates New Directions Paperbook Amazon.com
3: **The Secret Source of Google's Power**
By rich skrenta, Topix.net Weblog April 04, 2004
4: **Fagan Finder > Searching > Graveyard**
Fagan Finder January 19, 2002
5: **Search Engine Players: A Brief History**
PHDSoftwareSystems 2002
6: **The Anatomy of a Large-Scale Hypertextual Web Search Engine**
By Sergey Brin and Lawrence Page, Computer Science Department, Stanford University 1997

7: **Chief Yahoos: David Filo and Jerry Yang**
By Mark Holt and Marc Sacoolas sun.com Sun Microsystems, Inc. May 1995
8: **The ODP: The Spirit of the Web**
laisha.com ODP History 25-Dec-2003
9: **Searching times**
By Jack Schofield, The Guardian, Guardian Unlimited July 8, 2004

8

Adventures in hypertext

"We can remember it for you wholesale"

When Brin and Page found a way of calculating both internal and external context in a document by measuring the number and direction of hypertext links, they added their names to the history of hypertext. This includes a remarkably select band of people; imagining and then engineering a technology into existence is pretty rare and hypertext has proved a real mindbender.

Linking documents through hypertext and then measuring those links using PageRank to determine relevance may now look simple and obvious. Millions of people use these links every day without even noticing that they are doing so. But it actually took fifty years from the introduction of the idea of linked documents to make it work in practice.

Vannevar Bush

Vannevar Bush, US WW2 chief scientist, was the first person to conceive of document linking in order to supersede systems like Dewey decimal. The Dewey system is used by libraries to class books into themed categories by an almost infinitely extensible numerical sequence.

Bush (no relation of the US presidents as far as I can discover) is one of those towering figures of American science and engineering on whose shoulders we all now stand. He is best remembered as the godfather, as his biographer calls him, of amongst other things, the Manhattan project to build an atomic bomb. At the end of the war he wrote an essay "As We May Think" [1] where he develops the concept of the "memex".

> The real heart of the matter of selection, however, goes deeper than a lag in the adoption of mechanisms by libraries, or a lack of development of devices for their use. Our ineptitude in getting at the record is largely caused by the artificiality of systems of

indexing. When data of any sort are placed in storage, they are filed alphabetically or numerically, and information is found (when it is) by tracing it down from subclass to subclass. It can be in only one place, unless duplicates are used; one has to have rules as to which path will locate it, and the rules are cumbersome. Having found one item, moreover, one has to emerge from the system and re-enter on a new path.

The mind works by association

The human mind does not work that way. It operates by association. With one item in its grasp, it snaps instantly to the next that is suggested by the association of thoughts, in accordance with some intricate web of trails carried by the cells of the brain. It has other characteristics, of course; trails that are not frequently followed are prone to fade, items are not fully permanent, memory is transitory. Yet the speed of action, the intricacy of trails, the detail of mental pictures, is awe-inspiring beyond all else in nature.

Man cannot hope fully to duplicate this mental process artificially, but he certainly ought to be able to learn from it. In minor ways he may even improve, for his records have relative permanency. The first idea, however, to be drawn from the analogy concerns selection. Selection by association, rather than by indexing, may yet be mechanized. One cannot hope thus to equal the speed and flexibility with which the mind follows an associative trail, but it should be possible to beat the mind decisively in regard to the permanence and clarity of the items resurrected from storage.

The Memex

Consider a future device for individual use, which is a sort of mechanized private file and library. It needs a name, and to coin one at random, "memex" will do. A memex is a device in which an individual stores all his books, records, and communications, and which is mechanized so that it may be consulted with exceeding speed and flexibility. It is an enlarged intimate supplement to his memory.

Google and the Mission

Bush produced engineering drawings of his proposals but his system was never likely to work because although it was based on a superior indexing system, which was to be the key to Google's power, it was designed to use microfiche to store and project the documents. Microfiche is a now rare and deeply obsolete method of storing archives on silver bromide film. Even today we would have some difficulty using OCR (optical character recognition) technology to retrieve text from an analogue medium like microfiche. Fifty years ago it would have required an almost infinitely tedious degree of manual indexing.

The death of analogue

But there was another deep problem, which may yet be a key to the future of interpreting meaning in text: the battle between digital and analogue computers. History is written by the victors and the global triumph of digital computers has meant that analogue computers have almost been written out of history.

Few people today have heard of analogue computers even though they were extensively used for massively parallel gun placing in the Second World War, and were responsible for destroying an estimated 70% of the V1 flying bombs aimed at London. As James Gleick describes [2] in his masterly *Chaos:* **Making a New Science** it was a Royal McBee analogue computer that gave Edward Lorenz the first evidence of "the Butterfly Effect" where tiny initial differences in weather patterns lead to huge cumulative climatic effects.

These results could not have appeared on a digital computer because they were approximations, which are unknown to the digital universe, where all problems are divided into an exclusive matrix of true and false, 0 and 1. Analogue computers model a problem as a totality and the precise figures used to calculate, which are at the heart of digital computers, are set, in a sense arbitrarily by the user so that it makes no difference to the calculation whether the result is 7mm or 7 million kms.

The future was digital

Bush developed one of the first analogue computers, the "Differential Analyzer" - a mainframe-sized series of gears and spindles. It was noisy, greasy and huge, but because it worked like a gauge or dial it was capable of speeds of calculation for addition, subtraction and multiplication, which were not matched by digital computers for decades.

His pioneering role in developing working analogue computer may explain Bush's subsequent deep hostility to digital computers, whose funding he blocked after claiming, correctly, that they would never make a contribution to the US war effort. The prototype Eniac mainframe, based on thermionic valves rather than gears and rotors, was only funded because of fast political footwork behind his back and came into operation after the war ended.

But in the UK that was a secret

For once the UK, with Alan Turing at Bletchley Park, was ahead of the US - building the first programmable digital computer in 1943, the Colossus, to break Wehrmacht Enigma codes. The Brits, true to our traditions, dismantled it after the war and slapped a top-secret classification on it, ceding almost all technological and commercial leadership to the US. (Doh!..) It is now being rebuilt as a historical monument to Turing and Bletchley: - "the cock that never crowed" as Winston Churchill called them.

In one of the great ironies of computer history, Bush employed the brilliant maverick Claude Shannon to look at the programming of analogue computers. Shannon, who later developed the first wearable computers in order to cheat at roulette, realized the significance of Boolean algebra for machine calculation. Boolean logic, developed by the English Victorian mathematician George Boole, uses only the twin states of true and false to make calculations using And, Or, Not and notOr.

These can be implemented efficiently by electronic switches which represent those conditions by being in an On or Off state. Semiconductors, which replaced the original radio valves, could place millions of such circuits on a slice of silicon lattice.

Once Intel and its competitors started to engineer these semiconductors, analogue computers disappeared from history. Although one designed and built by the Kiwi economist Bill Phillips, which modelled the post-war UK economy very efficiently using flows of water (with inflation pushing liquid out through a hole in the top), can still be seen in the Science Museum, London.

Google and the Mission

Nelson conceives hypertext

One commentator has described the shift to digital from analogue as the difference between Computer Science and Computer Engineering where absolute precision and accuracy replace the workable estimates of engineering. Analogue theory was weak and the quest for the memex all but disappeared. Most other aspects of artificial intelligence went unsolved.

Bush's challenge to produce a memex gathered dust until the mid-sixties when Ted Nelson the prophet, showman and visionary, developed the concept of hypertext and tied it to the still unresolved problems of copyright payments. His search for "transclusion" where *all* documents could be scaled, windowed and made subject to copyright payments so as to appear beside other documents with related contents, inspired a millennial programmers cult of total information called, initially, Xanadu88.

It was also one of the key ideas, which Larry and Sergey were reviewing at Stanford when they developed the concept of Backrub/Google. Like Sir Tim Berners-Lee they succeeded because they adopted highly specific and much narrower targets than Xanadu.

Publishing requires payment, usually

As a writer of some influential books, including the cult-hit *Computer Lib* [3], Ted was understandably concerned that royalties due from using somebody else's text should be paid, and this would be through micropayments made at franchised booths. These booths materialized more than 30 years later when operations like Cyberia, the first UK Internet cafe, were set up.

After the dot.bomb disaster caused Cyberia's failure, through no fault of the management, in 2004 it reopened as a successful, online, public, South Korean social, games and business centre, and there are seven, similar Internet cafes centered on different ethnic communities within ten minutes walk of my home in Hackney, east London, which has a high transient and student population. Ted's booths have prospered, but royalty problems remain, and he never saw any franchises.

Ted was said to be heavily medicated for severe attention deficit disorder which made him obsessive about the memex concept - replacing his own non-functioning, and other people's weak, memories with a perfect, scalable, permanent and complete record of all that is known and all that will be known. The idea was so over-arching, so grandiose and so compelling that the Xanadu88 project had the same impact as a religious cult on a whole generation of programmers, getting its first real money from a $5 million investment by Autodesk, a major player in CAD (computer aided design) software.

Xanadu88

Ted's vision demanded answers to crucial problems, many of which have yet to be answered. By asking these questions, he shaped the future of the Internet, but the repeated failure to implement his ideas caused the kind of anger and frustration more normally associated with the loss of a religious faith. As Shahrooz Feizabadi put it in his History of the Internet [4]:

> In my limited reading on the history of computing, I have not encountered any subject as passionately discussed as Xanadu. Its followers believe in it with almost religious zeal and its skeptics bash it with equal conviction.

He also quotes Nelson's summary of Xanadu's targets:

1.   Xanadu is a system for the network sale of documents with automatic royalty on every byte.

2.   The transclusion feature allows quotation of fragments of any size with royalty to the original publisher.

3.   This is an implementation of a connected literature.

4.   It is a system for a point-and-click universe.

5.   This is a completely interactive docuverse.

Loss of faith

In **The Curse of Xanadu** [5], Gary Wolf did a demolition job in *Wired*, which, Nelson concedes, is beautifully written, but he says, drips with bitterness, malice and misrepresentation. Wolf is easy to quote and makes some important points about the relationship between scientific vision and practical engineering, but it is the availability of Ted's original concept of hypertext which now makes it easy to view his point-by-point rebuttal [6]:

> Evocatively written and cunningly constructed, the piece claims to be the final obituary of Project Xanadu; but some might imagine that it was intended to harm the reputations of all the Xanadu veterans and alumni (some fifty of us), and particularly my own, charging falsely (amid a fusillade of personal slurs) that my early work on media design and hypertext were based on technical "ignorance" and "fantasy."

"A trivial simplification"

Ted Nelson can, and now does, take credit for being the inspiration behind much of what has subsequently become the Internet, although in 1995 he dismissed the WWW to Gary Wolf as "a good try. He said it is a trivial simplification of his hypertext ideas, though cleverly implemented." But both HTML and Google's ideas solved a couple of fundamental flaws in the philosophy of Xanadu88 which had doomed it to a half-life as a project which broke hearts and sometimes careers as it was always six months away from ever being finished and actually working.

In the same long and often excruciating piece by Wolf, Mark Miller, one of the lead architects of Xanadu was asked if the Internet was accomplishing his dreams for hypertext.

> "What the Web is doing is easy," Miller answered. He pointed out that the Web still lacks nearly every one of the advanced features he and his colleagues were trying to realize. "There is no transclusion. There is no way to create links inside other writers' documents. There is no way to follow all the references to a specific document. Most importantly, the World Wide Web is no friend to logic. Rather, it permits infinite redundancy and encourages maximum confusion. With Xanadu - that is, with transclusion and freedom to link - users would have had a consistent, easily navigable forum for universal debate."

Simplicity and reliability do seem to be the two things most lacking in the decades of research by the teams led and inspired by Nelson.

The final stages of Xanadu88 were an object lesson in that inspirational scientific ideas can only be engineered by keeping development priorities clean and clear.

"Maybe forgetting is good"

"There were links, you could do versions, you could compare versions, all that was true," Jellinghaus, one of its final recruits, told to Wolf, "provided you were a rocket scientist. I mean, just the code to get a piece of text out of the Xanadu back end was something like 20 lines of very, very hairy C++, and it was not easy to use in any sense of the word. Not only was it not easy to use, it wasn't anything even remotely resembling fast. The more I worked at it, the more pessimistic I got."

The young programmer's doubts were magnified by his dawning realization that a grand, centralized system was no longer the solution to anything. He had grown up with the Internet - a redundant, ever-multiplying and increasingly chaotic mass of documents. He had observed that users wanted and needed ever more clever interfaces to deal with the wealth of information, but they showed little inclination to obey the dictates of a single company. "The front end is the most important thing," Jellinghaus slowly understood. "If you don't have a good front end, it doesn't matter how good the back end is. Moreover, if you do have a good front end, it doesn't matter how bad the back end is."

Although he sympathized with the fanaticism of his colleagues, Jellinghaus also began to question whether a hypertext revolution required the perfect preservation of all knowledge. He saw the beauty of the Xanadu dream - "How do you codify all the information in the world in a way that is infinitely scalable?" - but he suspected that human society might not benefit from a perfect technological memory. Thinking is based on selection and weeding out; remembering everything is strangely similar to forgetting everything. "Maybe most things that people do shouldn't be remembered," Jellinghaus says. "Maybe forgetting is good."

Google and the Mission

Or essential

That is more than an interesting philosophical point. To write this book I have read, or skimmed, thousands or probably tens of thousands of related articles, many with RSS summaries provided by the publisher and supplied by Google as email newsfeeds.
To provide the titles of all of them would be little more use than providing none. Outside a newspaper like *Lloyds List* (shipping news), titles rarely tell you exactly what an article contains. On the Internet HTML titles are often meaningless. Robert X Cringely, who makes some of the most trenchant comments available on the Net, has most of his articles entitled **"PBS | I, Cringely . Archived Co"** if you save them. Not a lot of use in an electronic bibliography.

Hypertext enables me to include *some* of these in the electronic version of the book, those I consider to be the most prescient, best written, amusing, wrong or occasionally, plain stupid. But there is no AI program capable of doing this kind of editing where sifting and then forgetting is not just good, it is downright essential. To create significance a great deal of information has to be thrown away.

Titles no guide

Cringely's missing titles are probably the fault of their publisher, PBS (Public Broadcasting Service), rather than the length of Mac System 9 filenames, which is my default system and was also Cringley's usual operating system the last time I saw a reference. It is a common problem. *Wired*'s archive is perhaps the best collection of historic articles about IT anywhere, yet until recently all of them are, or were, entitled "Feature" in HTML. The web pages for forbes.com, one of the main outlets for Reuters on the Net, are or were entitled simply "Forbes".

All of these examples would probably have failed in Google's prototype Backrub system, which used only titles with hyperlinks to index the web. A major part of Xanadu's aim was to include *all* previous drafts and *any* related articles that anyone wished to add to the original piece (another outstanding problem which Larry and Sergey studied at Stanford).

"Completely interactive docuverse": reality checkpoint

It is still not clear whether this aspect of transclusion is practical or desirable. Owners of web pages do not usually want their sites changed by anyone else adding links to them. It is a criminal offense in most countries to attempt to change someone else's page and it is frowned on to include other people's pictures (since they are paying for the bandwidth - transmission time) and close to illegal to include other people's material (such as video) within your own without permission. The best sites now usually have a forum for discussion, but these are moderated because the anarchic principle of letting anyone add their contribution allows spam and porn to turned unmoderated forums into wastelands of commercial landfill.

It was probably inevitable that although the idea of hypertext was picked up and developed almost immediately after Ted proposed it (in 1965 at the ACM 20th national conference) these developments were vastly simplified and localized compared to his vision. Xanadu itself was never implemented, and it was also almost twenty years before a public version of hypertext became available.

Meanwhile, back at the drawing board

Lest I give the impression that nothing ever happens in IT outside Stanford, the earliest developers included Dr. Andries van Dam at Brown University for IBM and then Houston Space Center, Donald McCracken and Robert Akscyn and the Zog team at Carnegie Mellon University funded by IBM and deployed by the US Navy, and Doug Englebart of the Stanford Research Institute the legendary Menlo PARC research centre, funded by Xerox, whose team also introduced the first computer mouse.

Impressive as innovations, none of these systems were public. The honor of producing the first generally available hypertext system goes to Janet Walker for the Symbolics computer manual in 1985, some 17 years after Englebart, followed two years later by Bill Atkinson of Apple Computers when he introduced HyperCard which included a limited but workable series of hypertext anchors.

Bill Atkinson was responsible for much of Apple's best Mac code and insisted on the free distribution of HyperCard, as part of his "power to the people" ethos of English language computer programming, which he forced the post-Jobs Apple to give away in opposition to their exploitation of the Mac's very temporary monopoly of the GUI. (A true nerd hero and man of parts, Atkinson is now a nature photographer [7]).

Sir Tim Berners-Lee saw the potential of HyperCard lay rather beyond the buggy personal wordprocessors that a few Apple users were trying to build, and used it to create HyperText Markup Language as a daughter of the academic Standard Generalised Markup Language. HTML was unique in that it enabled users to add hypertext links to a document just like any other markup.

Hypertext plus markup = critical mass

Markup has been used for hundreds of years to instruct printers how to set text - to display it in bold or use a headline typeface. Apple and Adobe then developed a system of markup to instruct software how text should be displayed on a screen or sent to a printer.

HTML began [8] as a display language for text, so that particle research physicists at CERN could swap pages easily without having to faff around decoding them. Apart from simple text display it also had the crucial ability that you could click on a (text) link to open another document. It did not include pictures and Sir Tim certainly did not envisage it carrying trailers for Hollywood films.

He built it on a neXT machine, a now historic but pioneering pc that Steve Jobs had set up in competition with Apple after they kicked him out for being impossible to work for. (Later they found he was impossible to work without and had to call him back to remedy what Douglas Coupland referred to in *Microserfs* as their "charisma deficit" which was near fatal.)

"Can you hear me, Major Tom?"

The Web itself was much older than the World Wide Web which HTML created, and had been trundling along with common exchange calls but proprietary systems that did not talk directly to each other for a couple of decades.

I joined it in 1984 with Western Union in order to send emails on North Sea oil to my editors in Houston, Texas, using a 300 baud acoustic coupler which worked anywhere in the world except Italy. It also involved using a Commodore64 or a portable Brother electric typewriter with an RS232 plug because the corporate link (for a company whose lifeblood is technology publishing) was part of a layout system in Tulsa which had cost tens of thousands of dollars, but could never be got to talk to London. (Ever. Not a peep. Eventually the corporate software company responsible failed to adapt and went under. Hum. The BBC TV puppet satire show, *Spitting Image*, even had David Bowie singing about his RS232 at the time.)

Dialogue between (language) systems is critical to this whole story, which means that the failure of that dialogue was the real issue. If you were on CompuServe you were not allowed to talk to Western Union. The closest the system came to being universal or public were the newsgroups (subsequently bought by Google) and the Bulletin Boards. The BBs published a phone number, you called them and they showed you a common message board. They earned half the cost of the phone calls.

The porn driver

These newsgroups and BBs ranged from electronic spare parts to shoe fetishists. Porn was a major driver from the beginning, as with photography. (Bred in the bone? Well, Kurt Vonnegut tells the true story that immediately after Daguerre invented the first commercial system for photography, his assistant worked nights and secretly to produce daguerreotypes reflecting a shadowy girl and Shetland pony in its blackened silver mirror. Well, it was 19th century Paris and that was the local light industry.)

Sir Tim Berners-Lee crucially simplified all the conflicting systems on the Net by providing a common platform, which is voluntary and free (and accidentally unleashed a new tide of pornography). HTML is 'agnostic' - if it sees something it does not understand, it seeks to ignore it. It is entirely up to the author of a web page to decide what links to include. There is no central register of these links and it is always the visitor's decision as to what links they will click on and look at.

HTML took off because users liked its simplicity and freedom. Xanadu88 could never have provided this because it was so complex and would have had to be controlled centrally.

Google and the Mission

"Compulsive communicators"

David Attenborough has suggested that what distinguishes human beings, as a species, is that we are compulsive communicators. Once Sir Tim had provided a system for communication on the Web for free (or at most the cost of a local phone call), millions felt the need to use it to communicate by creating new, unindexed web pages. Build an information super-highway and we certainly did come and keep on coming, pushing our obsessions in front of us.

The trouble with the next phase of HTML was that an agreed indexing system could take (and has taken in the form of XML) years to develop. Before anybody knew it, HTML was already being used, unindexed, in tens, hundreds, and hundreds of thousands of new Internet domains.

The number of web pages grew exponentially once the NCSA/University of Illinois's Mosaic project had launched a free browser, who could read HTML, and when pictures came in, it went critical. Shortly after, Netscape 1 appeared - the dawn of the public Internet when Silicon Graphics founder Jim Clark, also late of Stanford, recruited Marc Andreessen from the University of Illinois's NCSA coding pool to found Mosaic Communications (later renamed as Netscape Communications).

Sir Tim provided just about all the foundations on which Netscape and subsequently Explorer were built. But these were implementations of HTML's underlying system, the first real extension of the technology itself was Google's realization of the power of indexing hypertext itself; adding that to the context map of the whole Internet to do something we all wanted - to Search the Internet faster and more efficiently.

Transclusion at Stanford

Brin and Page had studied Nelson's central objective - transclusion, as one of a series of "whacky ideas" at Stanford. Page had wanted to make his Yahoo!-based collection of site links dynamic, so that anyone could attach "clever remarks" to important sites. And the question Brin and Page now asked themselves was, what would make a page important? They then effectively superseded any need for a centralized system when they discovered that HTML hyperlinks could be used as a global, impartial, democratic reference point for all web pages.

Unless there were major advances still buried in the code of dead search engines, and now lost, the early Internet search systems did not see the significance of hypertext links. They might have been included in indexes of the word locations and the word counts for each web page, but that was it.

Brin and Page pointed out that there was only one exception, the World Wide Web Worm. They expalined that this engine looked at hypertext in order to index the existence of pages that it could not read, usually because they were dynamic, created 'on the fly' by the visitor's request, from a database.

The critical thing that Brin and Page came to see, and there is no record that anybody else did before them, is that hypertext provides (almost all) the external context that is easily available on the Internet, beyond the local domain of the web site itself, and can give enough information to list the relative significance of document contents. The relationships between documents for a single site can be found inside their urls (domain name address), but between different domains the only certain connection between web pages is their hypertext links. The relative strength of this connection can make all the difference to search.

Counting hypertext generates global context

Because every hypertext link is a voluntary bridge to another page, each page can have a 'citation' value based on the total sum of the citation values of all other pages from other web sites, which refer to that page. This gives Google a citation index for the whole web, which has a couple of big, big advantages over other systems.

A citation index is a gold standard in academia, because despite their endless feuds, academics have to recognize that the number of times a paper is quoted is a fair indicator of its significance (of course, that can be a negative significance if that paper has been discredited by those citing it).

Hypertext link code has to be correctly spelt and accurate to work at all, and sometimes the text in the link gives a better reference than the title of the piece it is referring to, as Brin and Page pointed out in 1997. These links do not have to be interpreted in the same way as a natural language text that says something like

"It is well worth having a look at so-and-so's piece..." which is still way beyond the capacity of our software to interpret accurately.

Context in human communication is so complex we only begin to understand a tiny fraction of it. But context between different sites on the Web is always indicated by the markup code of 'a href="http:...."'. That makes it possible to find the exact context of all Internet citations. If that mark-up is there, it is a link that is part of global context, because it is always required by any and all links to the other documents on the Net. If it aint there, then no global (Internet) context can currently be measured, only the local context which is unique to that particular web page or domain.

If you can calculate both local and global context, then you can rank the relative relevance of each page on the Internet to the sequence the words used in the user's search request. There are three contexts that have to be juggled: the document itself, the entire Web, and the user's own search terms.

As the Marconi prize quote from Sir Tim in the first chapter suggests, this provides a direct link back to Vannevar Bush's concept of:

> ...associative indexing, the basic idea of which is a provision whereby any item may be caused at will to select immediately and automatically another. This is the essential feature of the memex. The process of tying two items together is the important thing.

To make a Memex

Boolean logic and digital computers depend on true or false polarities of certainty and cannot calculate anything as ambiguous as association between ideas. Brin and Page's breakthrough was to see that HTML coding made it quite practical to index hyperlinks recursively and the contents of those hyperlinks would provide the associative indexing of relevance.

Hypertext is the key to the breakthrough success of both HTML and Google. Both Sir Tim and the Google guys admit happily that they realized that hypertext was very significant, but not quite how significant it would turn out to be. After all, ranking in a Google search involves up to an estimated [100] different parameters, of which PageRank is only one, albeit one of the most important.

Transclusion still dubious

In 2004 Google Labs returned to the idea of "transclusive" links opening multiple related windows from a single document - here the Google search list. This was a simplified version of an aspect of transclusion and results reported [9] by Jennifer Laycock of websearch.about.com were not very encouraging.

True to warnings, the feature is a bit buggy and can run rather slowly depending on a user's dialup speed. Despite accessing the Google Viewer on a T1 line, I still experienced a browser crash during a couple of my searches. In addition, site previews sometimes fail to load properly as the listings scroll by. While searching with the scroll time set to the default 4 seconds, I found that about 20% of the site listings failed to produce a screen shot.

This is purely experimental, but it breaks with Google's foundation standard of the simplest possible user-interface, so it is unlikely to become part of mainstream Search.

Plus the royalty problem

Xanadu itself may have failed but one of it central concerns: royalties - how information providers would get paid for their work, is still not solved. If I publish the whole of this book in HTML on the Internet - an obvious thing to do, given all the links to web pages - I simply won't get paid for the work that went into it, however hard I request donations or solicit advertising.

In the early days of dot.com mania it seemed bizarre that almost all the major print publications were giving away material on the Internet, which had cost them such a lot to publish on paper. They were really just following the herd, but the 'thinking' was that resulting traffic would generate enough generic advertising to make a profit. A sensible calculation involving eyeballs and public billboards would have told them that this was unlikely.

After facing near disaster by supplying its entire content for free on the Internet, the *FT* now follows the first-taste-is-free principle: when you search their site, if you want to see more than one article, you have to subscribe.

Google and the Mission

The UK's *Guardian* newspaper, supported by a large Trust and highly successful classified jobs advertising (in print) have managed to avoid charging, and supply most if not all their material on the Internet to readers who might otherwise buy the print version. They are now urging readers to subscribe to an enhanced online edition, which is still free.

Pro bono or for profit

To get the quote from John Hegarty in the first chapter, I had to subscribe, but everything else quoted from the *Guardian* has been straight out of Google. One reason that this paper may be slightly over-represented in the citations here is that apart from having first class science and business reporting, all of their material was free and online. But it is expensive to produce this and I know daily readers of the paper who rarely pay for a printed copy. That looks fragile as a commercial model.

Most publications are now having to follow the prudent path of Dow Jones, whose conservative nature caused them to do the sums and start with a subscription-only model. The great exception to the inevitable move to online subscriptions is the BBC. Like Google, the BBC provides a near-universal public service, supported by a UK license fee rather than contextual advertising. Small world, the BBC has also drafted in Stanford's Professor Lawrence Lessig to formulate his Creative Commons copyright scheme for the publication of their archive online, free for non-commercial use.

Despite complaints even from liberal commentators that the BBC's license fee is being used for the benefit of other nations, in early 2004 Caroline Thompson, the BBC director of public policy told me that the BBC would continue to publish all its online material for free, supported by the UK license fee and not by any subscription model, for the period of their next charter. Not surprisingly, the BBC site includes a custom-version of Google.

Save our newsfeeds

A Google News Alert on any news story featuring the word "Google" has provided this book with many thousands of newspaper and magazine stories from around the world - all with a neat little summary, information source and hypertext link sent as email. The mistakes were rare and of the [20] stories a day listed, many were interesting and some are critically important. All were free. Some newsfeeds only allow you to read a single file before you have to subscribe, and some insist on subscribing before you see anything. They generally then want a lot of personal information and their service would make the daily stream of specific news stories through Google turn into an undifferentiated flood of general news to be left unread.

This is the old royalty problem, identified by Ted Nelson back in the mid-Sixties. If information is free, who pays the royalties to the author or publisher? Google generally avoids the subscription model to provide a free service, but they could make an exception here. I would pay to subscribe once, with one set of personal info to Google, in order to be able to access *Fortune* or *Times* Newspapers stories on a newsfeed, like "Google", that I want anyway.

Placing the request through Google would mean no deluge of unwanted stories clogging my email and no repetition of signup. Google could share a realiztic subs cost with the information providers and if I want to subscribe to a full news service, from say Reuters, I can do that as well.

The demand from working journalists and financial analysts should make that model viable and help save our beloved newsfeeds from extinction, because without a business model, any free alternative would need to come from an organization of equivalent size to the BBC with similar skills and ideals, and it is hard to think of any other examples.

Footnotes

1: As We may Think - Section 6
By Vannevar Bush: The Atlantic Monthly, July 1945
2: Chaos: Making a New Science
By James Gleick, Amazon.com
3: Computer Lib/Dream Machines
By Theodor Nelson, Amazon.com
4: History of Hypertext 1.1.1 Memex
By Shahrooz Feizabadi, WWW - Beyond the Basics
5: The Curse of Xanadu
By Gary Wolf, Wired, The Conde Nast Publications Inc. Jun 1995

6:   Theodor H. Nelson Letter to the Editor, Wired
Theodor Holm Nelson
7:   Within the Stone
Bill Atkinson Photography
8:   Information Management: A Proposal
Tim Berners-Lee, CERN March 1989, May 1990
9:   Google Shares Two New Experiments with Public in Google Labs and research
By Jennifer Laycock: Ab Inc

9

Context - it all depends on what you mean by...

"I don't know what you mean by 'glory'", Alice said.

"Humpty Dumpty smiled contemptuously. "Of course you don't - till I tell you. I meant 'there's a nice knock-down argument for you!"'

"But glory doesn't mean 'a nice knock-down argument,'" Alice objected.

"When I use a word," Humpty Dumpty said in a rather scornful tone, *"it means just what I choose it to mean - neither more nor less."*

"The question is," said Alice, *"whether you can make words mean so many different things."*

Through the Looking Glass and What Alice Found There Lewis Carroll [1].

What is your point?

Alice was asking the right question, and our computers still have the same problem. We do not have a theory of how meaning (semantics) works which can be expressed with the sort of logic our computers use to run on or search with.

We do not know how meaning attaches to words or text or as, Alice asked, how words can mean so many different things. On our own pcs this is a nuisance, on the Internet it nearly became a

Google and the Mission

disaster, because it meant that it was almost impossible to ever actually find anything.

We have some very effective theories of grammar (syntax) - how words fit together - particularly for "classical" languages like French which follow very specific rules of structure. It is semantics, rather than syntax, which is still as mysterious as it was in the days when Lewis Carroll wrote **Through the Looking Glass**, setting out with nursery rhyme simplicity and logical reversals some of the questions posed by Plato 2,000 years earlier.

In a lecture [2] published as a video [3] by the University of Washington in their Computer Science & Engineering Colloquium Series, Urs Hoelzle explained why this remains the central issue for future development of Search technology:

"incredibly primitive"

> In a certain sense the current search engines, including Google, are incredibly primitive. They are purely syntactic: you type in a bunch of character sequences and it sort of looks for those character sequences in [web] pages.
>
> It has absolutely no idea what those character sequences mean. It is amazing that this works at all

Urs became Google's Chief Engineer in 1997 and then [4]:

> "developed the staff (along with Google's technology) to its current industry leadership position... In recognition of his contributions and his desire to focus more on technology development, Urs has been named the very first Google Fellow".

A new technology often precedes a solid theoretical understanding of *why* it works. (The magnetic compass was discovered in China many centuries before magnetism was understood, for example.)

Google's founders cracked the initial engineering of Search, even if the discovery itself was almost, but not quite, accidental as Larry has suggested, because its maths may reflect something quite fundamental about the deep structure of meaning. If it did not, it would probably not have worked any better than the score of other search engines on the market before 1997.

Backrub

Google worked "pretty well" even in its earliest manifestation: "*Backrub*" - which dealt only with titles and hypertext links - because, I believe, it established a mathematical relationship between internal and external features - global and local context. This opened up the possibility of computing the problem of meaning because Brin and Page had found a back door that no one had previously noticed: hypertext.

Google probably developed internal context - the relationship between the words in a document - further than it had ever been taken before. It took into account local features like type size, perhaps for the first time. But this was incremental; a huge amount of work had already been done on internal context. What was unique to Google was that it found a way of measuring external or global context - the relationship of one document to another - through hypertext, a feature of the text which was unique to the Internet.

Global and local

Hypertext links could provide a global context and measurable index of relevance, and the fact that millions of such links are chosen for inclusion on Internet pages, can give an objective map of a critical area of meaning on the Net: the external, global, and contextual relationship between one person's publication and other people's perception of its value.

That, Brin and Page discovered, could be combined with local context, mainly the frequency and proximity of words on a page, to provide a ranking for relevance. That rank is a number, so it can be used to sort pages, found with word search, by their relative, consensually-determined significance to the whole, as represented by a self-consistent sequences of numbers (PageRank). These values are not absolute, because the value of a link is determined by the number of other links to that link and that can change monthly.

Ranking relevance by recursion

A link from Yahoo! is worth more than a link from my aunt, as Hoelzle points out in the lecture above, not because of its obvious subjective difference, but because objectively, millions of other links point to Yahoo! and few if any point to the aunt's web site.

Page and Brin developed the engineering of this context-mapping at a time when the web was itself providing a huge new wealth of measurable context, previously only accessible to scholars, editors and librarians as printed books, manual indexes (indices) and mental constructs pulled from human memory - like Melville's poor sub-sub-librarian who introduces [5] *Moby Dick* with an Etymology of whales.

EXTRACTS (Supplied by a Sub-Sub-Librarian).

It will be seen that this mere painstaking burrower and grub-worm of a poor devil of a Sub-Sub appears to have gone through the long Vaticans and street-stalls of the earth, picking up whatever random allusions to whales he could anyways find in any book whatsoever, sacred or profane. Therefore you must not, in every case at least, take the higgledy-piggledy whale statements, however authentic, in these extracts, for veritable gospel cetology. Far from it. As touching the ancient authors generally, as well as the poets here appearing, these extracts are solely valuable or entertaining, as affording a glancing bird's eye view of what has been promiscuously said, thought, fancied, and sung of Leviathan, by many nations and generations, including our own.

So even Melville could not give any guarantees on relevance or accuracy. This problem really goes much further back than 1997, when AltaVista and its competitors were swamped by the sheer size of the Internet. With 2,420,000 documents containing the phrase "Bill Clinton" (Google April 2004) what makes some of those documents more relevant than others, if they have the same frequency of that phrase?

Prior to Google the only key was the number of times the words "Bill Clinton" (or "bill" + "clinton" which is not the same) appeared in the document in both the text and its invisible metatags. Thanks to Google the answer is now obvious, but if it was understood before Google, then it was certainly kept as a commercial secret.

Measuring the relevance of different arguments or statements is an issue which predates Marvin Minsky and John McCarthy's work in artificial intelligence, predates Alan Turing and his work on computability, and even predates Charles Lutwidge Dodgson the mathematician who, as Lewis Carroll, in *Through the Looking Glass* (1872) and *The Hunting of the Snark*, satirized theories of meaning, including Aristotelian syllogistic logic and the predicate logic then being developed from the theories of George Boole [6], whose Boolean logic [7] now runs on all working computers.

"True names"

The problem was probably first articulated in Plato's Socratic dialogue: *The Cratylus* (**Theory of Language**), where Alice, above, plays Socrates. Benjamin Jowett, regarded as Plato's greatest translator, summarized [8] it as follows:

> **Hermogenes...** expounds the doctrine that names are conventional; like the names of slaves, they may be given and altered at pleasure... Cratylus is of opinion that a name is either a true name or not a name at all... (Whilst Socrates infers that) nature, art, chance, all combine in the formation of language.

Which is fine and dandy, but leaves the question open so that 2,300 years later we still have no theory of the meaning of words; actually we have dozens starting with Plato's ideal forms, but none that holds to its logic sufficiently to be translated into binary logic that our computers will also reliably recognize.

Spoofing understanding

Somebody might object at this point that computers can understand meaning, they have seen it done by giving an Apple voice commands, for example. It is true that there are a couple of harmless deceptions out there, including the AskJeeves search engine which appears to respond to natural language questions. These can sometimes convince newcomers that computers are capable of learning meaning.

Giving a computer voice commands is a prime example. The software can recognize the core patterns of the sound of a spoken word, but they cannot understand its semantic content. These programs can recognize patterns, including partial patterns, but crucially they cannot manipulate individual elements within those patterns to create new meanings.

The standard test of artificial intelligence is the Turing Test, named after the great mathematician Alan Turing. He used the entirely empirical (and consequently somewhat misleading) idea that if the observer cannot tell if a machine or a human is making an intelligent response, then, such a machine must be regarded as having (artificial) intelligence.

Turing proposed that for a computer to demonstrate that it understands meaning, it must be able to take a word and use it correctly in a new context to communicate fresh information. This has yet to happen. Trying to define meaning outside of context in order to create rules of meaning that computers can follow has proved just about impossible; although, like nuclear fusion, a breakthrough is always promised as imminent. (The most recent claim was made by kozoru.com, whose credibility suffers because its web page suggests that boolean logic is a computer language.)

Define "red"

At its simplest level, the problem is that binary computers do not accept ambiguity, whilst natural language depends on it. In the digital world if red is a color; it cannot simultaneously be anything else. Not so in the real world. If "red" has no context (as the single word in a Google Search, for example) it has so many possible meanings that it effectively has no meaning. Google themselves provide the context for a search on "red' however, based on the most frequent uses in different pages. (RedHat was ranked as #1 - an interesting result because these guys supplied the technology with which Google was engineered.)

After Newton revealed the prism's spectrum was continuous, it also became clear that our actual division of the colors of the rainbow into red, orange, yellow, green, blue, indigo, violet is cultural not optical. There is an objective range of frequencies there, but they are continuous, not the discrete bands of color that we name.

Red can be associated with a certain range in the wave-length of light, but that often has little to do with "red" hair at least for any hair-color that does not come out of a bottle, while Australian blokes with red hair are invariably called "Blue". In West Indian patois, red means of mixed blood, as does "High Yellow" in Billie Holliday's song. Then there is the term "Red Indian" for Native American, which presumably indicates skin color, or the Chinese anthem The East is Red, which conflates a political philosophy with the color of a flag, and is a traditional symbol of good luck.

Or "fag" or "cucumbers"

In England, a slang term like "fag" can mean a cigarette or a junior private schoolboy who acts as a servant or (as in the US) a gay man. Take the meaning of 'cucumbers', which might be defined as 'green vegetable usually eaten sliced raw in salads or sandwiches'. (An additional meaning was intended by Alexander Pope when he sniggered to his Celia that cucumbers had to be sliced before being taken into a Seraglio.)

Both meanings were probably known to the highly-educated Jonathan Aitken, the former UK government arms procurement minister, who was recently imprisoned for perjury. According to his apologia *I was so proud*, when he arrived in prison, he was urgently urged [9], **"Take the cucumbers, mate, take the cucumbers".** He lived to regret not knowing that cucumbers:

> "...is rhyming slang where cucumbers equals numbers; numbers equals rule 43; and rule 43 is the rule that says any prisoner can apply to be taken into solitary confinement for his or her own protection.

> That is of course what convicted police officers, prison officers and sex offenders usually do " and my informant thought that any passing Cabinet minister would be very wise to take the same precaution."

But Google does get the point

Another bad mistake. It must be scant consolation for Aitken that a search on 'cucumbers rhyming slang' in Google found the reference immediately, starting with its translation into, don't ask, Italian ("... *Il Cockney Rhyming Slang e una lingua tutta a se! ... Cream Crackered, Knackered, Crown Jewels, Tools, Cucumbers, Numbers, Currant Bun, Sun, Currant bun, Son, ...*")

Google and the Mission

Aitken's address in Bradford cathedral, quoted above, came in third (but second on 'cucumbers slang') in Google. The alphabetic characters used by the word shape of "cucumbers" is almost irrelevant to its meaning, which depends on its context - prison or a Conservative tea-party, but also here, on its sound. It rhymes to hide as well as to show something, because ultimately rhyming slang, like the underground gay cant Bonar, was a language code designed to conceal things within a particular sub-culture. Still, context-mapping in Google demonstrably does get it.

(This meaning of cucumbers was new to me too, even though I was born in Lambeth, London and brought up on rhyming slang like "butchers" - butcher's hook = look, and had had plenty of experience of Rule 43 for Irish terrorist suspects when I was working for the NCCL - now Liberty, the British equivalent of the ACLU).

If we cannot define relevance, how can our computers?

This is as good an example as any of the problem that has beset artificial intelligence since Turing. The burden of research has tended to concentrate on the top-down application of rules: where the approach would be cucumbers = plural of cucumber, cucumber= long green vegetable, vegetable = fruit, root or leaves of (usually edible) plants. Close to the definition Aitken would have already known, and quite correct, but only in a particular context and no help at all in Belmarsh prison.

So even simple terms like "red", "fag" or "cucumber" cannot be usefully defined, outside of a specific context, never mind abstract words like "terrorism", or "love", which has [35] separate definitions provided by Google define:. Words like "form" and "class", which tend to be central to any formal logic, are just as varied in their possible meanings.

"Evidence cannot exist out of context" - Gil Grissom

New meanings can be found from new contexts rather than existing rules or previous meanings. Google can find these meanings "correctly" partly because it ranks relevance by mapping the relative physical distance between words. Crudely, the closer words are grouped together the more likely they are to be linked semantically and thus to share meaning. Aitken's web page puts "cucumbers', "rhyming slang" and "solitary" close enough for a Google Search to place it close to the top of its list. This reflects an observable structure of the organization of meaning in text by the relative proximity of different words.

Proximity apart, the remaining structures of meaning are still inaccessible in that we have never been able to reproduce them on our computers. To suggest that a rule-based theory of meaning may not even be possible could provoke a fatwah (or **"nice knock-down argument"**) by linguists and computer scientists but, to speak as we find, the lack of a usable theory of meaning has been a real pain in the posterior as far as computer software is concerned.

The reasons why artificial intelligence might have hit such a mighty logjam are discussed below, but a good example for now is document summary. If we had a computable theory of meaning then it should be possible to get a document, such as an email, summarized by software. Currently it cannot be done. Even Google has to do the next best thing and show you the passages from the document, which match your search.

Why document summary is a total dodo

BT and Microsoft both attempted a system of document summarization based on word and phrase frequency. Microsoft includes this with MS Word and BT launched a product called ProSum in 1997. Neither was used much. You can probably see why from the first part of the summary which Word generated from Chapter Seven:

Summary

CHAPTER SEVEN: Before Google there was...um, AltaVista

Dozens of search engines

The missing index

The Searching Graveyard:

faganfinder.com 4 surveyed the search engines developed in the last century: Even before the internet bubble burst, great search

tools have gone extinct. Other search tools still exist, but have changed. Raging Search

Open Text Index

AltaVista relied on an index of the word/phrase frequency and whole-word search terms.

AltaVista Timeline

December 1995 AltaVista launched altavista.digital.com. AltaVista.com.

Manual directory technology is very different from search engines, but Yahoo! As Brin and Page described it in The Anatomy of a Large-Scale Hypertextual Web Search Engine 6

Automated search engines that rely on keyword matching usually return too many low quality matches.

Yahoo!'Yahoo! Yahoo!

Yahoo! By 2000 Yahoo! were really struggling with their manual indexing and were using the Inktomi search spider to create an automated index for searches that fell through the gaps in their taxonomy.

Yahoo! gets Google

(In late 2003, a Yahoo! search on "Angel of the North" homed on the sculpture in the north of England, more effectively than any other search engine.

Yahoo! Yahoo!

Word frequency is the key because what Word is doing here is taking whole sentences containing words or phrases that it finds repeated elsewhere in the piece, and then running them together sequentially (in the same order as the original). It cannot deal with 'Yahoo!', where the (correct) exclamation mark is taken as a complete phrase (hence "Yahoo! Yahoo! Yahoo!"). It does not make sense, no one has ever admitted to finding a use for it, but it is sweetly done.

Counting word and phrase frequency is very useful, but actually tells you very little about the underlying meaning. BT found there was huge public interest in the proposal for ProSum, but not much in its actual results. As Keith Preston, Manager, BT Labs, Natural Language Group put it [10]:

Word frequency: frequently unreliable

"Their main strength comes from the use of statistical techniques rather than in-depth language understanding. This enables them to operate on a wide range of documents, almost irrespective of subject area and writing style. But this lack of understanding is also a limitation. As the quantity and complexity of information which we face continues to grow, we will need to develop systems which can understand language to an increasing degree - which is the main thrust of our current work".

The main problem is that important subjects are usually conveyed by a multiplicity of different words. People are taught to write English using pronouns (eg "he, she, it"), and synonyms for different words with similar meanings. (Google Web Definition: synonym - two words that can be interchanged in a context are said to be synonymous relative to that context).

Translate: 'a nap on a nag'

The relative and connected meaning of synonyms is beyond our current ability to compute, but an article about horse racing, for example, will often use half-a-dozen or more different words for horse. Any logic to detect, and then summarize that text must be able to see the relationship between horse, mount, runner, colt, filly, pony, yearling or whatever, or it will not see the meaning of the piece. Crucially this is what ProSum and similar programs cannot do.

This is also a judgment call for human editors. Pat Coyne, one of the editors of this book, has never forgiven one sub-editor for changing "nap" into "nag" in a *New Statesman* article on software used for betting forecasts.

Chatbots rely on the fact that you can reproduce the rules of syntax for a dialogue without the software having the faintest inkling of what its responses will mean to the human being on the other end. Detecting the relationships between nouns and pronouns (eg "I" and "Alice" in the first line of this chapter) is the starting point. To recreate these relationships, as syntax requires a transformation algorithm - initially provided by Joseph Weizenbaum in his famous Eliza program.

Chatbots and WMDs

Eliza is a simulation of "non-directive" or Rogerian therapy, an extreme form of Freudianism where the analyst must express no opinion whatsoever. The best current example of Eliza (named after Bernard Shaw's Eliza Dolittle in *Pygmalion*) is **A.L.I.C.E.** [11], which uses a sophisticated version of Weizenbaum's pioneering transformations to make apparently sentient conversation, and in 2003 won Loebner's Turing prize for the second time.

A.L.I.C.E. is worth trying out, if only for the charming way her eyes follow your mouse - making me feel guilty when it/she watched me closing her window - but Weizenbaum did warn that we can be determined to see intelligence in a program like his, even when it has none because it understands and remembers nothing but some powerful rules for changing syntax.

He was particularly concerned that Defense analysts would believe that it was confirming what they already believed, when it had no means to actually verify, only reply, usually with another question. Did someone mention WMDs? [12]

In 1988, Weizenbaum was presented with the Norbert Wiener prize for Professional and Social Responsibility. In the accompanying tribute [13], Terry Winograd wrote:

> Weizenbaum's *Computer Power and Human Reason* stands alongside Wiener's books on science and society as a powerful reminder that wisdom and technical mastery are not the same, and that we confuse them at our peril.

By their fruits... This is, of course, the same Professor Winograd who was in charge of the post-grad class where Larry and Sergey first worked together at Stanford.

But it mimics dialogue, not communication

Weizenbaum demonstrated that you could create an apparent dialogue between user and machine by detecting substantives and pronouns, and transforming I into you, Alice into she. (Crudely - "Michael is bothering me." can be transformed into "Why is he bothering you?" The psychological context helps, of course, because people generally like to talk about themselves, whether or not the person they are speaking to is responding - or even listening.)

But ranking the significance of those transformations as semantic rather than syntactic relationships would require a computable theory of their relative meanings, which in our case we simply do not have. When we do have a usable theory of meaning it will also need to include actions - verbs, possibly harder to evaluate than nouns and pronouns, or as Humpty Dumpty put it "They've a temper, some of them - particularly verbs, they're the proudest - ".

Why are the most common verbs irregular?

In most, perhaps all, languages the commonest verbs are irregular, they do not follow the usual rules for indicating person or tense. (Eg I am, you are, you were; I go, you went; compared to I work, you work, they worked). Saki has a short story where a linguist is teaching German to an elephant. Eventually the elephant loses patience and stomps his tutor to death. "Serves him right, he was teaching it irregular verbs" said the narrator. Mark Twain would have agreed, "Life is too short to learn German", he opined.

The more serious point is that this irregularity is the opposite of efficient. The more often a word is used, the less efficient it is to start to use another, irregular version of that word because it hides meaning more frequently than an uncommon verb. The reason why all human languages do this is perhaps because the thought processes involved derive from the way genetic information is transferred, rather than a logical model of communication, which can be translated easily into binaries.

This may be contentious; what is not is that language is mutable and the more isolated the linguistic group the faster their language changes. Sometimes this is simply because changing physical conditions require different terms to describe them: Eskimos *need* different words for different kinds of snow in order to survive in the Arctic. Text has become a verb in the last couple of years (eg the macabre *Guardian* headline: Girl texted dad names of killers) because mobile phones have a new functional ability - simple text messaging.

Google and the Mission

Polyvalent English

English is much more successful as a global trading language than French because, apart from being associated with economic power, English syntax is such a mixture of roots that it welcomes new words; for instance Hindi (eg bungalow or pyjamas/pajamas) or black American (eg bling) or technical (eg broadband or indeed, to google). French has a classical structure, believed to have been established fully and finally by the Encyclopaedists in the Age of Reason, and it formally rejects new words and grammatical changes, even though the fixed spelling of French and its changing pronunciation have been going their separate ways for a couple of centuries.

If English has flourished as the world's premier business and entertainment language because of its ability to change easily, that mutability is a special headache for the natural language processing of English text. Rich and flexible does not mean logical, or easy to compute, but exactly the reverse. Somehow that compulsion to change is going to have to be incorporated into any algorithm of meaning.

Primary patterns

Our tools for matching patterns are good and getting better. Sergey Brin's early Stanford paper [14] on *Extracting Patterns and Relations from the World Wide Web* is an elegant example:

> We begin with a small seed set of (author, title) pairs (in tests we used a set of just five books). Then we find all occurrences of those books on the Web. From these occurrences we recognize patterns for the citations of books. Then we search the Web for these patterns and find new books. We can then take these books and all their occurrences and from those generate more patterns. We can use these new patterns to find more books, and so forth. Eventually, we will obtain a large list of books and patterns for finding them.

We can use increasingly sophisticated programs to match not just fingerprints, but fragments of prints, to match sounds against words, or decipher muddy photocopied images into reasonably clean text. But when it comes to discerning meaning, our tools have been, at least until Google appeared, still extremely primitive. Google does not, and does not claim that it understands meaning. But as cited above: "**The perfect search engine**", says Larry Page, "**would understand exactly what you mean and give back exactly what you want.**"

When it comes to defining "understanding", there are difficulties, with "meaning" the definition gets a lot more difficult, and anybody who wants both defined "exactly" is shooting for the moon. After eight years of working together 24 hours a day, according to Page (sleep is for wimps, presumably) he and Brin probably understand each other as well as any two people on the planet, but it is unlikely Page ever understands "exactly" what Brin means because they each bring their own utterly unique context to any dialogue.

The frustration of Marvin Minsky

Professor Minsky has an extremely impressive academic history; in some ways he is responsible for the whole science of robotics, but he has become increasing frustrated with the lack of progress in the ability of machines to decode meaning and to actually start thinking. As he put it "**It is 2001, where is HAL?**" (Dunno, Marvin, erm, wasn't HAL your idea? You tell us.)

In 1951 he built the world's first "**randomly wired neural network learning machine**" called the Stochastic Neural-Analog Reinforcement Computer (SNARC). But he is not happy with the progress that has been made since. As a 2003 geek.com news story [15] had it: '**Marvin Minsky: AI "has been brain dead since the 1970s"- AI researchers are not pleased by Minsky's comments**'.

In his recent (2003) work he majors on multiple causality - single causality rarely exists outside the lab, but he is also engaged [16] in: **Unpacking the Suitcase of 'Consciousness'.**"We pack such big clouds of ideas into those compact suitcase words and hope that our friends will 'know what we mean', when we use words like 'self' and 'consciousness'.**

Minsky uses the word "suitcase" in the same way as Humpty Dumpty uses the word "portmanteau". In *Jabberwocky*, Humpty explains:

"Well 'slithy' means 'lithe and slimy'. 'Lithe' is the same as 'active'. You see it is like portmanteau, there are two meanings packed into one word."

New meanings get packed into words like 'cucumbers' all the time both by choice and changing physical circumstance, and it is their new context, which determines the new meaning, not our previous understanding of the word itself.

John McCarthy's context

John McCarthy, listed by Minsky along with himself and Alan Turing as the three most important people in AI, comes across as being extremely modest, whilst politely answering questions on basic AI for ordinary web-users, he has also been responsible for generating a whole new field of thinking about mathematical context. In 2003, a seminar on Context organized at Stanford covered 28 areas of context theory, from neuro-science to autonomous agents, all of which could probably trace a common ancestor published in 1996: John McCarthy's *A Logical Ai Approach To Context* [17].

Professor McCarthy and colleagues at Stanford have begun to address the question of what you need to create a mathematics of context, where a proposition is true in one context but not in another. (Cucumbers are vegetables, true, but not in prison.) Propositions may only be valid within a certain context and McCarthy and colleagues want to find the "lifting" rules that can make a proposition invalid in one context and valid in another.

Many of these ideas are tough and need to be read at source. Researchers often cannot know if the problem they are addressing is real or a boojum - the right answers to the wrong question, whereupon all of their endlessly hard work "will softly and silently vanish away, And never be heard of again", as Lewis Carroll put in the *Hunting of the Snark*. As a mathematician, Dodgson was haunted by this, and it is no coincidence that Minsky called his first major success in machine intelligence a SNARC.

Professor McCarthy has declined to define "context" itself, but I do wonder if "lifting" is a mathematical analogue of "learning": the reformulation of a concept when circumstances change and it no longer fits our empirical experience. (As an early learning example: "Mummy is always nice to me", can become "mummy is always nice to me, except when I make the baby cry". The context has changed, so the child has to learn to modify its original proposition.)

Today Stanford, tomorrow...

The mathematical study of context is creating the sort of interest at Stanford which is reminiscent of the introduction of fractal geometry, when all sorts of very specific questions, such as where new oil reserves lie, could be addressed and often answered using a new mathematical toolbox. Context is likely to have the same impact, but so far it is mainly confined to Stanford. The discussion on geek.com of Minsky's critique of AI cited above generated only two comments on context, one sarcastic.

The only thing (11:01pm EST Sat May 17 2003)

that will make AI work is context. context context context context

may I say it again

context

in all it's meanings and nuances - by whatever

Context (1:14am EST Sun May 18 2003)

context background circumstance situation framework milieu perspective environment setting surroundings settings condition locale incident fact event state position state structure support construction agenda scene viewpoint standpoint view atmosphere upbringing ambiance stipulation clause happening episode information detail reality truth verity experience incident occurrence result shape affirm arrangement organization configuration makeup constitution formation composition edifice etc.

I am certain that in some extrapolation of the word, context will make AI work"

(Love that 'etc'. - context is a suitcase word or what!) Clearly, a useful maths of context needs to be a lot more specific than just saying that context matters; it has to address the question of how meaning is structured.

Context and exchange - the foundation of anthropology

Such a simple idea - that meaning can be derived from context should make few waves in fields like anthropology, where the significance of context has been quite unavoidable since Bronsilaw Malinowski. Work on the context of meaning, rather than the search for the inherent rules of meaning, has been relatively rare in IT and related AI studies.

What Brin and colleagues at Stanford found in their work data-mining in, for example the US population census sample was that useful results could best be obtained by cross-indexing references and associations with other associations using vector calculus, where those quantities, often denoted by arrows, have a magnitude and direction but perhaps no fixed location. The most important consequence is that results can be sorted.

When Brin tried to apply the same to *A Tale of Two Cities*, he hit a wall. From personal experience, a text on its own without any external context, even one as long and self-referential as *Moby Dick*, does not contain enough parameters to make it possible to cross-reference it automatically for significant meaning. It is almost impossible to use maths to deduct relative significance from within any narrative text, which stands alone, beyond the auto-summarization systems mentioned above. It is hard enough with non-narrative text, such as the population census, or a print dictionary, which carries an obvious, repetitive structure and no implied meaning in the thread of a story.

The Butterfly effect

One of the key words McCarthy uses is monotonic: meaning very roughly "new data doesn't affect existing data". A major problem for Search engines before Google is that they were monotonic. A page was only ever considered on its own - how many unique words did it have, how many repeated words, was the address commercially interesting? Typing in "Bill Clinton" could find a high-ranking page containing only "Bill Clinton Sucks" because it was the page closest to matching exactly the search phrase itself (only one additional word).

Google introduced a non-monotonic index, where the text contents and links from a new page alters in a small but significant way the index for the entire web by adding its own two cents (or ha'p'orth) of additional context.

Making it happen

It was not that Sergey went to hear John McCarthy lecture on the maths of context, snapped his fingers - snat - and said "That's it, mapping transclusion through anchor tags and combining that with the relative location of specific words to measure global as well as local context in a non-monotonic index is the solution to Internet Search".

It was just that when Larry wanted to index annotations, Sergey was already primed by his own work at Stanford to look for directional patterns within context as a means of data-mining more efficiently. He knew all the nightmares of finding significance in real world data whilst Larry was a street commander when it came to using cheap pcs, RedHat Linux and distributed processing for speed of thought access times.

Only after they had cooked up the applied maths to measure relevance for yet another take on Yahoo!, did the pair of them realize that no-one was looking at hypertext context in Internet Search and maybe that was because no-one had thought about it in quite that way before. Stressing the significance of hypertext context to Internet Search may now look like a statement of the bleedin' obvious, but it was only obvious after Google showed how it could and should be done.

Footnotes

1: **Through the Looking-Glass and What Alice Found There**
By Lewis Carroll, Electronic Text Center, University of Virginia Library
2: **Google Linux Cluster talk By Urs Hoelzle--Media player archive...**
From: Subbarao Kambhampati 25 Nov 2002
3: **The Google Linux Cluster**
Urs Hoelzle (Google) University of Seattle, Washington, November 5 2003
4: **A new Engineer-in-Chief: Wayne Rosing takes the helm**
Google Friends Newsletter for January 31, 2001

5: MOBY DICK; OR THE WHALE
By Herman Melville, prepared By Daniel Lazarus and Jonesey for Project Gutenberg's archives
6: George Boole (1815 - 1864)
Kerry Redshaw, Brisbane, Australia 1996-7
7: What's So Logical About Boolean Algebra?
Kerry Redshaw, Brisbane, Australia 1996-7
8: CRATYLUS By Plato Translated By Benjamin Jowett
From N.S. Gill, About, Inc. A PRIMEDIA Company
9: The Prison Diary Of Jeffrey Archer
By Jeffrey Archer, Sunday Proust, Alan Research and Tom Perdoo
10: Interview with Keith Preston, BT Labs and research
By Adrian Mars Le Journal (cached) 16/01/2001
11: The A.L.I.C.E. AI Foundation
The A.L.I.C.E. AI Foundation 2003
12: These Weapons of Mass Destruction cannot be displayed
Empire Poker
13: Joseph Weizenbaum 1988 Winner of CPSR's Norbert Wiener Award for Professional and Social Responsibility
By Terry Winograd Updated Nov. 22, 1997, By Marsha Woodbury.CPSR
14: Extracting Patterns and Relations from the World Wide Web
Sergey Brin Computer Science Department Stanford University 1997
15: Minsky: AI "has been brain dead since the 1970s"
By Sander Olson: Geek.com Geek News
16: Part IV CONSCIOUSNESS
By Marvin Minsky, a draft (3/16/04) of Part IV of The Emotion Machine MIT
17: A Logical Ai Approach To Context
By John McCarthy, Stanford Feb 28 1996

10

Context and learning

OK computer, tell me...

In his Washington lecture, Urs Hoelzle describes the ultimate search query with a *Star Trek* paradigm: "**Hey computer tell me everything you know about whatever**". This is the natural language search which everybody is after: from Autonomy, BT, AskJeeves's and their over-enthusiastic sales people, some now defunct defense contractors, right the way up to Bill Gate's most important strategic objective for Microsoft.

Natural language is well under digital control, but only at the syntactic level - we cannot measure the semantics, what a text actually *means* rather than how it says it. Bluntly, before Google we could not build useful patterns of meaning from known word patterns or existing semantic rules. This has prevented us from being able to use the meaning of our work to organize it.

Between worlds

Brin and Page found that PageRank could create a bridge between the power laws of syntax and the parallel universe of semantics. They discovered almost, but not quite, by accident that hypertext could provide that bridge because it is a form of simple communication ('Look at this?') which has a clearly identifiable structure.

Other forms of communication do not have an identical and hence machine-identifiable structure. Within Internet text they can only be identified by a human editor, but not by software. Because hypertext is so easy to find with software, it enables us, or at least Google and subsequently competing systems, to count a specific strand of communication, for both its quantity and the value it contains (who/what is being addressed and how many times) and then sort billions of results usefully by that relative quantity.

This shocked Bill Gates because it is now so simple and obvious, - hence his comments about Search being remarkably low tech, but it is much easier to describe than to engineer, as Microsoft have been discovering. Brin and Page were the first to point out that their discovery that hypertext and hence PageRank could make a golden bridge between a visible syntax and a hidden semantics was only obvious, both to them and subsequently the rest of us, after they had found it.

On the frontier

This is still a frontier because as a measure of external context, PageRank and similar systems are restricted to the directional values of hypertext links and local context. This has proved extremely powerful, but it is only the beginning of our understanding of how context and meaning work even within the inherent structural boundaries of HTML/text documents on the Web.

When Urs Hoelzle said: "It is amazing that this works at all" he sounded like the inventor of the, now almost universal, derailleur gear for bicycles Paul de Vivie, who is reported to have said (in French): "It really should not work, but, it does". A derailleur works because the gearing system synchs with the way a loop of linked chain is able to move (its degrees of freedom are horizontal as well as vertical). Google and similar systems work because they synch with the physical reality of the way information flows on the Internet.

Power laws

Google can return strong results in a quarter of a second more than partly because its distributed database models the shape of text on the Internet. Google's target has always been that the way that information is stored must match the structure of the data. This is not a trivial undertaking, and explains what keeps Google's [60]+ Ph.ds busy.

Larry and Sergey also believe passionately that computers should adapt to meet the needs of the user, not the other way round. That meant constructing the Google database from the ground up around what is there, rather than fitting the data into the existing structure of a database - which is the route that software often tends to follow.

Google plots the shape of the (visible) Internet by indexing every word on every page with its relative locations. The result is a vast topology or multi-dimensional map of almost all the text on the Internet. This map grows, shifts and decays every time that Google reindexs it (usually monthly) in a 'data dance'. Yahoo!/inktomi/FAST and AskJeeves/Teoma's spiders now do something very similar.

Back to the source

Anyone seriously interested in the ideas behind the engineering of Google needs to read Brin and Page's *Anatomy* paper cited above. Although it may have changed considerably since 1997, most of the architecture looks highly scalable, and an educated guess says that the current version of Google still has huge functional similarities. However, it is best not to treat this paper as the key to Google's *entire* existing technology, as one group has done, or not unless you want to be greeted by cruel hoots of well-informed derision.

Crudely, Google's map reveals the patterns generated within an Internet Index. These patterns allow us to navigate rapidly through an enormous quantity of data. It has been known for decades that language syntax contains large statistical regularities, what Google showed was that, at least within hypertext, the semantics could also contain an analogous (or compatible) sequence of regularities, size-independent patterns of growth and decay.

These regularities are sometimes known as power laws, and can be predictive as well as descriptive. This is clearly useful for preventing traffic jams, but it can also be applied to less obviously physical activities like the volume of traffic that visits bloggers' sites, as Clay Shirky explains: [1]

Power laws relating to text are only just beginning to be understood. Fortunately, you can engineer them without needing fully to understand how they come to be, as Murray Gell-Mann explains in *The Quark and the Jaguar* [2].

Zipf's law remains essentially unexplained, and the same is true of a great many power laws. Benoit Mandelbrot... noticed that when word frequencies in actual texts written in natural languages are fitted by modified Zipf's law, the power can differ significantly from 1, with the deviation depending on the richness of the vocabulary in the text in question.

Scalability

The operation of scale-independent regularities was partly discovered and charted by George Kingsley Zipf. Zipf taught German at Harvard and, as Murray Gell-Mann points out, he combined some brilliant maths with public support of National Socialism in Germany. The Nazis subsequently made a vigorous application of Zipf's power laws to the populations of occupied Europe.

Microsoft's market share of the desktop and the observation that with 5% of the world's population, the US has 25% of the world's prisoners and produces 20% of global carbon emissions, could also be regarded as the result of power laws, but as Gell-Mann points out,

> an important lesson about the applications of behavioral science to policy: just because certain relationships tend to occur, that doesn't mean they should necessarily be regarded as always desireable.

Zipf's law can be summarized as that: if you rank a class of objects (cities, businesses, sandcastles) by size, then the rank of an object is inversely proportional to its volume. Zipf believed power laws were unique to social organization.

We now know that these laws can be found in purely physical relationships (Per Bak demonstrated this with sand castles) as well as being the results of social organization (traffic jams, for example), and that power laws echo significant statistical regularities in both the material and the social worlds.

As John Allen Paulos [3], professor of mathematics at Temple University, Philadelphia pointed out in the *Guardian Online*.

> There is even a power law in linguistics. In English, for example, the word "the" appears most frequently and is said to have rank order 1; the words of rank 2, 3, and 4 are "of," "and," and "to," respectively. Zipf's Law relates the frequency of a word to its rank order k and states that a word's frequency in a written text is proportional to $1/k^1$; that is, inversely proportional to the first power of k. (Thus "of " occurs half as frequently as "the", "and" a third as frequently as "the" - and "synecdoche" hardly at all.)

Frequency

The same scaling laws may apply to our use of meanings and ideas, but while they map the same underlying reality as syntax, they are not the same. If they were, then AltaVista's generation of word-frequency analysers, and probably ProSum and MS Word Summarize would have worked, and there would have been no great need for Google. Why and how meanings fall into particular kinds of patterns is still speculative, but its clear that they do. As in the discussion of synonyms earlier, a relevant article on horses may only use the word "horse" once. Google calculates its relevance not by frequency alone but by measuring the collective consensus of how significant that one word match of "horse" has become through a series of ranked, directional values based on its local and global context.

Mapping the mountains

The way such power laws reflect the shape of the geography or topology of the Internet enables extremely rapid shortcuts when navigating into the data stored on those four billion web pages. It is like mapping a mountain range by flying over it in a helicopter rather than climbing the passes on foot. The mountains are the sites with the highest concentration of links or the best directional values found in the contextual relationships between the search query and the page index.

Teoma have concentrated on showing those mountain peaks in the shape of the Internet data by listing them as topics on the right side of their window. That also clearly works very well, but although a successful development, it is not really an innovation so much as a refinement because it builds on the same mathematical foundation that Google first put in place and published.

Although Pittsburgh start-up Vivisimo.com is sometimes cited as a competitor because it also ("uniquely") clusters results, it works as a meta-searcher which does not search the Web itself, but instead searches the results of many of the other Internet search engines, except for some reason, Google. (Although a BBC search is an option, and that does use Google). That can produce fair results, but it depends on the quality of other people's initial search, and it could be excluded from them, if to take a random example, Microsoft did not want their results delivered second-hand.

Google and the Mission

Spellcheck - the movie

Google's Spellcheck is a giant little example of the power of contextual mapping. Unlike conventional Spellcheckers, which work with a pre-established word list, Google Spellcheck looks at whether, to judge from their map, a spelling in a particular context is unlikely, and thus probably wrong.

Because of its take on proper names and neologisms (new words) I have found that a Google Spellcheck is often far more useful than a standard Spellchecker. Its limits are that it only looks at a search query, which is traditionally restricted to ten words in Google, rather than a whole document.

This is a potential candidate for distributed services that extend beyond pure Search. Spellchecking was magic when it first appeared, but was still almost completely unchanged and unimproved 20 years later. The Spellcheck which runs by default in the MS Outlook email system is very useful, but if you make any changes to the underlined word, however wrongly, the Spellchecker is switched off.

In other words it tells you if your spelling does not conform to its pre-determined list and if you intervene, it ceases to function entirely for that word. It learns nothing useful from, and tells you nothing useful about, your intervention because MS Spellcheck, and just about everybody else, is looking at a fixed list of words, whilst Google are working with the context of those words on the Internet.

The Spellchecker as AI

Recently it pointed out my mis-spelling of "Marc Andreessen" as "Marc Andreesen". The second could be a perfectly valid search but it is also a common mistake which even human sub-editors would do well to pick up. That makes it the only piece of artificial intelligence that I am confident that I have seen working in public, after about ten year's search.

Google also seem confident that this is one of their significant successes, pointing out under Credo 10:

Great just isn't good enough

...Search works well for properly spelled words, but what about typos? One engineer saw a need and created a spell checker that seems to read a user's mind.

It does this by checking a probability for the collective consensus of the Internet for that spelling. It can then compare two related results, one of which is technically correct but semantically unlikely, to suggest that the "real" spelling is Andreessen. Google Spellcheck only suggests this, because nothing is more annoying than being automatically corrected by a system following a rule in the wrong context.

When it was first released, and before the Google spider(s) had time to register its significance, a search for the new engine blinkx.com suggested 'blinks', harmless as a suggestion, but bad news if it were to execute without asking first - as other systems have done in the not very distant past.

The Turing Test

At a simple level this example of Google's Spellcheck passes the Turing Test because it was unclear at first whether this was a machine-generated response, or had actually been programmed in by somebody at Google who (presumably having warmer memories of Netscape than I do) had made sure that Marc Andreessen was as easy to find as he is to mis-spell.

Of course it was a machine response, because Google Spellcheck then repeated the same trick for "Guardian" which I repeatedly mistype as "Gaurdian" (probably because the newspaper itself became known as the *Grauniad* after its, now generally undeserved, reputation for screaming literals - typing errors). In both cases, Google Spellcheck worked out that I was trying to search on a typing error, primarily by comparing frequencies for that word or combination of words.

The dawn of consensus intelligence

This is intelligent because it goes beyond sorting information and actually calculates, better than I did, what I really meant. That is a small, unpretentious, but revolutionary shift in the ability of machines to process meaning. It means that we can now get back additional, useful meaning from a computer enquiry, not just a re-ordering of the previous information, which is all our computers have traditionally been able to do. And that ability to add useful information was the acid test of AI as far as Alan Turing was concerned.

Its limits are the limits of the context itself. When I searched on 'msn.com loss', Google's Spellcheck enquired politely if I meant 'loess' - a kind of wind-deposited rock common in China and the backdrop for the desert scenes in the films *Crouching Tiger* and *Hero*.

This was a temporary result and disappeared a few weeks later. The problem was that nobody has had any great interest in msn.com losses. Until 2004 they were huge, but still disappeared within Windows' profits. Without public interest there are no hyperlinks, which means no PageRank. Instead it found a false positive in another spelling.

There are maybe other examples of AI, such as Sony's scientific work with the prototype Aibo robot puppy, or computer viruses which show worrying signs of primitive intelligence in their ability to adapt by learning their environments, but these are second-hand observations - Google's Spellcheck is easy to test at first hand.

All right then, virtual intelligence

Perhaps we should refer to this as virtual, or apparent rather than artificial intelligence. It is clearly not autonomously intelligent but it appears to be intelligent in a way that the usual suspects, such as the chatbots, do not. A Spellcheck may not be a very glamorous example of virtual intelligence, but remember that Internet Search was the opposite of glamorous in 1997. Developers tend to have their own ideas of glamour (and that does not often include clothes).

Google have made themselves the kings of context and with applications like Spellcheck can use the whole Internet to ascertain what you mean rather than what you actually say (or type). These are baby steps but it is still one of the first real examples of comparing syntax as a key to semantics.

Once we can map context, the next stage of development has to be machine learning, where our computers can establish new relationships between and within different contexts by assessing the likely meaning from its context.

Thing-um-a-jig

People can do this from birth, but apart from Google's Spellcheck, and possibly a few other unsung programs, computer programs cannot do this except by associating a mathematically valid but semantically dubious percentage of probability through what is called, rather misleadingly, 'fuzzy logic'.

A good example of how humans learn meaning from context comes from the story of the American student in Dublin who was told 'Stick the plug in the yoke'. He deduced from the context that 'yoke' was the local word for 'electric socket' and it was only after a lot of conversations at cross-purposes that he learnt that in Ireland a 'yoke' means, as in *The Hunting of the Snark* [4]:

"What-you-may-call-um!" or "What-was-his-name!"

But especially "Thing-um-a-jig!"

Sir Bill and the Holy Grail

Software that learns is a well-established objective for IT; Bill Gates has made the ability of software to adapt to the user - by learning their needs - his 'Holy Grail'. Current software adaptions to the user rarely consist of more than a skimpy little Preferences file that should, if that software's developers were more than half-awake, retain your last settings.

Wade Roush's *Search Beyond Google* [5] describes how others, most notably Mooter, are also trying to work with principles of learning which, although still wobbly, may point towards the future of Search technology. Mooter is trying to do for the Internet what blinkx.com is attempting on the desktop. You can judge for yourselves whether they work, but machine learning is unquestionably easier to describe than to do:

Mooter analyses the potential meanings and permutations of the starting keywords and, behind the scenes, ranks the relevance of the resulting Web pages within broad categories called clusters. The user first sees an on-screen "starburst" of cluster names.

...Then comes the learning part. To develop a more precise understanding of what the user is probably looking for, the Mooter engine notes which clusters and links get clicked and uses that information to improve future responses. Suppose a user enters the term "dog," clicks on a cluster called "breeds," and then spends a lot of time looking at sites about Schnoodles (a popular Schnauzer-Poodle mix). When the user clicks on a new search result, Mooter will personalize the ranking to reflect this apparent pattern of interest, which might, for example, lead to sites about "dogs" plus "breeds" plus "Schnoodles" appearing higher. A refined set of results appears on every page; the engine continues to adjust the rankings based on the user's behavior.

"The other side of the hill"

When we learn a new language, or even a skill, we usually work out the possible meaning of what we do not know from what we do know. According to the Duke of Wellington, quoted [6] by the Canadian Armed Forces in their definition of (military) intelligence:

> All of the business of war, and indeed all of the business of life, is to endeavor to find out what you don't know by what you do; that's what I called guessing what was on the other side of the hill.

"What is on the other side of the hill" presents special problems for digital computers because the engineering of Boolean logic through electrical circuits does not permit unknowns or undefined variables. When George Boole created Boolean logic, he used the apparently rigorous premise that "a thing is, or it is not", where "the law of the excluded middle" means that a statement must be either true or false. Claude Shannon's great contribution was to see that this can be represented seamlessly by a switch which is either On or Off, with no other state possible.

This may be a key to the reasons why artificial intelligence has made so little progress with decoding meaning using our current generation of machines. Since the demise of the analogue computer, computers look at information as something whose structure can be reproduced in purely binary (true and false) terms. This can work as well for images as for text. A Van Gogh painting treated as a finite disposition of color areas can be digitized into patterns of true and false so that the reproduction contains *almost* all the visual information in the original painting.

But whereas information can be split into binaries, there is no evidence extant that meaning can be ordered in the same way.

Lewis Carroll was pointing out the absurdity of this kind of logic with Humpty Dumpty's **"A word means exactly what I choose it to mean, no more and no less".** That may fit the intentions of the speaker but it will not fit the listener, whose understanding of the word will be based on a different memory and experience of its usage, or even, like the 'yoke' example, a misunderstanding of the meaning because of its initial context.

Mathematicians tend to agree that there are really only two numbers: 0 and 1, because all other numbers can be derived from those two. This binary world of two numbers appears to fit snugly with the fact that computers use entirely binary storage and access systems and can only operate in multiples of 1 and 0. But while Boolean logic recognizes only these two states, true and false, 0 or 1, the real world depends on a third value, not so much "possible" as one branch of mathematics describes it, but 'unknown', 'undefined' or perhaps at best: 'to be defined'.

Deducing meaning from unknowns or undefined elements of communication is not something that digital computers can deal with, since Boolean logic does not permit the storage or processing of undefined variables. At the most fundamental level these must be divisible into true or false elements.

Boolean logic is wonderfully powerful because it is finite and certain, but it cannot associate, accept any kind of ambiguity or store anything that is not completely fixed and defined (if only for a fraction of a fraction of a microsecond). This makes digital processing perfect for calculating interest rates but useless at making jokes.

Mathematics itself has long ago left the law of the excluded middle behind and H. Rechenbach's trivalent logic works with **"the true, the false and the undetermined".** There can be an almost infinite number of degrees between true and false, as any lawyer or politician is aware. This is known as modal logic and it envisages intermediate values of (n-2) where classical logic deals only with n=2, true or false, again. Modal logic with applications in physics and in linguistics has resulted in the theory of 'pragmatics', which as its name suggests, is probably not a million miles away from John McCarthy's "common-sense" AI.

Not for the first time, the technology moves at different speeds in different areas. A computer using base three is quite practical but the development of a trivalent successor to Boolean logic, with the same power, has probably yet to be developed. In the binary universe of digital computers this can be represented by the (semantically arbitrary values of) fuzzy logic. What cannot be represented in binary is the unknown number of unknowns in almost any natural language communication, along with the ambiguities, omissions, repetitions and errors described in the last chapter.

Georges Ifrah in his hugely comprehensive [7] *Universal History of Numbers Vol 111:* **The Computer and the Information Revolution** points out that computers do not have to use semiconductors, or even water, they can also be based on air or, at least in theory, on enzymes. They do not have to be binary, they can use base three or base whatever number you like. They do not even have to be exclusively analogue or digital, working machines have been created which are hybrids of both.

"A New Job in a Strange Town"

One of the conditions, which all computers must have, according to Ifrah, is the use of Boolean logic. If that is true, then we are likely to have a continuing problem in getting our data models to match the shape of information in the real world, and hence of getting computers to learn new significance 'on the fly' as humans do.

The point being that all environments contain elements, which, at least initially, we do not understand. Even for a spider or a wasp, the real world consists of the true, the false and the unknown. Surviving and reproducing successfully often has a lot to do with being able to process the unknown and hence unusable variables in our environment into the known and usable.

Putting the undefined into a new context where we can remember it easily or work with it requires a great deal of mental work. The older we get, and the more familiar our surroundings, the more we conserve energy by relying on memory, which requires little mental activity compared to learning something new by rebuilding our personal mental maps of context.

Notation, notation, notation

If learning requires the ability to manipulate and remember a *minimum* of three possible conditions (yes, no, don't know) rather than the two of Boolean logic's true and false, then something fairly radical has to happen at the level or initial, primary calculation that can convert a duality into a trinity.

It took the better part of a thousand years for a universal notation for 0 to be accepted and used, partly because of philosophical problems; for how can a sign, which is a something, represent a nothing? Without a notation for 0, there could have been no Newtonian physics, certainly no digital computers, and very little progress in mathematics.

The principle that everything can be derived from nothing was developed by Lao Tzu and the Chinese Taoists of two thousand years ago, with imagery like the cup, which is defined by the nothing it surrounds. Unfortunately they did not develop a symbol for zero and that prevented any development of the idea beyond the purely philosophical, leaving the mathematical discovery to the Indians and Arabs, as Harvard mathematician Robert Kaplan, has described [8] in *The Nothing That Is*: A Natural History of Zero.

Mavericks

Unlike 0 and 1, there is no single notation for undefined, there are an uncountable number of possible variables beginning with 'x' - itself selected by Rene Descartes' printers, apparently because they had run short of 'z's. Developers often use 'foo' as the expression of an arbitrary or unknown variable. Under Google: define 'foo' is an "Algebraic place holder" or "The first standard metasyntatic variable". (The term 'foo fighters' may be a corruption of the French 'feu' and another semantic coincidence.)

At this point an agreed name and notation for 'to be defined' as a single universal value like 0 or 1, might be useful as a way of thinking about and working with the unknown variables of communication. The term 'maverick' originally meant "an unbranded range animal (especially a stray calf); belongs to the first person who puts a brand on it". That makes 'maverick' a reasonable analogy for an unknown word, or phrase, piece of information or even facial expression within a communication whose meaning to the listener is derived partly from the context provided by the speaker and partly from the contextual associations in the memory of the listener which is realigned to make sense of it in the learning process.

The wide Sargasso Sea

It is possible that this problem could lead to the resurrection of analogue computing, but Ifrah points out that one of the great deficiencies of analogue computers is that they never developed any form of storage. If you wanted a record of the results from the water-based resolutions of Phillip's analogue computer mentioned above, you had to write it down. Since under Ifrah's definition, computers must be able to use stored information to modify current calculations, analogue computing has the same level of functionality as an abacus in this respect.

This would preclude using purely analogue computers, but some form of hybrid computer where the digital portion stores the result of the analogue processing may be due for a return to favor, at least for Vannevar Bush's original purpose of tracking associations of meaning.

If calculating meaning depends on providing a model of learning, and learning depends on distinguishing at the most fundamental level the known from the undefined, we have to find a means of processing undefined values in a defined, digital universe.

When studying this problem as a developer I looked at how to build a program that "learns" the structure of a print dictionary in order to convert it into a digital database, or "learns" what bandwidth or videoplayer a website visitor is using. Every time it was an issue of dealing with information undefined in the current context, I kept bumping into a "Rule of Three".

Rule of Three

There are actually many different rules of three, including: a statistical method of renormalizing, elegantly described [9] by Professor Mean (aka Steve Simon), a visual design rule that the eye/brain accepts objects grouped in threes most easily, the Wiccan (neo-pagan) belief that any good or bad action is returned to the doer threefold, Lewis Carroll's injunction from *The Hunting of the Snark*: "What I tell you three times is true" and the opposite observation from satirical author Stella Duffy that anything said once is true, twice is unsure, and if repeated three times will be false. (Her example - "I need some time on my own", repeated three times, means "I want some time with somebody else" - which sounds about right).

Google itself can be said to follow a Rule of Three because it depends on three things: the internal context of the words in the search enquiry, the internal context of the words in the found page, and the external contextual relationship of both to an index of all the available information on the Internet.

A triple recursion

One rule of three, which I have found to be unavoidable in any attempt to mimic learning in code, is a triple recursion, a logical loop within a loop within a loop. While you can have as many recursions as you want or need (although they can be hard to keep track of mentally) you can never have less than three when dealing with natural language. This minimum is required to transcend the Boolean limitations of true and false, because it enables any data to be treated as true, false and undefined (or past, present and future).

Testing current data against historic data (or known rules) requires a double recursion, but as soon as it hits a maverick - an unknown condition (which may be a mistake or a legitimate innovation) it requires a third loop. It can then be processed subsequently either as a known error, or as an unknown innovation, which can be added to historic data only once previous definitions has been updated or modified. That would make it analogous to human learning, where we often require a night's sleep (seriously) to understand changes in our environment. Following this process, the program will have learned something new, rather than simply trying to fit everything into the terms it started with.

One company, Meaning Master, who have been in negotiation with Google, have spent eight years parsing semantic associations (in English). Whether they are ultimately successful may depend on whether they are simply formalizing relationships which are already known to exist (by turning these into relative rules) or combining existing rules of usage with the ability of their programs to learn new meanings and new rules, without the tedious, expensive and prohibitively time-consuming need to identify manually a new sequence of semantic associations when a new concept or word appears - such as 'WMD', 'texted', 'cucumbers', 'bling' or 'googling'. This is not an occasional anomaly; it is the heart of the problem.

Since developers, apart from Google in their early, Arcadian, days at Stanford, have very good reasons for *not* publishing their methods, we will probably only be able to guess from their results whether they are achieving their purpose. If it does not incorporate a learning algorithm then it will fail like many similar attempts to process natural language that assumed semantics could be treated as a state, which is static, rather than a process which is subject to continual change.

Deep structures

Learning physical context is not the whole story of meaning. Context is also provided by our experience of social behaviour whose patterns are local and cultural, but their shape may reflect some universal human experiences.

Proverbs are probably common to all cultures and the meanings of many proverbs are shared amongst very different societies in very different contexts. The English say "**Never spit at heaven**", for example; the Samoans: '**Au e te anu, 'i lagi**' while on the opposite side of the world, the Rastafarian version follows Isaac Newton: "**You spit in the sky, it fall in your eye, what goes up, *must* come down.**"

The best examples of meaning with little or no context are probably music and maths. All known societies have music, but our understanding or appreciation of it is not always determined by the culture we were brought up in. The suggestion is that music, like the structure of proverbs, mirrors part of the deep structure of the human mind. Hence child prodigies, who are almost invariably gifted in either maths or music, can access and manipulate these deep structures without the need for any knowledge of the cultural context, which only time and experience bring. There has never been a significant poem or novel written by a child, because writing depends on manipulating meaning from learnt context.

We have the world outside; we have the context of our local language and culture, and the internal mental context of the communicating human being. Unique as each individual is, many of these patterns are universal. In Structuralist studies in ethnology, the case for such universal patterns is well established. Proverbs and myths can be shared by societies separated by half the planet without any evidence of a common ancestor. At the risk of depressing some women trying to do a hard job, the myth of the wicked stepmother is probably universal, and the genetic and social reasons for this are intuitively obvious. The context is merely being human.

Exile on murder mile

We do not know how to reproduce semantic structures on machines without human intervention. Their shape can probably be found, ultimately, in the way the patterns of our brains (or neural pathways) mirror the flow of turbulent liquids in the wider universe. This is such a minefield of exploding boojums, promising theories that have disappeared and taken their authors with them, that a proper discussion of the place of maverick information in the physical basis of communication had better be exiled to another book.

Footnotes

1: **Power Laws, Weblogs, and Inequality**
Clay Shirky's Writings About the Internet, Networks, Economics, and Culture mailing list, February 8, 2003
2: **The Quark and the Jaguar: Adventures in the Simple and the Complex**
By Murray Gell-Mann Amazon.com
3: **The formula for 'success'**
By John Allen Paulos The Guardian Guardian Unlimited July 22, 2004
4: **The Hunting of the Snark**
By Lewis Carroll: Project Gutenberg
5: **Search Beyond Google**
By Wade Roush TechNewsWorld MIT Technology Review March 2, 2004
6: **What is Intelligence?**
Canadian Forces Intelligence Branch(www.intbranch.org) 2001
7: **The Computer and the Information Revolution - Review**
By Roy Johnson, Mantex 2001
8: **The Nothing That Is: A Natural History of Zero**
By Robert Kaplan, amazon.com
9: **STATS (STeve's Attempt to Teach Statistics) - Rule of three**
By Steve Simon, edited By Linda Foland, Children's Mercy Hospital, Kansas City 12/04/2003

Google and the Mission

11

Lighting out for the Territories

Kick their ass and take their gas

US bumper sticker - reported 2004

||

Set a better example, for the yout' to follow

The Music of the Burning Spear

Three's company

Larry was right when he informed the SEC that Google is an unusual company. It is unusual to produce a paradigm-shifting technology. It is unusual to have an ethical system for the entire global information industry rather than just for your own company. It is unusual to have a business model capable of generating large profits from a free Internet service.

Showing strength in depth in all three, as Google has done, is not so much unusual as downright unique. Apple come closest, but they never cracked the (free service = no income) business dilemma of the Internet, and when Steve Jobs was relieved of his duties at Apple in 1985, a lot of the most idealistic and most motivated developers went with him. Ideals and ethics were downsized as profits soared, allowing Gates to develop Apple's nemesis: a comparable product at a better price.

Google has come through their IPO intact and still friends, with the next stage of their ambitions in the Free Territories of the Internet developing nicely.

Without recourse to ruthless business methods or performance-enhancing drugs they have won gold in the Internet olympics by delivering a free and uncorrupted Search service which everybody in the world loves (at least everybody who does not use ideograms) and made their company (and themselves) enormously wealthy. Only in America, probably, and charting the progress of this version of the American dream has been great fun.

The American Dream - local

Google is not a dream, it is the result of the meticulous engineering of some great maths, but hopes, dreams and material aspirations mean a lot to Americans, even the poorest - judging from rap lyrics, especially the poorest.

To come out of the cold north-east and with maybe just a sprinkling of real luck find gold in California by creating a global product through being more clever, more hard working, more ambitious, and finally, more honorable than anybody else, and without losing that Michigan mockery or telling feel-good lies through the sales team - that's a real American dream.

There's a story that when President Nixon saw a portrait of President Kennedy he remarked, **"He showed the American people what they could be. I show them what they are"**. Cassini's first full-viewfinder pictures of Saturn came in on the same day as Larry's IPO filing and the pictures from Abu Ghraib in Iraq. Our last, best, hope or our worst nightmare - America shows the human race what it is capable of, one way or another.

The American Dream - global

The US itself probably faces a choice. It can either use *force majeure* - its overwhelming physical, ultimately military, force to attempt to retain its access and/or control over dwindling global resources, or it can use its vast wealth and cultural optimism to create new resources, as Google and others in Silicon Valley have done. Microsoft can claim the same because it forced down costs to make pcs almost universal, but usually threw in *force majeure* for good measure.

Google is very American in the enormous scope of its engineering ambitions - it required some really big thinking to enable sorted documents to be found from a collection of four billion in a quarter of a second.

The Chinese are now doing it, too, and Google's American competitors are not slacking, but apart from the Norwegian FAST (now part of Yahoo!) European companies have not, for technological or political reasons, been able to work on that sort of scale. It is probably no coincidence that technological leadership comes from American, Russian Jewish and now Chinese developers.

Google and the Mission

They come from cultures and companies, which are obliged to think and then act, on a huge scale.

21st century Webocracy

The English are proud of the contribution made to the Webocracy of a near-universal library by Sir Tim Berners-Lee and Alan Turing. Turing certainly could think on a global scale and was then able to apply it to the local problem of wartime codes. Sir Tim came from the other end; he created a global form of communication by looking for one that worked locally, albeit in a high-powered research establishment. It was then NCSA in the United States, who took his work and made it global with the Mosaic browser,

Europeans, particularly English-speakers, have benefited considerably from Google's technology and its political experience that **Democracy on the web works**. But we are pretty much innocent bystanders, if something went horribly wrong and Google went for paid-inclusion tomorrow, there is not a darn thing we could do about it except maybe to switch to Teoma - which has recently earned $100 million from using Google's advertising, and might themselves not be able to stay pure. If you do not own the technology you lose any power to influence it.

State regulation of Search would be a disaster, because of the necessarily secret nature of the core code within Search engines, and the strong tendency of governments to try to control access to information they do not like. Self-regulation according to international standards is weak, but does work. The UN clearly cannot enforce its Human Rights Charter by anything except argument and bad press for those who break it, but it does provide a standard that civilized countries are expected to live up to.

We cannot prevent any major Search company from providing advertisements disguised as Search results, except by publicising it. Any nation that wishes to close down sites within its borders will have the right to prevent criminal activity, and some states will always claim that political dissenters are busy committing crimes. The only real weapon against this is world opinion and trade sanctions when all else fails. An international agreement on the individual's right to privacy would also not come amiss.

Stanford

Stanford can take credit for helping to provide Google not only with the initial technology (and many of the key staff) but also with a strongly thought out ethical approach to the use of that technology. Praise for Stanford in this book has been pretty much unmitigated, but since the dawn of the Web saw the first ARPA network connect them to UCLA, Stanford seems to just keep on getting it right. In the entire saga, their only apparent failure was some difficulty in helping Google raise the initial finance, but with Larry and Sergey's determination and knowledge of what they could do and the enthusiastic investment environment of the dot.com era, this was a fairly temporary hindrance. If anyone else deserves to profit from Google, then it has to be Stanford. According [1] to Ann Grimes, of the *Wall Street Journal*, immediately after the IPO:

> Stanford is left with 7,574 shares of Class A Google stock and 1,650,289 shares of Class B stock, according to Securities and Exchange Commission filings. Those holdings are valued at $179.5 million. The university's trustees sold 184,207 shares, earning a quick $15.6 million.

> The university owns key technology used by Google that was developed at Stanford. Google paid the university in stock and cash for an exclusive licensing partnership, plus annual royalties. That agreement expires in 2011.

For British universities these kind of sums are eye-watering, but hey, like their graduate students, Stanford did the prep and come out of all this *summa cum laude*. I cannot help wondering whether, like Snoopy, Condoleezza Rice ever misses the old puppy farm, back in the days when she was the youngest, the first female and first non-white Provost of Stanford?

And the Mission continues. Professor Lessig is now using his work at Stanford on the *Creative Commons* [2] to help the BBC handle copyright on assets released without charge to a global public.

First we'll take Manhattan - classified and foreign

Google hit the mother lode when Sergey developed contextual advertising because it makes it more cost effective to advertise specific products on Google's window to the Internet than in magazines or the endless supply of print supplements to newspapers.

Those supplements are worth billions in classified advertising, which the publishers are going to see slip sliding away in the direction of Google, Yahoo!, msn.com and baidu.com. Starting in Dallas, the American print media are already feeling the wind, as advertisers start to investigate long-standing circulation claims. *Le Monde*, with France's biggest circulation, is in even deeper trouble having lost twice over, first by misjudging its own Internet investments, and then by losing a huge slice of readership to two successful freesheets and other Internet news sources.

A cheaper and more efficient technology is always going to win out against a traditional industry, and it is inevitable here as an increasing mass of individual advertisers realize the cost effectiveness of the medium. That actually happens fairly slowly, according to the major Internet companies, because those responsible for advertising budgets hate risk and need to see others succeed before they move. But the plates are shifting and the whole world's classified advertising is starting to move over to the Internet, because the technologly is finally ready for it.

Like Apple, and then Microsoft, Google moved into a foreign language service almost immediately after they became a serious player. The scope for developing contextual advertising in the [80]+ languages for which Google already provides Open Search represents a huge potential source of future income. Aside from non-alphabetic languages, like Korean, it is not the biggest and most exciting technical challenge, but it can help ensure that Google is still around in 50 years.

MS threat recedes

Google's share price rise of 40% in less than a month after the IPO, taking it to the top of Google's own original valuation, is quite steep, but unlike Netscape's quadrupling in a day, it is probably not life-threatening. Leverage needs to be kept low if, like this writer, you believe that the whole Internet and IT sector is overdue for a serious correction.

The main factor behind the rise was probably Microsoft's admission that they had no immediate date set for the release of WinFS/Longhorn. That means, as any IT stock analyst can probably tell you, that Microsoft will not have their own "Google-killing" desktop Search out in less than three years, and possibly longer. This looks painful for Microsoft, but do not underestimate Bill's pride and stamina in the long run. It certainly takes away any immediate threat from Microsoft and the share price rise was a rational response.

Microsoft's embarrassment may have an honorable cause. Bill has reinvented himself as the 21st century Andrew Carnegie, with an enthusiasm and thoroughness that is hard not to admire. *Fortune's* August 2004 list of the 25 most powerful businessmen in the US, put Bill third after Lee Scott and Warren Buffet, and declared:

> Just as Gates is showing geeks how to mature gracefully, Microsoft is showing tech companies how to deal with middle age... When he decides - through the Bill and Melinda Gates Foundation, at $27 billion in assets and growing - that AIDS should become as distant a memory as Netscape, researchers the world over pay attention.

We certainly do, and millions may have cause to be grateful.

This may leave Microsoft without Bill's legendary ability to reduce developers to tears by deconstructing their code. Steve Ballmer, teasing aside, is probably one of the best Chief Executives going, but his background is Procter & Gamble, not C++, and that may make it hard and sometimes impossible for him to gauge how well software development is going, when only a developer of Bill's experience could ever make a fully informed call.

Remember that all the considerable brains involved with Ted Nelson's Xanadu project were always convinced that they were only six months away from delivering a completed product. Writing code often generates that kind of false optimism because the logic can look easy until you take the software out into the real world, where real users and real conditions cause it to fall over.

Although I joked about FUD at the time, the reality was probably that something very similar happened to Microsoft WinFS project. It looked great until they took it out in the rain.

Only the beginning

Even the finest technology takes at least three or four years to get to the bottom line and Google will have to heed Larry's own advice and avoid being spooked by any technology bandwagon around a new service or product. But really, it looks like this is only the beginning of Google's big adventure, because they have only started to compute meaning using context. They have proved that their technology works, and now they intend to extend it as far as they can go with it.

Because of their strongly version one point zero approach, that probably means that they will do best when working out their own new solutions to old problems, and will probably be middling poor at catching on to other people's innovations outside Google itself. That has also been a consistent problem at Apple, and it is probably partly inevitable with any world-class engineering team. At Apple it is known as the Not Invented Here (and hence of no interest) Syndrome. Microsoft just loves other people's ideas, but can still be self-absorbed enough to miss major trends, for a while, at least.

Learning and Spam

Learning has a lot of commercially valuable applications, as Bill has been pointing out for a long time. He is characteristically ahead of the game on this, but the rest of the world will catch up eventually.
Any work with the meaning of the contents of text runs into the learning problem very quickly. MS Word, for example, contains a superb dynamic indexing system. This means that you can revise and change a document and Word will update the pagination of its index automatically, saving days of tedious work correcting it manually.

But that is only half the job. Before it can index, Word needs a Concordance file of the terms to search for and how they should be listed. There is no software to create a Concordance file by going through a document and calculating which words are most important and what their synonyms are.

Frequency alone does not cut it, though it can be helpful, because of the stopwords' problem described above. Nor is there any easy or cheap way of working out that "engineer" is also conveyed by "engineering, engineered, engineers, Engineering, well-engineered, Engineer, Engineer-in-Chief" which are all quite different words with no connection, as far as Word is concerned.

Since this may be the next important step for search technology it is worth exploring how it might apply to spam. Google defeated spam for years by using PageRank, but now that the link farms and spammers have themselves learnt how to manipulate PageRank, at least temporarily, Google and its peers may need to defeat spam with software that learns what makes spam, spam.

The software would need to learn rather than simply to be instructed, because any rules (such as spam contains obscenities) will generate false positives. ("Who put the **** in Scunthorpe?" was the kind of problem which defeated the early spam/obscenity filters.)

Even if you can create a complete and universal rule system defining Spam on Tuesday, the spammers will have learnt how to subvert it by Wednesday. One current technique is to break words up into innocent fragments (eg: "s eeho tt eens!"). What's needed is a way of learning new techniques as they appear.

"Exterminate all the brutes"

This problem is made worse because there are often actually relatively few links needed to influence or create a page rank of useful significance for any given page. That makes it relatively easy to spam fictitious pages with links to other domains.

My own attitude to link-farms is close to Colonel Kurtz's - **"Drop the Bomb - Exterminate Them All!"**. I appreciate the risk of significant collateral damage, but anybody whose business depends on one free Internet Search outlet - without other advertising - is probably doomed anyway.

Google's response similarly lacked finesse; they attempted to crush the spammers with the hobnail boots of probability theory rather than with their usual roller hockey blades. The fault may lie in the technology used: Bayesian probabilities.

The glass bead game

Bayesian probability theory was conceived in the 19th century to prove the existence of God, or failing that, to cheat at cards. Very crudely, it works like this. You have a vase containing an unknown number of black balls and white balls. You want to estimate how many of each it contains. You pull out a handful, count them and then use that result to guess how many of each color are in the vase. You repeat the exercise and modify each estimate from the previous results. And so on and on. Eventually, of course, you have counted all the balls and their colors, but long, long before then you will have a statistically valid estimate of the proportion of black to white.

For fixed, finite sets, like fingerprints this can work CSI-style well. Fingerprints don't change after they are measured, but the significance of web pages, like all natural language texts, can. The Bayesian world is fixed; the number of balls in the jar does not change. Web text pages are not constituents of finite sets and are subject to continual change.

False positives

The problem may be partly false positives, as Seth Finkelstein [3] suggested. Statistical connections can occur purely through chance, and then be normalized to give an entirely false reading. Since this technology is heavily used by the intelligence services, that matters. (Think of the bug that turned poor Buttle into Tuttle in *Brazil*.) But the real problem is that human ingenuity and commercial greed will probably always better machine logic.

The best way of countering spam-farms is probably to apply a stronger technology of learning, and Google is probably already doing just that. If you can learn the specific structures of spam you can identify and destroy it without harming innocent bystanders.

Like its competitors, Google already 'learns' the visible Internet in the sense that it reindexs the Internet every month or so. Albeit compressed and encoded, these indices hold a sequence of individual records of billions of pages over [6] years. The trick will be to find an efficient method of 'learning' the significance of the changes to pages between indices, specifically to target spam-farm structural and contextual signatures.

Learning signatures

Like any other form of communication, spam-farms have their own structures and context, which may mutate like an Aids virus, but can still probably be identified through a characteristic signature. Link farms that consist of pages that are empty of anything save lists of links to other domains have obvious structures and are probably already being targeted by Google and other Search sites. Spammers that slip links into innocuous-looking pages of text or convert the search words into a generic ad, will provide a context whereby the (dynamic) text does not match its links in the same way that a real page does.

Mentally, we do this kind of learning and editing all the time. If we can recognise spam by its heading without needing to read every specific message (or meaning), we need software that can begin to do the same. Mozilla's open-source Firefox browser is said to be good at this and there may be an important advance in that code.

Customer care & pr

Possibly because of the areas I am researching, the amount of Spam seems to be receding, and there appear to have been fewer complaints about it in the Web's Google fora. This would be good news because it impacts very sharply on public perceptions of how successful a Google Search actually is. Beyond the number of unique visitors to Google.com, user satisfaction is hard to measure, as Urs Hoelzle has noted.

One potential vulnerability here, which Microsoft is putting a lot of thought into on their own account, is that Google are primarily concerned with the satisfaction of the user. As a chronic user obviously I approve, but there may be a need to think equally of advertisers as customers. They do pay more than 90% of the bills, after all.

The thing to avoid is the kind of high-handedness and duplicity, which Apple has sometimes been accused of in the past. Advertisers with Google need to feel loved, want to be consulted regularly, listened to and generally taken seriously using the technology that can make that fast and efficient on the Internet.

More than 150,000 advertisers will need scarce resources, particularly on the management side, but if Google do not do this, and there have been a few grumbles, then they will find that a company like Microsoft becomes actually very good at it, and that really would be a fatal mistake. As long as Google maintains its engineering standards it will win plaudits, but keeping the main service free depends entirely on its advertising income.

The refusal to hire a glossy marketing department may be a luxury, but it is something of a relief if one has ever had to deal with corporate pr. Google already use Businesswire press releases and it would help keep observers happy if they made these as regular and as meaty as commercial confidentiality allows. The alternative is press speculation, which will probably happen anyway, but a smoother machinery for killing it off might make life easier. A regular press release will do this if it contains hard information which insiders, like searchenginewatch.com, trust enough to use for tracking progress and then dismissing fairy stories.

The free and paid territories

Central to Google's business model is that it targets only the free parts of the Net. This simplifies life by taking out the most difficult dynamic pages, and also avoids passwords and fees. This should probably not be regarded as sacred because, as with Google Alerts, there can be increasingly good reasons for Google to work within the walled gardens of the subscription-only parts of the Web.

In Fall 2004, Reed Elsevier, one of the world's largest academic publishers, wanted to negotiate a paid Search service from Google for their enormous proposed library of online university papers. The proposal was that both would split the joint subscription charges.

It was not clear whether this is actually going to happen, Reed Elsevier have their own problems with Open Access (Source) publishing, but it is a straw in the wind since this is one of the largest and most important sections of the paid Web, rather than Google's usual hunting grounds of the entirely Free Web.

In October 2004, Larry and Sergey went to the Frankfurt Book Fair to launch Google Print, which searches books for keywords and then shows titles and text that publishers want to put on line. They had already signed up Houghton Mifflin, Blackwell and Oxford University Press.

I can only wish them the best of British luck with this one. They have the technology, no question, and the book trade needs rationalising. With a shelf-life of less than three months for new titles, wastage is very high and a large proportion of all books published, at least in the UK, are subsequently pulped. Bookshops are supplied by reps using a model established in the 19th century. DTP (desktop publishing) and Adobe's Acrobat have transformed the printing technology and costs, but the rest of the industry is highly irrational, based on the love of books, low salaries, negative margins and a technophobia which can be utterly frustrating.

After attempting to print out a free copy of Lawrence Lessig's *Free Culture*, Michael Skapinker at the *FT* proposed an interesting model of providing books free online and selling the print versions. This is close to the model for this book, which provides the (hypertext-laden) electronic version free to purchasers of the print book, which is supplied as Print on Demand - no storage, no wastage, no dog-eared returns from the bookshops. There may be an interesting future development in financing books by including Google's contextual advertising. (Wartime Penguin paperbacks used to contain ads for Mars bars, which were unobtainable under rationing. Oh the power of the brand - even in those dark days).

Sadly it is not really practical for a book like this, but some books, such as the classic *Readers' Digest* guides, are natural candidates for contextual consumer advertising online. The kind of advertising which would not cause publishers to set fire to themselves in protest would be advertising of other books, since the rules of competition are quite different from other consumer goods. How long it takes the (British) publishing industry to accept such ideas and develop them is another matter entirely and Google Print will need oodles of patience. That's a promise.

To be human = to make mistakes

The danger with "bigging up" Google, as the kids used to call it, or celebrating their successes, is that at some point they will make significant mistakes. As the mighty Anthony Quinn, aka Zorba the Greek, put it, "**I am human, and because I am human, I made mistakes**". Google's pilots and employees are human, it tries to be an unusually human corporation, and so it is inevitable that they will make mistakes.

Google may already have made some serious, as well as some relatively trivial, mistakes. But what those mistakes might be, I am not sure anybody has actually identified. Management can look chaotic, and paperwork that should have been done is sometimes not done, but none of that looks potentially fatal - more the problem of over-rapid growth made inevitable once the brand achieved critical mass on the Internet.

Too much too soon?

I suspect that if Larry and Sergey got the chance to do it all again, they might wish they had handed out share options a lot more slowly and been able to stay a private company for much longer.

But that really is hindsight. In its first three years, before the implementation of contextual advertising, Google was in trad dot.com mode of burning investment money without any certainty of income.

Unlike the dot.coms, most of whose engineering was abysmal, Google had some of the best engineers in the world. Pay rates had gone into the stratosphere, and the only way of getting world-class work out of world-class developers was to hand out equity. It was part of the ethos that those who kept the faith and sweated in the vineyard would have their work rewarded when the money finally came in.

Split share governance

Unlike the outside world, Google's employees could see all the money being generated before the IPO, and it was reasonable that people who had been producing beautiful work through years of extreme effort - because you do not get that quality of engineering any other way - should want to see some cash. From the CEO down, their salaries were not that high.

So more than anything else, the public sale of the company through an IPO was the penalty of success; a penalty which they have partly pulled back through a fierce two-tier share voting system that leaves them as much in control as Murdoch or Gates.

That won them 0.2(sic) out of 100, the lowest score tested for corporate governance, in one report. That report looked like it might have been part of the campaign to short Google's share price before the IPO, by panicking retail investors out of the market, but it was actually published a couple of days after the IPO, unless, of course, they missed the deadline.

When James Murdoch at BskyB announced a 65% rise in operating profits in 2004 and a long-term strategy for the company, the City of London knocked 25% off the share price on the same day. Google should not be surprised in future at similar treatment from Wall Street for similar reasons, which are not determined by economic logic. Google should maybe even consider teaming up with James Murdoch to propose a governance structure for companies with two-tier share ownership systems, if only to show that fee parties and obscene expense claims will never tolerated in either company.

Rothschild's warning

Sir Evelyn de Rothschild, who as former chairman of the merchant bank NM Rothschild Ltd. can properly be regarded as an expert on capitalism, believes the problem of corporate integrity is extremely serious. Writing in the *Guardian* in July 2004, he warns [4]:

> Capitalism, or at least the corporate personalities and structures that define it for most of us, may be under threat from itself. The collapses of businesses in the US and Europe in a cloud of alleged fraud have shaken confidence in the financial system.

> ...One check on abuses comes from the culture of family businesses. These companies account for nearly a hundred million jobs across the EU. Many have been going for generations, and those who are bringing in outside professional help but still maintain control have proved to be very successful.

> The need to balance regulation, supervision and cooperation has never been greater. To achieve that balance will require an emphasis on ethics as much as on short-term returns. Leadership from government, the corporate community and commentators for a higher standard of ethical behavior may go a long way to reversing the damage and keeping greater regulation out of the markets. Without that leadership, it may be difficult to restore confidence and growth.

Google and the Mission

Gambling with the college fund - oil and IT

From a less lofty viewpoint, it looks like the problem is partly the gambling instinct. This is clearly very strong in the US, with its well-founded cultural faith in any leap in the dark, but it is probably equally strong in China and England and the best efforts of the Chinese Communist Party or the Salvation Army in the 20th century do not seem to have not made a heck of a lot of difference to either culture's love of betting.

Gambling in Las Vegas may only harm the gambler or their family; gambling in oil or IT, by speculating in the shares, costs lives and jobs. A lifetime's saving in a pension fund should not be a speculative investment, and an industry should grow because people want its products, not simply to provide short-term capital gains.

Google may not succeed in their long-term ambitions, which includes the long-term value of their company, but like Microsoft they are setting the right example. That is, if you believe that America cannot afford to behave like a gambler when it comes to one of the main sources of its current and future wealth.

The same applies to the US education system. Eisenhower had the authority, and the Soviet threat, to make a thirty-year investment in education politically viable. His successors may not have that stature. If American workers are less educated and less skilled than Indians and particularly the Chinese, more of whom will be online by 2006 than US citizens, the logic of globalisation is going to give America a lot of problems with maintaining its living standards and its expectations of material abundance.

Cult Google?

It took a tremendous amount of bottle - self-belief - to go up against Wall Street with a completely contrary set of beliefs and principles. It is hard to think of anybody who has ever beaten Wall Street in a nice knockdown argument, so it would not be surprising if that entailed an almost religious belief in one's objectives. Somehow it is not hard to imagine Larry and Sergey and the whole Google team on a *Blues Brothers*-style Mission from God.

Apparently there is dark talk in Silicon Valley of Google becoming a quasi-religious cult. (I have also noticed that people in San Francisco do not really appreciate jokes about the Reverend Jim Jones and his Kool-Aid.) But thus far Google have been saved from any sign of priggish self-righteousness, or tendency to lose touch with the real world, by a steady supply of excellent jokes.

Of all the ten of thousands of web pages on Google and Internet Search, I have read, the following [5] from Google themselves is still the best and worth quoting in full. (If you don't find it funny, you will probably never understand what makes Google tick.)

Our Technology - PigeonRank

The technology behind Google's great results

As a Google user, you're familiar with the speed and accuracy of a Google search. How exactly does Google manage to find the right results for every query as quickly as it does? The heart of Google's search technology is PigeonRank™, a system for ranking web pages developed by Google founders Larry Page and Sergey Brin at Stanford University.

Building upon the breakthrough work of B. F. Skinner, Page and Brin reasoned that low cost pigeon clusters (PCs) could be used to compute the relative value of web pages faster than human editors or machine-based algorithms. And while Google has dozens of engineers working to improve every aspect of our service on a daily basis, PigeonRank continues to provide the basis for all of our web search tools.

Why Google's patented PigeonRank™ works so well

PigeonRank's success relies primarily on the superior trainability of the domestic pigeon (Columba livia) and its unique capacity to recognize objects regardless of spatial orientation. The common gray pigeon can easily distinguish among items displaying only the minutest differences, an ability that enables it to select relevant web sites from among thousands of similar pages.

By collecting flocks of pigeons in dense clusters, Google is able to process search queries at speeds superior to traditional search engines, which typically rely on birds of prey, brooding hens or slow-moving waterfowl to do their relevance rankings.

When a search query is submitted to Google, it is routed to a data coop where monitors flash result pages at blazing speeds. When a relevant result is observed by one of the pigeons in the cluster, it

Google and the Mission

strikes a rubber-coated steel bar with its beak, which assigns the page a PigeonRank value of one. For each peck, the PigeonRank increases. Those pages receiving the most pecks, are returned at the top of the user's results page with the other results displayed in pecking order.

Integrity

Google's pigeon-driven methods make tampering with our results extremely difficult. While some unscrupulous websites have tried to boost their ranking by including images on their pages of bread crumbs, bird seed and parrots posing seductively in resplendent plumage, Google's PigeonRank technology cannot be deceived by these techniques. A Google search is an easy, honest and objective way to find high-quality websites with information relevant to your search.

Data

PigeonRank Frequently Asked Questions

How was PigeonRank developed?

The ease of training pigeons was documented early in the annals of science and fully explored by noted psychologist B.F. Skinner, who demonstrated that with only minor incentives, pigeons could be trained to execute complex tasks such as playing ping pong, piloting bombs or revising the Abatements, Credits and Refunds section of the national tax code.

Brin and Page were the first to recognize that this adaptability could be harnessed through massively parallel pecking to solve complex problems, such as ordering large datasets or ordering pizza for large groups of engineers. Page and Brin experimented with numerous avian motivators before settling on a combination of linseed and flax (lin/ax) that not only offered superior performance, but could be gathered at no cost from nearby open space preserves. This open space lin/ax powers Google's operations to this day, and a visit to the data coop reveals pigeons happily pecking away at lin/ax kernels and seeds.

What are the challenges of operating so many pigeon clusters (PCs)?

Pigeons naturally operate in dense populations, as anyone holding a pack of peanuts in an urban plaza is aware. This compactability enables Google to pack enormous numbers of processors into small spaces, with rack after rack stacked up in our data coops. While this is optimal from the standpoint of space conservation and pigeon contentment, it does create issues during molting season, when large fans must be brought in to blow feathers out of the data coop. Removal of other pigeon byproducts was a greater challenge, until Page and Brin developed groundbreaking technology for converting poop to pixels, the tiny dots that make up a monitor's display. The clean white background of Google's home page is powered by this renewable process.

Aren't pigeons really stupid? How do they do this?

While no pigeon has actually been confirmed for a seat on the Supreme Court, pigeons are surprisingly adept at making instant judgments when confronted with difficult choices. This makes them suitable for any job requiring accurate and authoritative decision-making under pressure. Among the positions in which pigeons have served capably are replacement air traffic controllers, butterfly ballot counters and pro football referees during the "no-instant replay" years.

Where does Google get its pigeons? Some special breeding lab?

Google uses only low-cost, off-the-street pigeons for its clusters. Gathered from city parks and plazas by Google's pack of more than 50 Phds (Pigeon-harvesting dogs), the pigeons are given a quick orientation on web site relevance and assigned to an appropriate data coop.

Isn't it cruel to keep pigeons penned up in tiny data coops?

Google exceeds all international standards for the ethical treatment of its pigeon personnel. Not only are they given free range of the coop and its window ledges, special break rooms have been set up for their convenience. These rooms are stocked with an assortment of delectable seeds and grains and feature the finest in European statuary for roosting.

What's the future of pigeon computing?

Google continues to explore new applications for PigeonRank and affiliated technologies. One of the most promising projects in development involves harnessing millions of pigeons worldwide to work on complex scientific challenges. For the latest developments on Google's distributed cooing initiative, please consider signing up for our <u>Google</u> <u>Friends</u> <u>newsletter</u>.

This is essence of Google. A cult? No, cults never have *any* sense of humor about themselves.

A Mission? Undoubtedly, yes. If it is going to maintain its priorities and preserve its secrets Google is going to have to be quite tribal. The strength of an IT company seems to be down to the strength of its own internal culture. Companies like Intel, Apple, Microsoft itself, all need a close-knit sense of joint purpose and strong leadership to work successfully (even if this also probably reflects America's increasing tendency to gated communities).

Do no evil - to Google

Following Google's famous injunction, and the experience that most people do evil without meaning to, this book was written with the simpler ambition of doing no evil to Google. It is based entirely on freely available public documents, obtained in almost every case by a simple Google search, and my own work in neighboring fields. If Microsoft have not worked all this out for themselves, then they really do need Bill to kick their arses, because FAST, Teoma and the spam-farmers certainly have already understood most of what is happening.

There should not be anything here which is any use to a spammer, and precious little for those attempting the often-dubious art of 'Search Engine Optimisation'. In a couple of cases I have refrained from discussing publicly any of the system's possible security vulnerabilities, and trust that Google is now well aware of them.

Google is broken - yeah, right

One group believe that they have found Google's fatal mistake and claim that Google's index is now full and consequently Google itself is broken and is dieing. Unfortunately, the same group – googlewatch.com have already been campaigning against the 'undemocratic' nature of PageRank for a good while and this has earned them the reputation of wearing tin foil hats to keep out the microwaves from space.

Their attack on Google's method achieved a lot of coverage at a time when nobody could think of anything bad to say about the company, and journalists were looking for a quick show of impartiality. But anybody seriously interested could see that it was nonsense: if you have several million references to Bill Clinton and no system of measuring hyperlink references to those pages, then you would have to list them on the basis of either a random number generator (very common in the early days of the Net) or possibly date the document was posted. Worse results than AltaVista are guaranteed.

Although no one took them seriously, they had noticed one potentially significant thing. The number of pages that Google was indexing rose rapidly in 2003, but stayed stuck on four and a bit billion for most of 2004. The reason, probably, is that during 2004 Google were despamming furiously and had decided that a dynamic url address (usually as Urs pointed out through a session cookie) with the same content did not constitute another ten thousand possible pages, but one.

If they then found that they were indexing a lot fewer pages in total, they probably did not want to provoke 'Google fails - Internet full!' headlines from newspapers that should know better. Google must be pretty weary of all that after their IPO and by November 2004, their pagecount had doubled to more than 8 billion.

The End

Googlewatch' were convinced that because Brin and Page had set an initial index size not far off four billion, in 1997, it was now full. They promptly got a lot of mail from people whom Google had indexed only a couple of days after they had posted up their pages, so Googlewatch decided that Google must be throwing away previously indexed pages to make room. Frankly, having listed all other probable difficulties to the SEC, Google were unlikely to forget to say that the index was now full and would no longer scale.

An educated guess says that (inside the relevant objects) they will be using nested arrays so that a [4.2] billion entry index itself can consist of 4.2 billion arrays which can hold another 4.2 billion arrays and so on to a Cantorian conception of infinity. If they could not scale, their index would have been full a long time ago.

Similar conclusions fueled a cruel satirical site from SlashNot.com. "You're right, you're right", they told Googlewatch. "Y2k is come again, the Sky is falling, Google is full, the Internet is about to collapse and we are retreating to the basement with 16 Linux servers in order to archive Google's contents and recreate the civilization now doomed to crash to extinction above our heads".

"It's true", said another observer, "the Internet has come to an end. I have seen the last page".

Footnotes

1: Why Stanford Is Celebrating The Google IPO
By Ann Grimes, The Wall Street Journal (Montana Associated Technology Roundtables) August 23, 2004
2: Creative Commons
By Professor Lawrence Lessig, creativecommons.org
3: Google Bayesian Spam Filtering Problem?
Seth Finkelstein November 26 2003
4: Capitalism is a danger to itself
By Evelyn de Rothschild, Guardian Unlimited July 13, 2004
5: PigeonRank
Google Inc. April 1st 2004

Webthreads

Our website http://**fleetworks.info** contains an electronic version of this text with links to the following 600 articles, which is free to purchasers of this book. Some of the issues dealt with are complex, and have been skimmed over to keep this book short enough to be readable. The idea of **Webthreads** is that any researcher, developer, journalist or student can jump into the middle of almost any of these issues within two or three mouse clicks.

Since work began on this book in late 2003, some of these pieces have been placed behind subscription accounts, so we will be seeking permission from their publishers to include them as cached copies on the website and possibly in a printed version for a hardback version of this book.

AI

Interview with Keith Preston, BT Labs and research
By Adrian Mars Le Journal (cached) 16/01/2001
Artificial Intelligence
Yahoo! Directory 2004
The Hunting of the Snark
By Lewis Carroll: Project Gutenberg
Marvin Minsky Intro
Game Developers Conference 2001 Dr. Dobb's TechNetCast
Consciousness
a draft (3/16/04) of Part IV of The Emotion Machine By Marvin Minsky MIT
The A.L.I.C.E. AI Foundation
The A.L.I.C.E. AI Foundation 2003
The Nothing That Is: A Natural History of Zero
By Robert Kaplan, amazon.com
The Quark and the Jaguar: Adventures in the Simple and the Complex
By Murray Gell-Mann Amazon.com
Perspective of Mind: Douglas Hofstadter
Beatrix Murrell Stoa del Sol
Historical Background - Plato , Aristotle and Descartes
Robert Stainton Department of Philosophy Calteon University
STATS (- STeve's Attempt to Teach Statistics) - Rule of three
By Steve Simon, edited By Linda Foland, Children's Mercy Hospital, Kansas City 12/04/2003
Humpty Dumpty Theory of Language
P.D. Magnus
Minsky: AI "has been brain dead since the 1970s"
By Sander Olson: Geek.com Geek News
The formula for 'success'
By John Allen Paulos The Guardian Guardian Unlimited July 22, 2004

Google and the Mission

What is Intelligence?
Canadian Forces Intelligence Branch(www.intbranch.org) 2001
From irony to skepticism
Niels Helsloot 1992
Attack of the Two-Headed Scientists
By Charles Mandel: Wired News Lycos Jun. 11, 2003
Through the Looking-Glass and What Alice Found There
By Lewis Carroll, Electronic Text Center, University of Virginia Library

AOL

AOL loses Ted Turner and $99 billion
By Jim Hu: Staff Writer, CNET News.com CNET Networks January 30, 2003
Google turns up on CompuServe search
By Jim Hu: CNET News.com CNET Networks March 25, 2002
AOL, Microsoft's peace a sign of times
By Jim Hu: CNET News.com CNET Networks May 30, 2003
AOL exercises Google warrants
By Jim Hu, CNET News.com May 7, 2004
AOL has right to buy nearly 2 million Google shares
Reuters news.com
Is this the end of Netscape?
By David Becker CNET News.com CNET Networks May 29, 2003
Would AOL drop Google, just like Yahoo did?
By Bambi Francisco: CBSMarketWatch.com AlwaysOn 02.25.04
AOL lays off 375 in Mountain View
By Elise Ackermann: mercurynews.com The Mercury News Wed, Dec. 10, 2003
AOL Time Warner Reports $100 Billion Loss
By Stephen Taub, CFO.com Economist Group CFO Publishing Corporation January 30, 2003
Time Warner Ditches AOL Name
By Keith Regan EcommerceTimes.com ECT News Network September 19, 2003
AOL Secures Google Shares
WebProNews

AdWords and AdSense

7 Scary Google Adsense Truths
By Christopher Knight, Ezine-Tips newsletter July 13, 2004
Google-like technologies could revolutionize TV, other media
By Stefanie Olsen: CNET News.com CNET Networks, Inc. April 29 2004
Google unveils new pay-for-play plan
By Lisa M. Bowman: CNET News.com CNET Networks February February 20, 2002
Google's ad plans provoke grumbling
By Stefanie Olsen, CNET News.com May 17, 2004
Yahoo! Accepts Anti-Pollution Ads Rejected By Google
Sam Haswell: Oceana 2/26/04
Draining the Rivers of Gold
By Mick O'Regan: Radio National (Australia) ABC 14 August2003
Google's Ads -- and Minuses
Alex Salkever BusinessWeek Online The McGraw-Hill Companies Inc. March 9, 2004

The Next Context
By Pamela Parker: clickz.com Jupitermedia Corporation April 16, 2004
Google Does About-Face on Banner Ads
By Keith Regan, ECT News Network, Inc. 05/13/04
Google and Newspapers
By Carl Sullivan: Editor and Publisher February 17, 2004
How Google Is Revolutionizing the Ad Game
David Kirkpatrick FORTUNE Wednesday, March 17, 2004
No Pop-up Ads on Google
Google Inc. 2004
Search Engine Marketing - In a Funk?
By Lisa Wehr: Internet Search Engine Database 02-09-2004
Collateral Damage Why Most Internet Advertising Doesn't Work and What Little Does Work Is Killing Us
By Robert X. Cringely, I, Cringely, pbs
Quigo Launches Innovative New Content-Targeted Advertising Platform for Advertisers and Publishers
Quigo Technologies, Press Release, June 21, 2004
Quigo to Challenge Google AdSense, Contextual Advertising
Search Engine Journal 3/2/2004
Google AdSense Tracker Tool Released
Search Engine Journal
Kanoodle's ContextTarget Hopes to Challenge Google and Quigo
Search Engine Journal 3/16/2004
Contextual Ads Gain Momentum
By Shari Thurow: Search Engine Watch Jupitermedia December 23, 2003
Microsoft set to take on Google
By Alan Kohler: The Sydney Morning Herald February 5, 2004
AdWords Advice From Google
By Garrett French: WebProNews
Does Googles Improved AdWord Relevancy Affect You?
By Chris Richardson, WebProNews 2004-07-06
Channel Tracking Now In Google Adsense
WebProNews
AdWords
Google Inc. 2004
Google Adwords- Pricing and Billing
Google Inc.
Google AdSense - Overview
Google Inc. 2004
AdSense
Google Inc. 2004

Apple

OK, Mac, Make a Wish
By Steven Levy Newsweek Feb. 2 2004
Apple Throws Spotlight on Search
By Sean Gallagher eweek.com Ziff Davis Publishing Holdings Inc. June 28, 2004
Mac hits 4% of Google usage
MacDailyNews Friday, March 19, 2004
WWDC: Live Steve Jobs keynote coverage
By Nick dePlume, Think Secret The dePlume Organization LLC. June 28 2004

Google and the Mission

AskJeeves

AskJeeves to join Excite
By Richard Waters in San Francisco and Amy Yee The Financial Times Ltd March 4 2004
About AskJeeves
AskJeeves, Inc.
Deal boosts AskJeeves
By Ellen Lee: Contra Costa Times Mar. 05, 2004
AskJeeves Profit Soars on Google Listings
By: Brian Morrissey: DMNews.com Courtenay Communications Corporation April 28, 2004
AskJeeves Buys Desktop Search Company
By Matt Hicks eweek.com Ziff Davis Publishing Holdings Inc. June 9, 2004
AskJeeves CEO: Technology Matters in Web Search
By Matt Hicks eweek.com Ziff Davis Publishing Holdings Inc. July 9, 2004
AskJeeves to Acquire Direct Hit
AskJeeves, Inc. Jan. 25, 2000
AskJeeves: What's the Future of Search?
By Andy Beal: Search Engine Watch February 25, 2004
Teoma - Search with Authority
teoma.com
Teoma Adds Style to Jeeves' Substance
By Andrew Goodman: Traffick.com Page Zero Media and Siteopedia.com April 2, 2002
Teoma: Owner AskJeeves has relaunched
Internet News April 2, 2002
AskJeeves, Google extend ad links deal
CNET News.com July 26, 2004

Autonomy

Bayes' theorem
Wikipedia
Autonomy Corporation
businessweekly.co.uk December 2003
Rating review rattles Autonomy
By Neil Hume The Guardian Guardian Unlimited

Blogs and Usegroups

Google Acquires Deja's Usenet Archive
Google Inc February 12, 2001
Google buys remaining Deja.com business
By Paul Festa CNET: News.com CNET Networks February 12, 2001
Microsoft aims to make blogging big in Japan
Reuters CNET Networks, Inc. August 04, 2004
Google Overhauls Blogger
By Chris Sherman, searchenginewatch.com May 10, 2004
Google Buys Pyra: Blogging Goes Big-Time
Dan Gillmor weblog.siliconvalley.com
Google Tests New E-mail Groups
By Matt Hicks. Ziff Davis Publishing Holdings Inc. May 12, 2004

Google to Bloggers: Get Your Ad Share
By Matt Hicks, eweek.com, Ziff Davis Publishing Holdings Inc. August 25, 2004
Google buys Blogger web service
By Neil McIntosh: The Guardian Tuesday February 18, 2003
Google To Penalize Blogs?
Mediajunk: Michael Heraghty
Google Announces the Official Google Blog
Search Engine News 5/11/2004

Brin, Sergey

Extracting Patterns and Relations from the World Wide Web
Sergey Brin Computer Science Department Stanford University 1997
Interview with Sergey Brin, Google Co-Founder
Jeremy Allaire's Radio 1/6/2004
A meeting with Sergey Brin
Red Herring, Inc.
Danny Sullivan interviews Sergey Brin
By Greg Jarboe: Search Engine Watch Jupitermedia Corporation October 16, 2003
Exclusive: Sergey Brin interview
By: Sachin Kalbag Mid-Day Multimedia September 10, 2003
My favorite books
By Sergey Brin
Near Neighbor Search in Large Metric Spaces
By Sergey Brin: Department of Computer Science, Stanford University November 1995
Sergey Brin
By Sergey Brin: Department of Computer Science Stanford University
Sergey Brin of Google at PC Forum 2003
By Cory Doctorow
Google Co-Founder Lives Modestly, Emigre Dad Says
By Adam Tanner Reuters April 26 2004

Cassini

Cassini Interplanetry Trajectory
NASA Jet Propulsion Laboratory, California Institute of Technology Curator: Alice Wessen Webmaster: Lori Sears JPL Clearance:CL02-2452
Cassini-Huygens Mission to Saturn and Titan
NASA Jet Propulsion Laboratory, California Institute of Technology Curator: Alice Wessen Webmaster: Lori Sears JPL Clearance:CL02-2452
NASAs Cassini Enters Saturn Orbit
NASA, Gray MidAmerica TV Interactive Media, LLC

China

Brain buzz that proves Chinese is harder to learn than English
By Tim Radford, Guardian, June 30, 2003
Netease and Google forge strategic partnership
By Mure Dickie, The Financial Times July 6 2004
Baidu president takes on Google
Shenzhen Daily www.chinaview.cn 2004-03-29 10:41:59
A blatant attempt to curry favor with China
China Reform Monitor American Foreign Policy Council, Washington, D.C. March 26, 2001

Google and the Mission

CHINA: Google sharpens mainland pitch
By Sidney Luk: By Sidney Luk February 12, 2004
Google Adds Chinese AdWords Service
By Brian Morrissey: dmnews.com Feb.12,2004
Google, Yahoo Accused Of Irresponsible Chinese Censorship
By Brittany Thompson, WebProWorld.com 2004-07-28
Baidu grabs search engine market
By Liu Baijia China: Daily 2004-02-02

Desktop

Blinkx to Launch
John Battelle's Searchblog July 19, 2004
The Secret Source of Google's Power
By rich skrenta, Topix.net Weblog April 04, 2004
Google Experiments With Local Filesystem Search
By timothy News for nerds slashdot.org May 19 2004
Google Moves Toward Clash With Microsoft
By John Markoff, The New York Times Company May 19, 2004

Directory

The Semantic Web: An Introduction
Sean B. Palmer: informesh.net 2001-09
Galaxy: The Internet's First Searchable Directory (Since 1994)
galaxy.com Logika Corporation 2004
Gurunet - The Ultimate Reference Tool
gurunet.com Atomica Corporation 2004
The ODP: The Spirit of the Web
laisha.com ODP History 25-Dec-2003
Google Updates Google Directory
Search Engine Journal 3/15/2004

Froogle

Yahoo to launch product comparison service
By Stefanie Olsen: CNET News.com September 22, 2003
Israel's Shopping.com to hold IPO at $400m value
ISRAEL21c.org March 28, 2004
Marketing with Googles Froogle Product Search Engine
By Loren, The Search Engine Journal 5/15/2004

Genesis

Internet Killed the Video Star,
By Mark Cohn and Ken Martin, Atom Films, AtomShockwave Corp.
Search firm gets $25 million influx (Google Launch)
By Bloomberg News CNET News.com June 3, 1999
Markets plunge in frenzied sell-off
By Sam Ames CNET News.com CNET Networks April 14, 2000
The Marc Andreessen Interview
By Thom Stark, 1995
Congressional Efforts to Increase Funding for Science Education Program
By Audrey T. Leath American Institute of Physics FYI Number 58: May 9, 2002

Burning Chrome,
By William Gibson, 1996-2004, Amazon.com, Inc. or its affiliates
Microserfs
By Douglas Coupland. amazon.com
Just Java
Peter van der Linden, Sunsoft Press, Prentice Hall 1996
Chaos: Making a New Science
By James Gleick Amazon.com
Only the Paranoid Survive: How to Exploit the Crisis Points That Challenge Every Company
By Andrew S. Grove, Amazon.com
The Strategic Alliance between Nazi Germany and America's Most Powerful Corporation
By Edwin Black, amazon.com
Labyrinths
By Jorge Luis Borges, James E. Irby, Donald A. Yates Amazon.com
Joseph Weizenbaum Winner of CPSR's Norbert Wiener Award 1988
By Terry Winograd Updated Nov. 22, 1997, By Marsha Woodbury.CPSR
Can You Work in Netscape Time?
By Tom Steinert-Threlkeld: Gruner + Jahr USA Publishing November 1995
How We Got Started: Gordon Moore, Intel
Fortune Small Business Time Inc. September 13, 2003
Can Google Grow Up?
By Fred Vogelstein: Fortune Time Inc Dec. 8, 2003
AOL to Drop Netscape
By Sheri R. Lanza: Information Today, Inc. August 3, 2004
The Computer and the Information Revolution - Review
By Roy Johnson, Mantex 2001
Bill Gates Stanford Dedication 1/30/96
microsoft.com Microsoft Corporation
Roughing It
By Mark Twain, Alan Eliasen for the Mark Twain Library
Searches Where Less, Not More, Is Better (Google Launch)
By Peter H. Lewis: nytimes.com The New York Times Company September 30, 1999
Google Keeps Search Simple (Google Launch)
By Andy Wang nytimes.com The New York Times Company October 6, 1999
Pair Evaded Family Academic Legacy to Found Google
By Adam Tanner, Reuters, Apr 27, 2004
Opsware INC. On the record: Marc Andreessen
San Francisco Chronicle December 7, 2003
Google Search Appliance
Information Technology systems and Services, Stanford Univesity December 12, 2003
Google's Endless Summer
By Andrew Goodman Traffick.com 8/28/2002
The IBM Link to Auschwitz
By Edwin Black villagevoice.com Village Voice Media, Inc. October 9th, 2002
The Godfather
By G. Pascal Zachary, Wired, The Conde Nast Publications Inc. Issue 5.11Nov 1997

Gmail

Google co-founder promises Safari compatibility with Gmail
By Mat Honan and Jim Dalrymple: maccentral.macworld Mac Publishing April 26, 2004
Google's Gmail could be blocked

Google and the Mission

BBCi BBC News 13 April, 2004
Is Google the future of email?
By Declan McCullagh: CNET News.com April 12, 2004
Google denies FBI interest in Gmail
CNET News.com April 30, 2004
Is new Gmail an opportunity or threat?
By Paul Andrews: The Seattle Times Company April 19, 2004
Google to Launch Free Mail Service?
Slashdot 2004
Google's Gmail To Offer 1GB E-mail Storage?
Slashdot March 31 2004
ExtremeTech Reviews Google's Gmail Beta
By Jim Lynch slashdot.org May 09 2004
Read My Mail, Please
By Paul Boutin slate.msn.com Microsoft Corporation April 15, 2004
Gmail Requires The Least Personal Info
WebProNews iEntry 2004
Feedback for: Welcome to the Google Desktop?
By Danny Sullivan: ClickZ Network, Jupitermedia Corporation
Google's Brin Talks on Gmail Future
BySteve Gillmor: eweek.com Ziff Davis Publishing Holdings Inc. April 23, 2004
Google's Gmail headache grows with trademark claim
Forbes.com Reuters 04.07.04
A First Look At Google's Gmail
By Arik Hesseldahl: Forbes.com Inc. 04.12.04
Google email lacks privacy, EU groups allege
Reuters International Herald Tribune Tuesday, April 6, 2004
The i-Technology World Remains Giga-Baffled By Gmail
linuxworld.com April 2, 2004
Google set to sort out free email
By Will Knight NewScientist.com news service 01April04
Google May Change Gmail Advertising Model Due to Complaints
Search Engine Journal 4/14/2004
Google Gmail - User Review and Preliminary Impressions
By Bob Matsuoka: Search Engine Journal 4/15/2004
Google Advertisers Like Gmail, But Want Lower Rates
The Search Engine Journal 5/11/2004

Google Info

Google Groups: googleguy
Google
Google keeps board a Silicon Valley family affair
Reuters, Forbes.com Inc. 04.29.04
google.public.support.general FAQ
By Tomi Hs April 24th, 2004
Google Offices - Worldwide
Google Inc
Corporate Information: Who's Behind Google
Google Inc
Some disturbing results
googleblog Tuesday, May 11, 2004
A new Engineer-in-Chief: Wayne Rosing takes the helm
Google Friends Newsletter for January 31, 2001

Google chooses Dublin Gasworks site for Europe
By Gretchen Friemann: The Irish Times Apr 14, 04
Business India Google R&D centre in Bangalore to start operations soon
Business News India Pehla Technologies, The Vijay Aditya Group May 5, 2004
The Google Support Newsgroup FAQ
By Garrett French WebProWorld,
Google To Set Up Research And Development In Japan
WebProNews iEntry, Inc.2004

Hypertext

Plato's Cratylus translated by Benjamin Jowett
From N.S. Gill, About, Inc. A PRIMEDIA Company
Theodor H. Nelson Letter to the Editor, Wired
Theodor Holm Nelson
History of Hypertext 1.1.1 Memex
By Shahrooz Feizabadi,www Beyond the Basics
Transclusion
Wikipedia 5 Jan 2004
Google Linux Cluster - Urs Hoelzle(Media player archive)
From: Subbarao Kambhampati 25 Nov 2002
Vannevar Bush
By Marc Berrnier, Adventures in Cybersound
Computer Lib/Dream Machines
By Theodor Nelson Amazon.com
Within the Stone
Bill Atkinson Photography
Where our hyper-media really should go!
Ted Nelson Engelbart's Colloquium Bootstrap Institute
HyperCard
Wikipedia
Metadata: Our Savior
By David Cohen Sponsored By MSN Sales Jupitermedia Corporation March 3, 2004
The Google Linux Cluster
Urs Hoelzle (Google) University of Seattle, Washington, November 5 2003
As We may Think - Section 6
By Vannevar Bush: The Atlantic Monthly, July 1945
MOBY DICK; OR THE WHALE
By Herman Melville, prepared By Daniel Lazarus and Jonesey for Project Gutenberg's
archives
META Tags
ilovejackdaniels.com bBlog November 3, 2003
George Boole (1815 - 1864)
Kerry Redshaw, Brisbane, Australia 1996-7
What's So Logical About Boolean Algebra?
Kerry Redshaw, Brisbane, Australia 1996-7
Claude Shannon (1916 - 2001)
Kerry Redshaw, Brisbane, Queensland, Australia February 2001.
Data, Know Thyself
By Robert X. Cringely, I, Cringely, pbs
Internet Radio is DeadLong Live Internet Radio!
By Robert X. Cringely, I, Cringely, pbs
Short History of Hypertext
Jakob Nielsen's Multimedia and Hypertext Sun Microsystems

Google and the Mission

Information Management: A Proposal
Tim Berners-Lee, CERN March 1989, May 1990
Tim Berners-Lee
W3C
X A N A D U
wired archive
The Curse of Xanadu
By Gary Wolf, Wired, The Conde Nast Publications Inc. Jun 1995

IPO

FT: Google Considers Launching Online IPO
By Richard Waters: Financial Times Yahoo! Inc. October 23 2003
Hollinger Int'l seeks $1.25 bln in revised lawsuit
By Martha Graybow Reuters Yahoo! Inc. May 7 2004
Motley Fool's Google forum
The Motley Fool 4/29/04
Wall Street bonanza hopes fade as Google delays float
By James Doran January 29, 2004 January 29, 2004
Why Wall Street wants Google to fail
By Jim Juback, moneycentral.msn.com, Microsoft 2004
Google IPO? Don't do it!
By Mark Hulbert: CBS.MarketWatch.com April 29, 2004
Who rules -- Google or big media?
By Bambi Francisco, CBS.MarketWatch.com May 4, 2004
Google's IPO risks another bubble
By George Colony: CNET News.com February 13, 2004
IPO VIEW - What am I bid for a Google Dutch auction?
By Steve James: Yahoo! India News:Technology Reuters Dec 26, 2003
Google files for $2.7 billion IPO
By Paul R. La Monica: CNNmoney Cable News Network April 29, 2004
Bankers, "Sex in the City" gaga for Google
Random Access CNET: News.com CNET Networks January 6, 2004
Yahoo IPO closes at $33 after $43 peak
By Rose Aguilar: CNET News.com April 12, 1996
Google seeks to break the mould with $2.7bn IPO
By Richard Waters and David Wells: ft.com The Financial Times April 29 2004
letter from Google's founders
Larry Page and Sergei Brin ft.com The Financial Times April 29 2004
The web's amazing floating platform
John Naughton: The Observer May 2, 2004
Competition In The Dutch Flower Markets
Ajit Kambil of New York University and Eric van Heck of Tilburg University
Google's $2.7 Billion IPO Is Biggest Test of 'Dutch Auction'
Bloomberg L.P. April 30 2004
Google IPO To Happen, Files For Public Offering
By Danny Sullivan: Search Engine Watch April 29, 2004
People gaga over Google IPO prospects
By Griff Witte: The Washington Post The Seattle Times Company January 14, 2004
Still More Google IPO Speculation
slashdot.org April 18,2004
Yahoo, Google and Internet math
By Scott Thurm, The Wall Street Journal, baltimoresun.com May 17, 2004

Google: What Lies Beyond Search?
By Scott Kessler, Standard & Poor's Equity Research Services, Businessweek, The McGraw-Hill Companies Inc. JUNE 11, 2004
Google's populist IPO mixes upsides with pitfalls
By Shannon Buggs: Houston ChroniclePrinter May 31, 2004
Google Files For $2.7B Public Offering
By Susan Kuchinskas ClickZ News April 29, 2004
MS IPO: money porn
By Mike O'Sullivan Corp Law Blog
The Greatest IPO Ever: comment
Barry Ritholtz, Rob Corp Law Blog
Fraudulent analyst research
edgarsnyder.com Edgar Snyder and Associates 2003
Google IPO has risks, even if you're feeling lucky
By Jonathan Stempel: Reuters, Forbes.com Inc. 04.29.04
Google co-founder Page mum on IPO plans
Reuters, 02.26.04
CEO Pay Meets Its Match
By Geoffrey Colvin: Fortune, Time Inc August 2004
Google IPO Central
google-ipo.com Feb 2004 (unaffiliated to Google)
Capitalism is a danger to itself
By Evelyn de Rothschild, The Guardian, Guardian Unlimited July 13, 2004
Google IPO is legacy of Quattrone
By Andrew Ross Sorkin and Landon Thomas Jr. NYT the International Herald Tribune April 27, 2004
News Corp. To Pick Delaware
INCUSA.com Registered Agents, Ltd. 2004
Readers respond with their Google bids
By Bambi Francisco Investor's Business Daily, Inc. 5/7/2004
Goldman may lose $100m Google fees
By Simon English: Telegraph Group 04/05/2004
Google May Have Pre-empted Regulators on Public Offerings
By Floyd Norris:The New York Times Company May 4, 2004
Form S-1
As filed with the Securities and Exchange Commission on April 29, 2004
AN OWNER'S MANUAL FOR GOOGLE'S SHAREHOLDERS
Copyright 2004 Fran Finnegan & Company All Rights Reserved.www.secinfo.com - Mon, 2 Aug 2004 16:30:48.16 GMT - Help at SEC Info
"An IPO is not on my agenda"
ByAndy McCue: silicon.com CNET Networks January 29 2004
Analysis: NASD charges are a reason to root for Google
By Neal Lipschutz SiliconValley.com Knight Ridder May. 18, 2004
Investors frothing over massive Google IPO
ByShawn Mccarthy: Bell Toronto Globe and Mail Globemedia April 30, 2004
Feds slap cuffs on Google stock scammer
By Jan Libbenga: The Register 12/03/2004
Want in on Google's IPO?
By Dawn Kawamoto: CNET News.com CNET Networks April 29, 2004

Labs and research

FedEx, UPS, Patents, airplane and FCC equipment
By Aaron Swartz: theunofficialgoogleweblog Jan 13, 2004

Google and the Mission

Google beefs up search hardware
By Stefanie Olsen: CNET News.com CNET Networks September 29, 2002
Search engines rise to next level
By Brian Bergstein The Seattle Times Company The Associated Press April 19, 2004
Topic: Exploiting the Google toolbar
By GreyMagic Software 08 Aug 2002
Simplicity and Enterprise Search
Google Inc 2004
About Google Toolbar Features
Google Inc
Search using Google without opening your browser
Google Labs Google Inc.
Google Shares Two New Experiments with Public in Google Labs and research
Jennifer Laycock: Ab Inc
CrossRef Launches Google-Powered Crossref Search
WebProNews
Google's Dave Girouard on the Future of Enterprise Search
By Alison Diana: www.EcommerceTimes.com ECT News Network 04/27/04
Google Steps Up Enterprise Development
eweek.com Ziff Davis Publishing Holdings 2004
Google -Search tips
By Jack Schofield, The Guardian, Guardian Newspapers Limited October 3, 2002
How Google Bursts the Pop-Up Bubble
Doug Barney Microsoft Certified Professional Magazine Friday: March 19, 2004
Google Database Components
By Greg R. Notess: Notess.com March 4-6, 2002
Power Laws, Weblogs, and Inequality
Clay Shirky's Writings About the Internet, Networks, Economics, and Culture mailing list, February 8, 2003
Google Alert Shows the Power of API Program
By Cory Kleinschmidt traffick.com 10/15/2003
The Google Toolbar and Search Engine Optimization
Alec Duncan: WebProNews
How To See What Pages Of Your Site Google Has In Its Index
By Tinu Abayomi-Paul WebProNews iEntry 2004
The Future Of Google Voice Search
WebProNews
Google To Search Scholarly Papers
WebProNews 2004

Local

Google to target Web surfers By city
By Stefanie Olsen: CNET News.com April 14, 2004
Google Weblog: Local Goes Live
Aaron Swartz (Google Weblog is not affiliated with or endorsed By Google, Inc.)
Google Connects Searchers with Local Information
BUSINESS WIRE March 17, 2004
Internet Searching Hits Close To Home
Neil Street: WebProNews

Maryland

Michael Brin
Department of Mathematics University of Maryland
Interview: Sergey Brin
TechKnow University of Maryland Fall 2003
We've Been Googled!
University of Maryland
Sergey Brin of Google from UMD
katz
Sergey Brin
Office of University Communications University of Maryland Electric Pub

Michigan

Alumni Profiles: Page By Page
Michigan Engineer Online Spring/Summer 2001
Forum on the Future II: "Usable IT Security"
College of Engineering, University of Michigan October 25, 2002
University of Michigan
Wikipedia.com

Microsoft

DR-DOS
Wikipedia.com
Google Challenges Microsoft Monopoly
By Mitch Wagner: informationweek.securitypipeline.com CMP Media April 12, 2004
CP/M History
The Online Software Museum
Ballmer the undaunted
By Ina Fried: CNET News.com April 7, 2004
MSN's quest for dominance
By Stefanie Olsen: CNET News.com April 1, 2004
Microsoft, Google may go head-to-head
By Jim Hu and Mike Ricciuti CNET News.com June 25, 2003
Google plays down Microsoft search plans
By Stefanie Olsen: CNET News.com April 8, 2004
Google and Microsoft Talked Takeover
Search Engine Watch Jupitermedia Corporation November 5, 2003
Microsoft sharpens tools
By Todd Bishop SEATTLE POST-INTELLIGENCER REPORTER March 27, 2004
Microsoft not ready to battle with Google
By Paul Andrews: The Seattle Times Company February 09, 2004
Ballmer rues Web-search decision
By Kim Peterson: Seattle Times March 26, 2004
Gates on Google: Davos Dispatch
By Tony Perkins: AlwaysOn 02.03.04
I Sing the Body Electronic: A Year With Microsoft on the Multimedia Frontier
By Fred Moody, Amazon.com, Inc
Microsoft faces host of patent suits
angelfire.com MSNBC 2002-Oct

Google and the Mission

MSN rivals Google with its own pop-up blocking toolbar
By Jennifer Whitehead: DigitalBulletin 27-01-2004
Search-Boosters For Your PC
By Stephen H. Wildstrom: BusinessWeek Online The McGraw-Hill Companies Inc April 26, 2004
So Many Pages, Such Feeble Search
By Steve Hamm, BusinessWeek Online The McGraw-Hill Companies Inc. JULY 16, 2004
Misperceptions give Microsoft hard time
By Shobha Tsering Bhalla, channelnewsasia.com MCN International Pte Ltd. 28 June 2004
Microsoft Takes on Linux in Ad Campaign
By Peter Galli: eweek.com Ziff Davis Media Inc January 5, 2004
Microsoft Promises 'Ten Times Better' Search
By Brittany Thompson Google Community (unaffiliated to Google.inc) Jun 29, 2004
Searching times
By Jack Schofield, The Guardian Guardian Unlimited July 8, 2004
Gates: Longhorn is 'a bit scary'
By Joris Evers: infoworld.com IDG News Service July 24, 2003
More Insight into MSN's Pending Search Technology
By Ross Dunn: Internet Search Engine Database 03-30-2004
CP/M The First PC Operating System
MaxFrame Corporation
All PDC Roads Lead to WinFS
By Mary Jo Foley: eweek.com Ziff Davis Media Inc October 24, 2003
Microsoft Reports Strong Third Quarter Revenue
2004 Microsoft Corporation.
Natural Deselection: Not Even Microsoft Will Last Forever, but They Plan to Try
By Robert X. Cringely, I, Cringely, pbs
Crazy After All These Years Does the Key to Microsofts Plan for Global Media Domination Involve Driving Judges Insane?
By Robert X. Cringely, I, Cringely, pbs
Shake Your Groove Thing - The Only Way to Beat Microsoft is by Ignoring Microsoft
By Robert X. Cringely, I, Cringely, pbs
Notes From The Comp.Compression FAQ
Ross N. Williams 1996-1997
Hotmail and Messenger Setback?
Search Engine Journal 3/14/2004
Microsoft needs geek appeal
By Andrew Donoghue: ZDNet (UK) April 26, 2004

Newsfeeds

The Google News EPpy Controversy
By Carl Sullivan Carl Sullivan, editorandpublisher.com, VNU eMedia Inc. May 21, 2004
RSS: Not Just for Bloggers Anymore
By Pamela Parker: clickz.com Jupitermedia Corporation March 26, 2004
RSS - A Primer for Publishers & Content Providers
By M.Moffat, EEVL Development Officer, eevl.ac.uk, 20th August 2003
Story On Iraq Disinformation Pulled From Google News
U.S. Foreign Aid Watch Tuesday, March 16, 2004
Microsoft goes after Google News
By Christopher R. Anderson Geek.com
Google Moves to Block RSS Scraping
By Ryan Naraine: internetnews.com Jupitermedia Corporation April 1, 2004

Yahoo, Google, and MSN Tackle The News
searchenginejournal.com

Open Search

Zittrain on the 'Google Death Penalty'
By Dave Winer: Apr 14, 2003
Google's chastity belt too tight
By Declan McCullagh CNET News.com April 23, 2004
Google, Censorship, and the Hostage Dilemma
David Veksler December 9, 2002
The cost of China's web censors
By Mary Hennock: BBC News Online 23 September, 2002
ADL Praises Google for Responding to Concerns about Rankings of Hate Sites
usnewswire.com U.S. Newswire 4/22/2004
IT: Federal censorware law CIPA, in Supreme Court
Seth Finkelstein 5 Mar 2003
Google revisits policy on hate sites
By Verne Kopytoff: sfchronicle.com San Francisco Chronicle April 23, 2004

Open Source

The secrets to MyDoom's success
By Mary Landesman About.com About, Inc February 2004
The little operating system that could
By Andrew Leonard Source Salon.com
Maverick Richard Stallman Keeps The Faith
By Andrew Leonard: salon.com 2000
NYT: The Valley v. MSFT, Round 2
John Battelle's Searchblog February 01, 2004
SCOvsIBM
DonMarti (revision) IWeThey 01 Dec 2003
Caldera Systems dances the Tarantella
ComputerWire 2004 01/09/2000
Caldera CEO steps aside to focus on UnitedLinux
By Todd R. Weiss ComputerWire Computerworld Inc June 27, 2002
Dell plus Sun equals VA Research
By Om Malik: Forbes.com 05.03.99
Lineo: Sparking the Embedded Revolution
By Robert McMillan: Linux Magazine March 2001
Interview with Google's Sergey Brin
By Fernando Ribeiro Corra: Issue 59 of Linux Gazette, November 2000
IBM Throws Knockout Punch at SCO
By Jay Lyman, LinuxInsider 03/31/04
Interview with Google's Sergey Brin
Jason Schumaker: Linux Journal September 2000
Nutch: About
The Nutch Organization
A Brief History of Free/Open Source Software Movement
Chris Rasch openknowledge.org Dec 26 17:54:46 MST 2000
OSI Position Paper on the SCO-vs.-IBM Complaint
Eric Raymond, Rob Landley Open Source Initiative 2003-08-22
A quick history of Open Source
David Lane Openz 2002-2203

Google and the Mission

A Fight to the Finnish - Why Linux Quite Appropriately Scares the Bejesus Out of Microsoft
By Robert X. Cringely, I, Cringely, pbs
Caldera buys SCO for $145m
ByJoey Gardiner: silicon.com CNET Networks August 02 2000

Overview

The Secret Source of Google's Power
By Rich Skrenta, Topix.net Weblog April 04, 2004
More Than 6 Billion Items
Business Wire February 17, 2004
The trouble with viral campaigns
By John Hegarty, Bartle Bogle Hegarty, The Guardian, October 11, 2004
All Eyes on Google
By Steven Levy: Newsweek MSNBC.com
The Future of Search
By Andrew Goodman Searchenginewatch.com July 22, 2004
Welcome To The Google Desktop?
By Danny Sullivan: searchenginewatch.com Jupitermedia 2 April 2004
Google Named Brand of the Year
By Brian Morrissey: By Brian Morrissey Jupitermedia February 11, 2003
Psychoanalysis in the Web
Jorge Luis Borges automatically translated from the Spanish - Google
Google Is Searching for the Perfect Hit
AlwaysOn February 26, 2004
Google: Lessons for America's Innovation Policy
By Thomas Kalil, Center for American Progress, May 14, 2004
Larry Page: Good Ideas Still Get Funded
businessweek.com The McGraw-Hill Companies Inc March 13, 2001
How Good Is Google?
The Economist CFO Publishing Corporation October 31, 2003
Google may challenge Microsoft
By Chris Gaither: Los Angeles Times Apr. 15, 2004
Cre8asite Forums - Google
Cre8asiteForum Cre8pc.com
The Prison Diary Of Jeffrey Archer
By Jeffrey Archer, Sunday Proust, Alan Research and Tom Perdoo
The weakness of Google
The Economist Newspaper, Apr 29th 2004
Never settle for the best
Google Inc.
Google Web Search Features
Google Inc. 2004
The third era starts here
By Jack Schofield Guardian Unlimited Guardian Newspapers May 29, 2003
In Searching We Trust
By David Hochman: The New York Times
Google searching for ways to take over world
By Chris Gaither: Los Angeles Times Knight Ridder Apr. 19, 2004
The new "G" operating system
By Serge Thibodeau: rankforsales.com Rank for Sales 2004
Google Services and Tools
RateItAll Magellan

Review of Google Search Engine
By Greg R. Notess: Notess.com Oct. 01, 2003
Microsoft Acquires Yahoo!, Google in Blockbuster Search Deal
Stephen Wynkoop: Bits on the Wire, Inc. 1 April 2004
Whacked By Google: why the search engine war matters
David Rowan Times Online Times Newspapers Ltd. February 20, 2004
Emulating Google will be a struggle
By Colin Barker: Computing vnunet.com 22-04-2004
Google discussion
Joel Achenbach: Washington Post February 20, 2004
Google Answers User Questions
webpronews.com WebProNews 2004
Google vs. Evil
By Josh McHugh: Wired Digital, Inc. The Conde Nast Publications Inc. January 2003
The Jungle Book
By Rudyard Kipling: The Gutenberg Etext March 1995

Page, Larry

Google is not an anomaly:
By Larry Page, Google Seminar on People, Computers, and Design Stanford
University January 11, 2001
Google's Goal: "Understand Everything"
By Ben Elgin: BusinessWeek Online The McGraw-Hill Companies Inc. May 3, 2004
Google and Larry Page
j-bradford-delong.net Delong February 14, 2003
Re: web topology
Larry Page Stanford Wed, 26 Jun 1996

PageRank

When It Comes To Search Engines, Think Links
Neil Street WebProNews
Google bombing heating up
By Ken "Caesar" Fisher 01/22/2004 Ars Technica, LLC
The Google gods
By Stefanie Olsen: CNET News.com October 31, 2002
Google sued over site ranking
By Stefanie Olsen: CNET News.com CNET Networks October 22, 2002
The Anatomy of a Large-Scale Hypertextual Web Search Engine
Sergey Brin and Lawrence Page Computer Science Department Stanford University
Optimizing URLs for Google
By Brice Dunwoodie: cmswire.com Cylogy, Inc. - Content Management (CMS) Apr 19
2004
Google - Page Rank Question
Cre8asite Forums - Google
Waffle keywords
By Jerry Minchey: www.SearchEngineU.com eMedia PR Web April 13, 2004
PigeonRank
Google Inc. April 1st 2004
Google PageRank Algorithm Explained
By Harjot Kaleka: Internet Search Engine Database 04-05-2004
Google PageRank Updates Every Day?
googleguy-says

Google and the Mission

After Florida, Search Marketers Have More To Handle Than Hanging Chads
By Kate Kaye MediaPostCommunications March 03, 2004
Do What I Mean - If Web Searches Are Going to Get More Accurate, It Might Require a Technology Like MeaningMaster, Which Was 20 Years in the Making
By Robert X. Cringely, I, Cringely, pbs
What Happened To My Searches On Google?
By Danny Sullivan: What Happened To My Searches On Google? Jupitermedia Corporation December 7, 2003
PageRank = High Rankings?
Anthony Parsons: WebProNews
Is Hilltop Good For Google Users?
By Gord Collins: WebProWorld 2004
Crawler Insights From Google And Yahoo!
Garrett French: WebProNews

Paid Inclusion

FTC wants paid search to shape up
By Evan Hansen, Stefanie Olsen: News.com June 28, 2002
Search sites work to clean up their act
By Stefanie Olsen CNET News.com CNET Networks August 19, 2002
AskJeeves denounces paid inclusion
Stefanie Olsen CNET News.com March 2, 2004
How the search engines sold out
By John Naughton: John Naughton July 7, 2002
LookSmart Changes To Cost-Per-Click Listings
Danny Sullivan, Editor: searchenginewatch.com
Paying for listing with search results
By Hiawatha Bray: Boston Globe, Globe Newspaper Company 3/8/2004
MSN Demarcates Paid, Organic Search; Google Tweaks AdSense
Janis Mara: ClickZnews (Formerly Internet Advertising Report) Jupitermedia Corporation
Watchdog forces Freeserve to clarify sponsorship
By Heather Tomlinson: Guardian Unlimited Guardian Newspapers Limited June 17, 2004
Inktomi: Paid Inclusion Programs
Inktomi Corporation 2003
Do You (Pay To) Yahoo?
laisha.com Yahoo News 25-Dec-2003
Yahoo Launches Fee-Based Content Program
By Jay Wrolstad NewsFactor Network March 2, 2004
Overture Pay-Per-Click Search Advertising Match Types
Search Engine Journal 3/13/2004
Planning a Search Engine Marketing Campaign
Search Engine Journal 3/15/2004
Will The Government Intervene In Paid Online Advertising?
By Garrett French: webpronews.com WebProWorld 2004
Don't Underestimate Search Advertising
WebProNews

Personal

Kaltix and personalized search
DocBug Media Technology at August 13, 2003

Searching for the personal touch
By Stefanie Olsen: CNET News.com August 11, 2003
Google takes searching personally
By Matt Hines CNET News.com March 29, 2004
Blending the Best of Google and Amazon
By Chris Sherman: Search Engine Watch April 21, 2004
Onfolio providing bookmarks on steroids
By Christopher R. Anderson: Geek.com Geek News Tue Mar 16 2004
Google Acquires Kaltix Corp.
Google Inc Sept. 30, 2003
Allaire Founder Debuts Online Research Tool
By Tony Kontzer: Information Week TechWeb March 15, 2004
RSVP to cyberspace networking trend ASAP
PEGGY ROGERS: The Miami Herold Tue, Mar. 09, 2004
MSN Newsbot Search Engine Get Personal
Search Engine Journal - Search Engine News 4/19/2004
Searching With Invisible Tabs
By Danny Sullivan, Editor Search Engine Watch Jupitermedia Corporation December 2, 2003
Google makes attempt at connecting friends of friends
By Andy Ihnatko Chicago Sun Times March 9, 2004
Amazon's A9.com Taking Shape
By Danny Garon www.geekvalley.com W3Reports.com JP WebTech LLC
Search wars are about to get personal
By Stefanie Olsen: CNET News.com February 17, 2004

Privacy

Removing Your Materials from Google
O'Reilly Media, Inc
10 things the Google ethics committee could discuss
BBC News 20 May, 2004
Is Google good for you?
By Bill Thompson: BBCi BBC NEWS
Google is watching you
By Lawrence Donegan: The Observer Guardian Newspapers Limited April 4, 2004
Privacy group files Google Gmail complaints
By Lucas van Grinsven and Bernhard Warner Reuters Forbes.com 04.19.04
Google seeks consensus on privacy issues
Associated Press
It's time to take a stand for online privacy
By Liz Figueroa San Jose Mercury News, Knight Ridder June 14, 2004
Why we target Google
google-watch.org
Brad Templeton on 'The Gmail Saga' - Google vs Privacy?
By Brad Templeton:linuxworld.com IDG SYS-CON
I Search, Therefore I Google
By Lance Ulanoff: PC Magazine Ziff Davis Media Inc. November 26, 2003
The perils of Googling
By Scott Granneman: The Register 10/03/2004
Total Info System Totally Touchy
By Ryan Singel: Wired News Lycos, Inc Dec. 02, 2002
CPA Googles For His Name, Sues Google For Libel
Slashdot

Google and the Mission

California privacy law kicks in
By Stefanie Olsen CNET News.com July 6, 2004

Schmidt, Eric

Google chief forecasts future of search
Dawn Kawamoto: CNET News.com October 09, 2003
Eric Schmidt's lucky search
By Stefanie Olsen: CNET News.com CNET Networks August 8, 2001
What Eric Schmidt Found at Google
By Ben Elgin: BusinessWeek Online The McGraw-Hill Companies Inc. May 3, 2004

Search Engines

Inktomi: Eric Brewer
ByTed Smalley Bowen: infoworld.com InfoWorld magazine October 6, 2000
Lycos: Wired Digital HotBot
wired.com Lycos 1999
@Home buys Excite in $6.7 billion deal
By Sandeep Junnarkar: CNET News.com CNET Networks January 19, 1999
Web search results still have human touch
By Paul Festa: CNET News.com CNET Networks December 27, 1999
Terra Lycos bets on portal power
By Jim Hu : CNET News.com CNET Networks March 14, 2001
AltaVista: In search of a turning point
By Jim Hu: CNET News.com CNET Networks July 31, 2001
Search start-ups seek Google's throne
By Stefanie Olsen: CNET News.com CNET Networks August 28, 2001
Google searches for more euros
By Stefanie Olsen: CNET News.com CNET Networks August 30, 2002
Excite@Home files for bankruptcy
By Ben Heskett and Rachel Konrad: CNET News.com CNET Networks October 1, 2001
Nielsen NetRatings Search Engine Ratings
By Danny Sullivan, searchenginewatch.com July 14, 2004
Vivismo Clustering Engine
Vivismo Inc
Terra Lycos Looking To Sell Lycos Portal
WebProNews
Dipsie
dipsie.com
Topic Clustering
Fagan Finder March 17, 2002
Fagan Finder > Searching > Graveyard
Fagan Finder January 19, 2002
Competitors lining up to crash Google's party
By Reed Stevenson and Lisa Baertlein 03.22.04 Reuters - Forbes.com
Crimped By Dot-Bust, InfoSpace Finds Room
By Pete Barlas: investorideas.com ECON Investor Relations, Inc.1/13/2004
what is kozoru?
kozoru corporation, july 2004
Northern Light Web Search database discontinued
Northern Light Web Search UC Berkeley The Regents of the University of California Fall 2001

Silverstein, Craig

Spam

eBay affiliate spam pages on Google
AuctionBytes Forum Steiner Associates Feb 06, 2004
Bayesian spam filters
By Serge Thibodeau: isedb.com Internet Search Engine Database 12-05-2003
Federal charges: Man threatened Google
By Howard Mintz: Mercury News
Letter from Bill Gates to the U.S. Senate Commerce Committee Regarding Spam Hearings
Bill Gates Chairman and Chief Software Architect Microsoft Corporation Wednesday, May 21st, 2003
Google Bayesian Spam Filtering Problem?
Seth Finkelstein November 26 2003
Gates: A Spam-Free Future
By Bill Gates: washingtonpost.com The Washington Post Company November 24, 2003
Google's Promises For The Future
WebProNews

Stanford

Formalizing Context
John McCarthy 1997
CONTEXT'03 (4th International Conference)
Stanford June 23-25, 2003
Context Research Home Page
Stanford 2003
Creative Commons
By Professor Lawrence Lessig creativecommons.org
Searching the Web
Arvind Arasu Junghoo Cho Hector Garcia-Molina Andreas Paepcke Sriram Raghavan Computer Science Department, Stanford University 1999
Terry Winograd: Professor of Computer Science
Stanford University September 12, 2003
Google's Early Hardware
By CmdrTaco: Slashdot on Sat Apr 03
Global InfoBase
Stanford July 7th 2003
Hector Garcia-Molina
Department of Computer Science Stanford University
Uniquely Google
By Rich Scholes: e-BRAINSTORM Stanford's Office of Technology Licensing (OTL) March 2000
Copy Detection Mechanisms for Digital Documents
By Sergey Brin: James Davis, Hector Garcia-Molina Department of Computer Science Stanford University 1996
The Stanford WebBase Project
Stanford University
A Logical AI Approach To Context
John McCarthy Stanford Feb 28 1996
John McCarthy's Home Page
Stanford
Context 2003: Full Papers
By Michael Ley: Dec 4 DBLP 2003
Why Stanford Is Celebrating The Google IPO

By Ann Grimes, The Wall Street Journal (Montana Associated Technology Roundtables) August 23, 2004

Trademarks

Google plans trademark gamble
By Stefanie Olsen: CNET Networks April 14 2004
Trademark search wars find new battle
By Lisa M. Bowman: CNET News.com CNET Networks February 8, 2002
Google Drops Restrictions on AdWords
By Jeffrey Rohrs: Search Engine Watch April 15, 2004
French insurance giant fights Google ad strategy
The Seattle Times The Associated Press, Knight Ridder/Tribune Information Services and Bloomberg News April 26, 2004
Judge won't toss out Google, Overture suit
By Declan McCullagh: zdnet CNET News.com April 6, 2004

Trust

Google co-founders to establish foundation
Reuters 29 February, 2004
Google To Launch Foundation, Expand Google Grants
Search Engine Journal 3/2/2004

WMDs

These Weapons of Mass Destruction cannot be displayed
Empire Poker

Yahoo!

Yahoo! Renewed
By Michael S. Malone: Special to ABCNEWS.com Internet Ventures July 172004
Yahoo! Co-Founder to Sell 8 Million Shares
The Associated Press. Yahoo! Pte Ltd. May 29 2004
Yahoo! Vs. Google: Algorithm Standoff
Slashdot 2004
Yahoo! founders thank alma mater with endowment
By Greg Lefevre, Cable News Network, Inc. March 6, 1997
Nothing compares to Yahoo!
By Paul R. La Monica: CNNmoney January 13, 2004
Overture sues Google over search patent
By Stefanie Olsen and Gwendolyn Mariano: CNET News.com April 5, 2002
Yahoo co-founder Filo muses on the early days
By Stefanie Olsen CNET News.com December 3, 2003
Overture's Gamble
By Brian Morrissey: internetnews.com Jupitermedia Corporation February 19, 2003
Dropping Google No Drawback in Yahoo's Big Q1
Computer Business Review ComputerWire April 08, 2004
Google, Yahoo Make Nice over Patent and Stock Disputes
By Matt Hicks. Ziff Davis Publishing Holdings Inc. August 9, 2004
FAST Data Search
Fast Search and Transfer ASA 2003

Google and the Mission

Yahoo! Inc. (NASDAQ: YHOO)
Hoover's Online Hoover's, Inc. March 30, 2004
Yahoo Goes Local
InformationWeek.com CMP Media LLCAug. 4, 2004
Yahoo! Pursues Invisible Web Content for Its Search Engine
By Barbara Quint: Information Today, Inc March 8, 2004
Inktomi: Web Portal Solutions
Inktomi Corporation 2003
Yahoo! to Buy Overture
By Brian Morrissey internetnews.com Jupitermedia Corporation July 14, 2003
Yahoo CEO Says Web Big Enough for Yahoo and Google
Reuters.com Apr 27 2004
Yahoo Intros New Search Robot - Yahoo! Slurp
Search Engine Journal 2/17/2004
Chief Yahoos: David Filo and Jerry Yang
By Mark Holt and Marc Sacoolas sun.com Sun Microsystems, Inc. May 1995
Yahoo! Sinks Under Rising Valuation Concerns
By George Mannes: TheStreet.com 01/15/2004
How Yahoo! Plans To Tackle Google
Brittany Thompson, WebProWorld.com 2004-08-04
Newspaper sites take up paid search ads
By Sylvia Carr, Silicon.com August 25, 2004

Index

BBC, 103, 177, 182-183, 209, 224-
225, 250, 257, 261, 263
Newsnight, 24
Bechtolsheim, Andy, 139-140
Berners-Lee, Sir Tim, 26, 55, 116-
117, 145, 170, 176-177, 184, 224,
252
Bertelsmann, 92, 101
Black, Edwin, 92, 97, 249
blinkx.com, 107, 156, 158, 211, 213,
248
blogs, 35, 56, 74, 94, 107-109, 115,
131, 138, 153, 161, 207, 246-247,
253
Bookmark/Favorite, 115, 146, 153,
163, 261
Boole, George, 130, 169, 189, 204,
214, 251
Borges, Jorge Luis, 124, 145, 164,
249, 258
Library of Babel, 145
Ultima Thule, 145
Boston, 137, 260
Bowie, David, 177
Brand, 3, 4, 7, 14, 18-19, 21-22, 24,
27, 32, 34, 36, 41, 45, 49, 53, 67,
73-74, 79, 86, 96, 99-101, 105,
112-113, 125, 132, 152, 217, 233-
234
Brazil -the film, 97, 230
Brin, Professor Michael, 24, 121,
133-134, 141, 255
grandmother, 134
Brin, Sergey, 1, 3, 5, 10, 14, 19, 24-
25, 27, 29, 34, 43, 51-52, 56, 75,
84, 87, 89, 96-97, 107, 112, 116,
121, 126, 129-131, 133-135, 137,
139-142, 145, 147-148, 150, 153-
154, 160-161, 164, 166, 178-180,
187-188, 194, 198-199, 202, 204-
207, 237-239, 241, 247, 250, 252,
254-255, 257, 259, 264
broadband, 105, 198
Brown, Gordon, 130
Brown University, 137, 175
browsers, 12, 18, 44, 47-48, 64, 68,
72, 108, 115, 122, 125, 146, 151,
178, 181, 224, 254
BT, 66, 193-194, 204-205, 243
ProSum, 193-195, 209
Buffet, Warren, 9, 43, 46, 227
Berkshire Hathaway, 8
Buggs, Shannon, 37, 253

Bush, Vannevar, 91, 97, 129, 136-
138, 142, 166, 168-170, 180, 183,
218, 251
Memex, 167, 180, 183, 251
Microfiche, 168
Businesswire, 113, 232
Caldera, 77-78, 257-258
California, 6, 28, 121, 153, 155, 223,
247, 261-263
Cambridge, University of, 4, 143
Canada, 8, 41, 95, 214, 221, 243
Capitalism, 3, 41, 43, 47, 235, 242,
253
Carnegie Mellon University, 175
Carroll, Lewis, 185-186, 189, 200,
203, 215, 218, 221, 243-244
Alice, 28, 185, 189, 195, 197,
203, 244, 247
boojum, 200, 221
Charles Ludwidge Dodgson, 189,
200
Humpty Dumpty, 185, 197, 199,
215, 243
Jabberwocky, 199
Looking-Glass, 203, 244
Snark, 189, 200, 213, 218, 221,
243
Casper, Gerhard, 135
Cassini, 1, 10, 28, 223, 247
Huygens, 1
censorship, 95, 112
CERN, 176, 184, 252
China, 15, 22-23, 30, 33, 42, 83, 92,
95, 112, 122-123, 127, 186, 191,
212, 217, 223, 236, 247-248, 257
Amnesty, 92
dissent, 22, 92, 224
Hong Kong, 23, 92
Taiwan, 23
Churchill, Sir Winston, 92, 169
Cisco, 140
Clark, Jim, 48, 178
Clarke, Charles, 130
clients, 8, 25, 50, 94, 155
customer, 13, 15, 88, 92, 95, 231
Clinton, President Bill, 141-142,
158,188, 202, 241
CNet, 17, 29-30, 61, 84, 111, 126,
244, 246, 248, 250, 252-255, 257-
263, 265
CNNMoney, 39, 72
code, 62, 66-70, 77-78, 83, 90-91,
94, 108, 111-113, 116-117, 125,

Google and the Mission

www.ingramcontent.com/pod-product-compliance
Lightning Source LLC
Chambersburg PA
CBHW051046050326
40690CB00006B/614